"This is one of those books you need to rea[d] so dear, so gifted, so black, so singular in so m[any ways, and to] miss the story of her life is to miss a huge part of ours. She left us way too soon, and yet the gift of her presence, so briefly among us, is still felt in the art she left behind. But not only in the art, but in the life. A life at last made comprehensible by this loving, attentive, thoughtful book."

—ALICE WALKER

"*Looking for Lorraine* is phenomenal. I didn't know how hungry I was for this intimate portrait until now. It feels as though Ms. Hansberry has walked into my living room and sat down beside me. What an honor and joy to read this. The writing is whip-smart, yet lovely and clear-eyed. What gifts this book, Ms. Perry, and Lorraine Hansberry are to the world."

—JACQUELINE WOODSON, National Ambassador for Young People's Literature and National Book Award Winner for *Brown Girl Dreaming*

"This powerful and profound book is the definitive treatment of a literary genius, political revolutionary, and spiritual radical—Lorraine Hansberry. Imani Perry takes us beyond the widespread misunderstandings of Hansberry's complicated text into the zone of artistic greatness and moral courage—where Lorraine Hansberry belongs!"

—DR. CORNEL WEST

"Imani Perry's magnificently written and extremely well-researched *Looking for Lorraine* reclaims for all of us the Lorraine Hansberry we should have had all along, the multifaceted genius for whom *A Raisin in the Sun* was just the tip of the iceberg. Though Hansberry's life was brief, her powerful work remains vital and urgently necessary. One can say the same of this phenomenal book, which hopefully will lead more readers to both Hansberry's published and unpublished works."

—EDWIDGE DANTICAT, author of *Brother, I'm Dying*

"*Looking for Lorraine* by Imani Perry feels like sacred text. A love letter to who James Baldwin affectionately called sweet Lorraine. Thank you for your diligence, Imani. It is a joy to savor your words."

—WELL-READ BLACK GIRL

"Perry seeks to deepen our appreciation in this richly dimensional portrait of a brightly blazing artist, thinker, and activist. . . . Mining writings private and published, collecting memories, tracking the reverberations of Hansberry's personality, words, and actions, and, at times, entering the narrative, Perry illuminates with arresting impact Hansberry's thoughts, feelings, and revolutionary social consciousness."

—DONNA SEAMAN, *Booklist* (STARRED)

"An intimate portrait of the artist as a black woman at the crossroads . . . Perry infuses the narrative with a sense of urgency and enthusiasm because she believes Hansberry has something to teach us in these 'complicated times.' Impressively, she tells her subject's story in a tightly packed 200 pages. Perry also smartly delves into the inspirations for Hansberry's brilliant *A Raisin in the Sun* and engagingly explores Hansberry's profound friendships with James Baldwin and Nina Simone. . . . Throughout this animated and inspiring biography, Perry reminds us that the 'battles Lorraine fought are still before us: exploitation of the poor, racism, neocolonialism, homophobia, and patriarchy.'"

—*Kirkus Reviews* (STARRED)

"A work of scholarship and love . . . Perry takes us into [Hansberry's] interior life with a deft hand and a richness of language that makes every page of this book a pleasure to read. . . . [A] wonderful biography of the radical Lorraine Hansberry."

—NORMAN STOCKWELL, *The Progressive*

"A must-read for fans of black and queer history, literary, biography, and women's history."

—*Library Journal* (STARRED)

"Perry mines Hansberry's life, her indefatigable radicalism, and her queerness, and she prods us to consider what this fuller portrait of a categorically transgressive figure reveals about the state of social justice today."

—BRANDON TENSLEY, *Slate*

"This impassioned study by Perry, a scholar at Princeton, yields a fascinating portrait of the influential black playwright and activist, who died young in 1965, cutting short a life of unusual promise."

—*The New York Times*, 100 Notable Books of 2018

"Imani Perry gives Hansberry the recognition she deserves. . . . A fascinating account of a woman whose talent and intellect changed the shape of mid-20th-century art."

—BUZZFEED, Best Nonfiction Books of 2018

"Perry provides a genre-defying portrait of Hansberry."

—*The National Book Review*

"While structured around examinations of Hansberry's journals, manuscripts, and the early radical newspapers for which she worked—and her own invaluable lit scholar soundbites on those—Perry is as committed to the unknown as she is to dutiful research, and she tastefully intertwines her own biography."

—SARAH FONSECA, *Lambda Literary*

Looking *for* Lorraine

Looking *for* Lorraine

THE RADIANT AND RADICAL LIFE
OF LORRAINE HANSBERRY

Imani Perry

BEACON PRESS

BOSTON

BEACON PRESS
Boston, Massachusetts
www.beacon.org

Beacon Press books
are published under the auspices of
the Unitarian Universalist Association of Congregations.

23 22 21 20   8 7 6 5 4 3 2   (pbk.)
23 22 21 20   8 7 6 5 4 3   (hc.)

This book is printed on acid-free paper that meets the uncoated paper
ANSI/NISO specifications for permanence as revised in 1992.

Text design and composition by Michael Starkman
at Wilsted & Taylor Publishing Services

Gwendolyn Brooks, "kitchenette building" from *Selected Poems*,
published by Harper & Row. Copyright © 1963 by Gwendolyn Brooks.
Reprinted by consent of Brooks Permissions.
Richard B. Moore, "For Lorraine Hansberry," reprinted by permission.

Frontispiece and photo on page 206: David Attie
for *Vogue*, 1960; reprinted by consent of Eli Attie.

Library of Congress Cataloging-in-Publication Data

Names: Perry, Imani, author.
Title: Looking for Lorraine : the radiant and radical life
of Lorraine Hansberry / Imani Perry.
Description: Boston : Beacon Press, 2018. | Includes bibliographical
references and index.
Identifiers: LCCN 2017055552 (print) | LCCN 2017058768 (ebook) |
ISBN 9780807064504 (ebook) | ISBN 9780807039830 (pbk. : alk. paper)
| ISBN 9780807064498 (hc. : alk. paper)
Subjects: LCSH: Hansberry, Lorraine, 1930-1965. | Dramatists, American—20th
century—Biography. | African American dramatists—Biography. | African
American women civil rights workers—Biography.
Classification: LCC PS3515.A515 (ebook) | LCC PS3515.A515 Z84 2018 (print) |
DDC 812/.54 [B] —dc23
LC record available at https://lccn.loc.gov/2017055552

For her brilliance

CONTENTS

INTRODUCTION Lorraine's Time   1

CHAPTER ONE Migration Song   9

CHAPTER TWO From Heartland to the Water's Edge   27

CHAPTER THREE The Girl Who Can Do Everything   43

CHAPTER FOUR Bobby   60

CHAPTER FIVE Sappho's Poetry   79

CHAPTER SIX *Raisin*   97

CHAPTER SEVEN The Trinity   117

CHAPTER EIGHT Of the Faith of Our Fathers   136

CHAPTER NINE American Radical   150

CHAPTER TEN The View from Chitterling Heights   175

CHAPTER ELEVEN Homegoing   186

CONCLUSION Retracing, May 2017   199

ACKNOWLEDGMENTS   207

NOTES   209

INDEX   219

Lorraine's Time

For some time now—I think since I was a child—I have been possessed of the desire to put down the stuff of my life. That is a commonplace impulse, apparently, among persons of massive self-interest; sooner or later we all do it. And, I am quite certain, there is only one internal quarrel: how much of the truth to tell? How much, how much, how much! It is brutal in sober uncompromising moments, to reflect on the comedy of concern we all enact when it comes to our precious images![1]

—*Lorraine Hansberry*

FOLLOWING HER LEAD, I too am putting down "the stuff" of Lorraine Hansberry's life. In my hands, the narrative comes from the sketches, snatches, and masterpieces she left behind; the scrawled-upon pages, published plays, and memories: her own and others from people who witnessed and marveled at, and even some of those who resented, her genius.

But why did I believe this book, less a biography than a genre yet to be named—maybe third person memoir—had to be written? The obvious answer is Lorraine Hansberry was the first Black woman to have her play produced on Broadway and the first Black winner of the prestigious Drama Critics' Circle Award. That first play, *A Raisin in the Sun*, is the most widely produced and read play by a Black American woman. It is canonical, not just in Black American literature but also in American arts and letters. She is an important writer. And Lorraine Hansberry is an important writer who has had far too little written about her, about her other work, about her life. Hers is a story that remains in the gaps despite the fact that she was widely influential. Her image in the public arena has a persistent flatness, even now as more people know about the details of her life. Knowing only two dimensions is our misfortune. She sparked and sparkled. Now, in the digital age, to so easily hear her voice, to look at the many photos that pop up on Google Images, to search newspaper archives for her incisive comments and her teasing wit is to feel the crackling excitement of her persona. Her eyes are alight. Her voice veers between the studied artifice of elocution and the drawled vowels and rhythm of the Chicago South Side to, finally, the slurring speech of the terminally ill. Elegance in one photo gives way to the boyish charm and mussed hair of another. It isn't hard to see there was a great deal of there there.

Lorraine died young. That is undoubtedly one reason we know too little. The life cut short has cast a pall over remembrance. The question "What if she had lived?" echoes. What else wasn't done? Poor remnants of an unfinished life lie dormant, at least that is what many critics have told us. And then there is the way the play itself, canonized neatly as the story of a Black family fighting Northern segregation, is set into the narrative drama of the twentieth century United States, the march toward freedom. Like Selma, like Washington, *A Raisin in the Sun* sits static.

Static things don't breathe. Or live.

But Lorraine did. Deeply.

I call her Lorraine rather than Hansberry because she is just one of a number of Hansberrys whose names you ought to know. I can't just call her Hansberry—the surname of her uncle, her mother, her father, her grandfather—because I might mean any one of those notable figures. In thirty-four years, the briefest life of the great Hansberrys, she left a lasting impression. She was an artist and an activist. She was strident and striking, an aesthete, and, as John Oliver Killens called her, "a socialist with a black nationalist perspective."[2] Born at the dawning of the Great Depression, she was one of those great artists whose life rode the wave of some of the most pivotal and complex moments in American history: World War II, McCarthyism, civil rights. Lorraine was right in the thick of it, trying to make sense of it all.

There are enticing details: She was a Black lesbian woman born into the established Black middle class who became a Greenwich

Village bohemian leftist married to a man, a Jewish communist song-writer. She cast her lot with the working classes and became a wildly famous writer. She drank too much, died early of cancer, loved some wonderful women, and yet lived with an unrelenting loneliness. She was intoxicated by beauty and enraged by injustice. I could tell these stories as gossip. But I hope they will unfold here as something much more than that.

Legacies and traditions are funny matters. They are so often pruning devices. For example, to write about Lorraine is to write about the remarkable legacy of Chicago, and more broadly the Midwest, in the history of Black art in the United States. She followed in the footsteps of so many greats: Richard Wright, Gwendolyn Brooks, and Ralph Ellison. She set the stage for so many more, like August Wilson and Toni Morrison. When I say that, I imagine what comes to mind for some readers are those laminated posters of famous Black writers. This one might read "Great Black writers of the Midwest" and have elegant photos with their names written in cursive. But to write about Lorraine in the way I intend to here, and to think of her as part of the tradition, is not that kind of gig. Like the ones who came before, she lived an artist's life, a flesh and blood life, with a great deal of difficulty and little in the way of respectability once she committed fully to who she was. She did things that were politically dangerous. She was brave and also fearful; experimental and superb. She failed and hurt. Her tradition, then, cannot be reduced to the picture of greatness. It has to entail the vagaries of imagination and the many circumstances that excite it.

By the mid-twentieth century, Chicago Black artists, working in the shadow of the University of Chicago, which had decades of studying poor Black people as one of its many validating archives, had been grappling with what could be called "sociological conditions" for a very long time. Poverty, racism, segregation, mob violence, overcrowding, so many people in such little space—for Black Chicagoans these things existed amid factory smoke and meatpacking plants, entrails on the ground, and grime in the cracks. The exploration of big human questions about love and meaning always had material conditions as a backdrop. That was the Chicago tradition into which Lorraine was born. She too struggled over the social and political meanings of dreams and their deferral, rejecting absolute bleakness and anything too romantic or abstract. Instead, she looked for what was real about the human experience under captive conditions.

Lorraine's searching was one for her own life and also for her art. She stood in the collective tradition of the Black artist, but also in a family tradition of the Black activist and public servant. Her father's father, Elden Hansberry, was a history professor at Alcorn College. Her father, Carl, an Alcorn graduate, was a civil rights activist and a real estate entrepreneur. Her mother, Nannie, was a teacher and a ward leader. Her uncle William Leo Hansberry is known as the father of African Studies and worked as a professor at Howard University. She grew up surrounded by their interlocutors: lawyers, physicians, activists, intellectuals, businessmen. Their expectation was that all their children would grow up to do something of significance that would not just be a sign of personal excellence but also achievement for the race.

That was a huge expectation. And it was one that Lorraine exceeded. Not only would she distinguish herself among artists of her generation, she would also think her way into the vanguard of issues that would come to the fore of American and global thought in the years after her death: feminism, postcolonialism, LGBTQ rights and lives, Black nationalism and liberation. She was before her time, and it is also fair to say she died before her time. I hope to capture that here. The title of this book is an homage to Isaac Julien's impressionistic 1989 memorial film *Looking for Langston*, which was dedicated to Langston Hughes and to the queer Black Harlem Renaissance world. As he looked for Langston in footage, language, and imagination, I look for Lorraine in words, ideas, and imagination.

Although this is not a traditional biography, it is close enough to admit the truism that all biography is autobiography, at least in part. My own connection to Lorraine began with my father. He, a Jewish man, born into the Brooklyn working class in 1943, adored her. He often bragged that he shared her birthday and that of Malcolm X and Ho Chi Minh. He was born under the sign of the bull and the freedom fighter. That man who loved egg creams, long walks, Karl Marx, the Brooklyn Dodgers, and the Cuban revolution also loved Lorraine.

My father informally adopted me in my infancy, when he was partnered with my mother. He was a New Yorker who migrated to Chicago (with a brief yet life-changing time in my birthplace, Alabama). Lorraine was a Chicagoan who migrated to New York (with deep meaningful roots in Mississippi and Tennessee). Lorraine was a Black woman who loved and left, but still held close, a Jewish communist named Robert Nemiroff. My father was a Jewish communist who loved and was left by a Black woman. I am her daughter by birth, his by love, one whom he held close until his last breath. Robert watched Lorraine die. We watched my father die.

My dad adored Lorraine for her radicalism, for her unflinching truth telling, and for being a seeker. My dad was also taken by beauty and poise. From the time I was young, he would take me to see productions of *A Raisin in the Sun*. And we watched the film versions together. He built her into my coming of age.

I lived in a kitchenette apartment for part of my youth, although it was in Harvard graduate student housing, not the South Side of Chicago. (In our apartment in Chicago we had a galley kitchen, though other details were reminiscent of the Younger family's place in *A Raisin in the Sun*.) I am deeply familiar with the interstices of Lorraine's life: the rare air of higher education and leftist intellectuals, and yet also up close to working-class, salt-of-the-earth living, a life bohemian and migratory, yet deeply Southern. It resonates with my own. When I was in school, she was one of the few Black women who everyone seemed to know once existed. Lorraine provided a bridge between my riotous collage of a private life and the larger white world I occupied, a world that failed to account for, or even recognize, the complexity of my identity. She was seen, even when I wasn't. And that mattered. I always had her, even when I knew relatively little about her, as someone who was at least a little bit "like me." Maybe that was part of my father's gift too. Role models are important, notwithstanding how trite it sounds.

A 1977 yearbook—it belonged to one of my aunts—has been sitting on my grandmother's shelf in Birmingham, Alabama, for as long as I can remember. Now, many years after her death it remains. In it are several pages devoted to photographs of a student performance of *To Be Young, Gifted and Black*, Robert Nemiroff's experimental posthumous play about Lorraine Hansberry's life, collaged from her own writings. In the yearbook, most people are wearing large Afros, with some beehives thrown in. Hot pants, leotards, and bellbottoms are the style. Unapologetic Blackness, ostentatious even, is all over the pages. They've always made me happy. Though I can only faintly remember the sounds of that time, back in the recesses of my memory, I spent enough hours listening to Nina Simone's ode to Lorraine, "Young, Gifted and Black," that I hear it when I open the yearbook.

What I'm looking for in the pages is something of my past and Lorraine's legacy. The exercise is bizarre and exquisite. Writing about her now, many years past my childhood encounters, is a temporal oddity. She died at thirty-four; I am forty-four as I write these words. I will always be older than she ever was. She was born in 1930, I was born in 1972; she will always be generations ahead of me. As a woman of my generation I look to her to understand the historic past and the bloom of lost youth at the same time.

Even though I read all her published work as I came of age—*To Be Young, Gifted and Black*, *A Raisin in the Sun*, *Les Blancs*, *The Sign in Sidney Brustein's Window*—and was therefore more familiar with her writing than the vast majority of readers, I would guess, Lorraine's life remained largely invisible to me until I was well into adulthood. But then in 2007, while a fellow at Princeton, I began spending afternoons in the microfiche room, reading Paul Robeson's *Freedom* newspaper. Lorraine's name all over the paper caught my attention.

My father was still alive then. I started a little project about Lorraine, really about the community of thinkers who mentored her and made her work possible, but I didn't tell him about it. I'm not sure why, beyond the fact that this discovery was something private for me: I reveled in her words, words that I was fairly sure people I knew hadn't read. A talk that later became an unpublished essay led me down a road that other scholars had also begun to take, to begin to fill out the details of Lorraine's life. Scholars Cheryl Higashida and Mary Helen Washington have written brilliantly about her role in the Black Left. Judith Smith has compellingly placed her work in the context of mid-twentieth-century civil rights. Kevin Mumford has written powerfully about her queerness. The eagerly anticipated comprehensive biography by the preeminent Hansberry critic Margaret Wilkerson will settle so much that is unsettled about Lorraine, and Tracy Strain's 2017 documentary *Sighted Eyes/Feeling Heart* is a visual masterpiece of a composition that brings Lorraine to life. Soyica Colbert and Monica Miller will bring their brilliance to Lorraine's corpus. This list isn't comprehensive. There are more, all building her story.

And then there is this book, something that fell into my consciousness, a percolating surprise. I want to honor her labors. I was always given the impression that, because Lorraine died so young, so much of what she was supposed to do was left undone. But the archive, appropriately housed at the Schomburg Center for Research in Black Culture in Harlem, tells a different story, the one that journalist Izzy Rowe shared at her death: "Though she lived but a few years in the full bloom of womanhood, she accomplished the full measure of living and left behind an immortality which will live out the life span of even generations yet to be born."[3] Joi Gresham, the executor of Lorraine's estate, has given us the gift of its vastness. So much is done. And from it my story of her has emerged, the story of an artist and intellectual of a particular sort, no less passionate than she was probing, but consistently both. It is a story that disrupts her obscurity and the manner in which she has remained hidden in plain sight, not simply with expanded details of her life but as a portrait of the artist. This is more like composition than an archaeological dig (though a great deal of digging through thousands of pages was involved). I try to catch a likeness of her. The urgency with which she lived, especially in her final days when she was literally running out of time, was infused with a sense of the possible. Peace, justice, love, beauty—she believed they could all be achieved, and that we ought to reach for them. And so, in these complicated times, not only a time in which, were she alive or reincarnated, she could be an out lesbian and loudly unconflicted about her myriad identities, but also a period in which her impolitic and incisive tongue would likely have prevented her from a great deal of recognition, I think she has something to teach us. The portrait here is, then, as much homage to her as it is gift to myself, and to you. That we might see the stuff of our lives in hers. So much has yet to be done and she can help us do it.

Time insists in a multitude of forms. The urgency of her time and its particularities must be understood within the deep sense of possibility that she maintained, a sense that characterizes youth in general and in particular those for whom justice seeking is their life work. We are running out of time, the earth is ravaged, our bodies are indefinite; Lorraine reminds us to make use of each moment.

This book is then also a portrait of the artist as a woman at that crossroads. Ahead of her time, Lorraine's witness and wisdom help us understand the world, its problems and its possibilities. In her lonely reckonings, her impassioned reaching for justice, and the seriousness of her craft, she teaches us how to more ethically, more lovingly, witness one another today. There is something quieter but no less important too. In these pages I want to catch a likeness of her to give the reader a sense of the sweet and intimate parts of her: what made her smile and raised her ire, what drove her passions and how she loved.

CHAPTER ONE

Migration Song

Why was it important to take a small step, a teeny step, or the most desired of all—one GIANT step? A giant step to where?
—*Lorraine Hansberry*[1]

THE WEATHER WAS COOL, blue sky and bluster. Lorraine was born in May. Her mother, Nannie Perry Hansberry, gave birth in Provident, the first Black owned and operated hospital in the nation. It was a fitting location. Carl and Nannie, like thousands of others, had departed from the Deep South decades prior and built their lives in the Windy City. Chicago was a destination of Black hope and aspiration. The Hansberrys were strivers. And Lorraine was the last of their four children. She came into something special.

Their life, like that of most Black Chicagoans, was on the South Side. But Carl and Nannie were distinguished in their community: They were college educated. Carl had graduated from Alcorn State in his native Mississippi and Nannie, from Tennessee State University in her home state. Nannie was a teacher and a ward leader for the Republican Party. Carl was a successful real estate entrepreneur, a man known as the "kitchenette king" in the *Chicago Defender*. He earned this designation by routinely purchasing three-unit apartment buildings and chopping the units into ten smaller sections, each of them with a partial kitchen attached to the living room. The kitchenettes allowed Carl, and the other investors who followed suit, to provide housing for Black residents who, due to widespread housing discrimination, were squished into far too small a terrain. Quite simply: the South Side was bursting at the seams, and Carl found a lucrative solution to the problem. As a result, the Hansberrys were, at least in the eyes of the community in which they lived, wildly successful.

And yet, like the vast majority of their skinfolk, they were shuttered into the ghetto. The Great Depression had cast an already poor community into desperation. The waves of migrants from the South slowed, and the people relied on each other even more intensely. Lorraine would remember her early years in this way:

> The honesty of their living is there in the shabbiness: scrubbed porches that sag and look their danger. Dirty gray wood steps. And always a line of white and pink clothes scrubbed so well, waving in the dirty wind of the city. [. . .] Our south side is a place apart . . . each piece of our living is a protest.[2]

Living on South Parkway and Forty-Fifth, the Hansberry family was knitted within a fabric of migrants. They occupied the same building as their tenants. Many of the adults worked in the stockyards of the smoky industrial city that was at once a center of global exchange and a site of intense segregation. Chicago was known for business, from gangsters to gilded captains of industry, and the hardscrabble lives of its laboring residents. The Black migrants from Southern farms traded terror and cotton fields for crowded units with hallway toilets and a slightly greater taste of freedom.

Lorraine, though a bookish and interior child, was part of the throng of children playing on those wooden back porches of Chicago apartment buildings and on the burning concrete of Chicago blocks. Her recollections of childhood were often sweetest when she remembered summertime:

> My childhood South Side summers were the ordinary city kind, full of the street games and rhymes that anticipated what some people insist on calling modern poetry. . . . I remember skinny little South Side bodies by the fives and tens of us, panting the delicious hours away.

A favorite game was the childhood classic Mother, May I, the choreography of which Lorraine described tenderly:

> One drew in all one's breath and tightened one's fist and pulled the small body against the heavens, stretching, straining all the

muscles in the legs, to make—one. . . . giant . . . step . . . Why was it important to take a small step, a teeny step, or—one giant step? A giant step to where?[3]

Some steps Lorraine was expected to take as a child of the Black middle class, in particular, isolated her. They discomfited her, and even made her suffer. In one of the most poignant recollections of her youth she recalled the terrible error her parents made in sending her to school in a lavish white fur coat in the middle of the Great Depression. Wearing it, Lorraine thought she looked exactly like someone wearing one of those dreadful rabbit suits meant to entertain children. She detested those big human rabbits. Her parents thought it was lovely. Lorraine explained their delight, in part, by saying that she was the only child who did not come from the "Rooseveltian atmosphere of the homes of the thirties." Her parents had not yet defected like other Black folks from the traditional Black Republican Party affiliation that reached back to Reconstruction. President Franklin Roosevelt's social safety net was not entirely in line with the Hansberrys' politics. Carl was a capitalist. When Lorraine showed up at school in that fur coat, her classmates gave her a good walloping. She understood why. She too reviled the fancy coat and soon all symbols of affluence. Her providential birth became a source of shame. Though a little girl, she knew, as someone intimately connected with her people, people who had so little in comparison to her family, that her classmates had good reason to resent that coat when food was often scarce and both work and housing were hard to come by.

The gap between Lorraine and her parents was pronounced in other ways. From her perspective, Carl and Nannie approached parenting in a utilitarian fashion. All four children were well fed, clothed, and provided for. But there was no coddling. When sick, the children were nursed back to health with appropriate remedies and attention, but not much affection. The Hansberry children were expected to be good and were matter-of-factly taught clear values:

We were also taught certain vague absolutes: that we were better than no one but infinitely superior to everyone; that we were the products of the proudest and most mistreated of the races of man; that there was nothing enormously difficult about life; that one succeeded as a matter of course.[4]

Carl and Nannie's parenting style might have had something to do with class or generation, or merely disposition. Even though her parents were good parents, for Lorraine the emotional distance hurt. She yearned for affection. That, along with her being the youngest and a bother to her older siblings—Mamie was seven years her senior and Perry and Carl Jr., nine and ten years older respectively—contributed to an early sense of loneliness.

Though Lorraine rebelled from her parents' politics and, as far as she was concerned, the coat incident was one of those early signposts of such rebellion, and she resented their emotional distance, the lessons about race and racial loyalty that she learned from them took root. Most of all: one must never betray the race. Notwithstanding their status, Carl and Nannie's striving was not primarily self-aggrandizing. They were "race people" in the old-fashioned sense of the word: respectable representatives who believed that every success and every failure was either championing the race or shaming it. Carl's entrepreneurialism was consistently connected to fighting against Jim Crow practices. His greatest fight began in 1937, the year Lorraine turned seven years old. Carl set his sights on a brick building for purchase at 6140 South Rhodes Avenue. This one was different from his previous purchases. The home was covered by a racially restrictive covenant, a private land agreement in which neighbors in the area had agreed to not sell to African Americans and other "undesirables." Such agreements covered the majority of Chicago real estate at the time. But a personal dispute between one homeowner who served on the board of the Woodlawn Property Owners Association and the rest of the board led him to sabotage the neighborhood by selling his home to a Black purchaser, Carl Hansberry. Carl was well aware that his purchase would lead to a legal battle. He enlisted the support of the National Association for the Advancement of Colored People (NAACP) in advance and received a mortgage from the Supreme Life and Liberty Insurance Company, a Black-owned outfit that was often involved in Black politics in the city.

The case that resulted from Carl's bold move sits somewhat dully in constitutional law textbooks today. But behind it was a harrowing story for the seven-year-old Lorraine. As an adult, she described the event in an unpublished letter to the *New York Times*. Carl, she said, spent a great deal of money and time working on the case with the NAACP. She, her mother, and siblings occupied the home and lived under siege. Outside their door a howling white mob lay in wait. She and her siblings were hit, spat upon, and cursed out as they walked to school. In the evenings, her mother protected the home with a German Luger pistol while Carl was often out of town working with the team of lawyers, fighting for their right to be there.

In an interview with the *Chicago Tribune*, Lorraine's sister, Mamie, recalled that a chunk of cement was thrown through the window by a member of the mob. The cement almost caught Lorraine's head. It was thrown with such force that after it shattered the glass, and nearly hit the seven-year-old girl, it landed at the living room wall and lodged itself tightly into the plaster. "That was a grotesque sight to see that lodged in the wall," Mamie told the *Tribune*. "You know that somebody doesn't like you, doesn't want you there."[5]

Any reader familiar with Lorraine's most famous play, *A Raisin in the Sun*, will sense that this episode, and Lorraine's near-death experience in the midst of it, is an undercurrent of *Raisin*'s story of a Black family that buys a home in a white neighborhood in Chicago. But in truth, the Hansberry experience was not unique. There were literally hundreds of cases across the Midwest of white mob violence in response to individual efforts to integrate. The consequences were destroyed property, lost homes, trauma, and sometimes death. Unlike the South, in which the racial hierarchy was marked in a plethora of other ways, from segregated train cars to lynching, in Northern cities real estate was the border of racial status.

Before writing *A Raisin in the Sun*, Lorraine reflected on her own childhood experience multiple times in fictional form. Lorraine habitually worked through her ideas, memories, politics, and passions by writing vividly imagined fictional scenes. They are a key to revealing her interior life.

Unlike in *Raisin*, the violence in these creative vignettes was always immediate. In one, the protagonist is a migrant from Macon,

Georgia, a working-class man who has tired of fighting rats in the ghetto and simply wants to give his wife a little house. "What the hell is a Negro suppose to do? [. . .] I have fought rats til I'm all but crazy and I said by the time my baby came I was going to have some kind of little house for her and I am."[6] His peers, however, are worried about him leaving his pregnant wife, Clarise, at home to face the white mobs while he's at work. Clarise, he says, sits at home with a German Luger on her lap, like Nannie Hansberry did. When one of his coworkers suggests getting police protection, he scoffs, "Police don't mean nothing. They white ain't they?"[7]

The failure of police to protect Black residents in the face of white mobs was to be expected. What Lorraine meditated upon, with some frustration, was gender. In her not too thinly veiled critique of her father, and in the words of her fictional protagonists' peers, she was troubled by the burden upon her mother, or any Black woman for that matter, who had to face bloodthirsty violence. Her disposition reflected her era, in which the masculine ideal was one of protector and provider, but it also reflected her sensitivity to the general reality that Black women were not afforded protections from the meanness of the world but rather called to face them up close.

In another experimental vignette, which Lorraine wrote in 1950, a white mob attacks a group of Black people getting into a car in front of their home. In this one, the Black people fight back. A person in the mob smashes their window; they retaliate by calling her a "whitebitch." Twenty people surround the car, the Black driver attempts to drive into the crowd. The fantasy of retaliation and what satisfaction it might afford is disrupted again by a police officer who attacks.

The girl is dragged from the car. An officer, whom the girl calls with bitter sarcasm "a good uncolored," stands above her and spits, "Get up, nigger." She spits back, "Who, your mother?" He pulls her up and kicks her face, breaking her nose and knocking out a tooth. The girl says, "I wondered if the good uncolored was smiling. If he had gaps."[8]

Lorraine's impressionistic renderings of the violence of the "good uncolored," an ironic turn of phrase if ever there was one, tells the reader that the "coloreds" were the human ones, the normal and decent ones. But the "uncolored" were a haunting other, devoid of morality or decency. And that is, of course, how they must have seemed to a young Lorraine.

She repeated the trauma in fiction, sometimes impressionistically and sometimes realistically. In the most intimate of the vignettes in which she conjured up her childhood terror, Lorraine herself appears in the first person as the little girl named Sarah who is almost hit by a brick. She is surrounded by her mother, her aunt, and a family friend named Mr. Rector, who is a World War II veteran. The kind, gentle, and disabled man feels a murderous rage. It is directed toward his racist fellow citizens, for whom he once killed in France. Then the rage turns to anguish: "Mr. Rector was calmer, the steel was gone from his eyes and there was water in them. I was seven . . . and men did not cry . . . but somehow there was water in Mr. Rectors [*sic*] eyes. . . . Bitter little Mr. Rector. He sat there and wept his soldier's tears. No one tried to comfort him."[9]

When the police arrive, the sense of pained impotence felt by Mr. Rector is paired with their willful disregard. They examine the home and take notes. Though they touch the window with the gaping hole, they repeat that there is nothing to worry about because "no one was hurt." It reads as though Lorraine was writing from memory.

When Sarah's mother asks the police to stay until her husband arrives, the cop, a large man, responds,

> Look lady I don't care about your husband, I've got to take the brick to headquarters. [. . .] I don't give a damn about none of this. I'm here because I was sent. [. . .] I don't know what you folks are all excited about anyhow. [. . .] Some people throw a rock in your window and you act like it was a bomb. [. . .] Jesus, these people wouldn't have bothered you noways, if you was in your own neighborhood.[10]

Her maternal rage belies a steely insistence. She tells the officer that despite the fact that her baby was almost murdered by the racist mob, "we are not moving." Lorraine wrote two different endings to this story. In both, the father comes home. In one, the girl falls asleep listening to the Southern accent of her father; in the other it is her mother's voice, "The soft slurring made crisp in places by association with those who spoke in sharper accents. I went to sleep with his voice in my ears."[11]

The South was never far from Lorraine's consciousness. People were always coming from "down home" and telling stories about down home, and she even traveled to her mother's birthplace in Tennessee around the time of the brick incident. Along the ride Nannie directed her children, from the car, to look at the hills of Kentucky. She told them that her father, their grandfather, had escaped to them when he was a boy. A runaway slave as a child, he was protected by his own mother. She kept him alive by wandering into the forested hills in the middle of the night, leaving food and other provisions. Lorraine found the hills beautiful.

As a motif in her life, the South was a reminder of the struggle her parents had undertaken and how much labor remained. It was also her "root" and the source of her people's routes, as it were. Once they arrived in Tennessee, Lorraine intuited that her grandmother's tender and aged posture bespoke something that slavery, Jim Crow, and all the ills the migrants fled, had never been able to arrest or beat out of them. She was old, wrinkled, and resilient. She made teacakes and rocked in her rocker and talked about the past, about slavery, constantly. Lorraine's grandmother died soon after their visit.

Migrants are rarely spoken of in the same manner as immigrants, but they share a great deal, particularly when it comes to the obligations of the second generation to make sense of how they came to be there, among those who spoke in sharper accents, becoming one with a sharp accent.

Lorraine described her fictional character Sarah dreaming about playing with the brick, turning the near-death object into a toy. A feature of trauma is repetition. Lorraine made the event into art. It is perhaps an understatement to say that this childhood event traumatized her. Of course it would. But in particular it shaped her ideas about gender and race. As her father was embarking on his respectable and righteous crusade, she, a girl of seven, was beginning to understand the world. In the North, like the South, they were at once fugitives from injustice and resilient and insistent Americans.

As white mobs illegally threatened the Hansberry family, the

Woodlawn Property Owners Association went the legal route with their racism and filed a claim in circuit court to force the Hansberry family to leave the property. The Hansberrys were soon evicted from the property they owned at 6140 Rhodes Avenue. But Carl would not be defeated. With the legal support of Truman Gibson Jr., he spent three years in the courts arguing for his property rights. Their case reached the United States Supreme Court, and *Hansberry v. Lee* was decided on November 12, 1940, when Lorraine was approaching ten and a half years old. The resolution was bittersweet. The Hansberry family prevailed. They could take possession of the property. Several more blocks of the city were opened up to Black residents. But the court reached this decision only because the racially restrictive covenant had been improperly executed as a contract. It hadn't had enough signatories to be binding. The Supreme Court refused to take up the issue as to whether racially restrictive covenants violated the Equal Protection clause of the Fourteenth Amendment to the Constitution. It would be eight more years before the court would tackle that question.

In reflection years later, Lorraine would describe her father as a "real American type American" who believed in struggling for equality "the respectable way."[12] And yet it was clear to her, as a child, that such efforts were rarely rewarded in kind. Her encounters with the forces of Jim Crow were hardly ones in which white Americans demonstrated themselves to be respectful or "respectable" when it came to their Black fellow citizens. Their public life as a family—and they had a more public life than the vast majority of American families of any race—was demanding, taxing, and even in victory shaped by the rules of a Jim Crow society.

But when Lorraine was immersed in life "behind the veil" (to borrow a term from her future mentor W. E. B. Du Bois), a great deal of society's ugliness receded from view and the world of Black Chicago was an extraordinary place. In the 1930s, Chicago was in the midst of a Black Renaissance. It was the center of the blues and gospel music industries. The greatest acts and choirs resided in or came through Chicago, and the records were pressed and distributed in the city. The Chicago Black press was robust. Newspapers and periodicals, including the *Chicago Defender*, the *Chicago Sunday Bee*,

Negro Digest, and *Negro Story Magazine*, were all published in the city. These periodicals provided local, national, and international news of the Black world and also a venue for a crop of young writers to publish their work. Groups of writers working in collectives also flourished. These groups had emerged in Chicago in two primary ways: the Communist Party had established them as part of their cultural policy efforts, and the Works Progress Administration had too. Perhaps the most important project in the 1930s for Black Chicagoans was the Negro in Illinois project of the WPA, which enlisted dozens of workers to study the world of Black Chicago under the directorship of Black sociologists Horace Cayton and St. Clair Drake. Among the writers who worked on the Negro in Illinois project were future literary luminaries Gwendolyn Brooks, Richard Wright, and Margaret Walker.

As Lorraine turned ten, life behind the veil took on a stunning public face when the American Negro Exposition opened. The exposition was held July 4–September 2, 1940. Truman Gibson Sr., one of Carl's business partners, served as its executive director. It celebrated the seventy-fifth anniversary of the conclusion of the Civil War and was billed as a sort of Negro World's Fair. Funded by a $75,000 matching grant from the WPA, it was an enormous collaborative effort. The exposition was held at the Eighteenth Street armory on the near South Side. Visitors to the exhibition entered a virtual city of Black American accomplishment. The center hall was dominated by a replica of Lincoln's tomb. The exposition included a temple of religion with material from ten denominations, and films were screened in North Hall. There was a live theater, displays for the Associated Negro Press, a federal government display, dioramas with images of historic Black figures, a social science booth featuring the renowned Black sociologist E. Franklin Frazier, and the Tanner Gallery, which was a juried art show featuring the largest display of African American art that had ever been presented.

A small child in a vast city of the race, Lorraine witnessed her world. She also saw the thousands of Black visitors who were eager to see themselves reflected. WPA and communist artists and intellectuals in whose tradition she would follow were part of the exhibition. They included Margaret Taylor Goss, Charles White, Horace

Cayton, Richard Wright, Langston Hughes, and Melvin Tolson, whose poem "Dark Symphony" was chosen to represent the exhibition. Tolson's high modernist, seven-part evocation of Black history and creative resilience concludes with an elegant and enthusiastic embrace of Americanism, civil rights, and socialism:

> Out of the dead-ends of Poverty,
> Through wildernesses of Superstition,
> Across barricades of Jim Crowism . . .
> We advance!
> We the Peoples of the World . . .
> We advance![13]

Walking through the exhibition, perhaps Lorraine felt the Rooseveltian atmosphere she described as suffusing the homes of her classmates and the cosmopolitan milieu of her own home. She already knew many of the figures celebrated as heroes of Black America. Her uncle Leo brought fellow intellectuals to her house. Her parents were friends and associates of many activists and leaders. She witnessed the interior workings of Black aspiration for the masses *and* for the leadership class, and in the exhibition she saw the ways those aspirations could be made to explode into the world. She must have imagined her own future in that throng.

Though she described herself as bookish and somewhat retreating, consistent with her family tradition, Lorraine was a leader as a child. She became president of both the Ivyettes and the Gadabouts clubs, social organizations that bourgeois Black people created for their children. However, as she recalled, these children of the elite were not the ones whom she sought out for friendship. Instead she was drawn to the throngs. Lorraine sustained the greatest admiration for the children of the working class. She found them appealing because, as she described it, "they fought back." She was taken by their demands for respect and willingness to make those demands physical: "The girls as well as the boys. They fought. If you were not right with them there they were after school, waiting for you, a little gang of them in their gym shoes, blocking off the sidewalk. Face to face with the toughest the dialogue began."[14]

Lorraine, though flourishing according to the rules of the bourgeois, stepped away from its standards of evaluation and mandates of respectability. She liked the rough and tumble self-regard of children who weren't afraid of conflict or assertion.

There is a certain poetry that in the year Lorraine turned ten, the year of the exhibition, and the year when the *Hansberry v. Lee* case was decided, Richard Wright's *Native Son* was published. It was a Chicago novel, identified as a protest novel by some, and an immediate best seller through the popular Book of the Month Club. Wright's unflinching depiction of Chicago's poor and Black South Side featured a deliberately unredeemable antihero in the form of Bigger Thomas. He was not, as Lorraine would describe her peers, self-possessed, clever, and proud. He was defined by his condition of oppression, so much so that any sense of self outside his circumstance couldn't be found. Wright's indictment of American racism in the form of a monstrous character elicited ire from many sectors of Black America. However, his literary brilliance shaped the legacy of Black Chicago and its writers, even those who were still yet to be, like Lorraine. Though it is unlikely that she read *Native Son* at age ten, she knew a Black Chicago writer, born in Mississippi like her father, had appeared on the national stage. It was another example of Black striving and achievement in her midst.

Lorraine graduated from Betsy Ross Elementary and matriculated at Englewood High School in 1944. During her years at Englewood, notwithstanding her love of reading and her gift for leadership, she wasn't an outstanding student. She described herself as "not . . . particularly bright. . . . I had some popularity and a premature desire, probably irritating, to be accepted in my circle on my terms."[15] Lorraine was average at most academic things: she received a C in stage design and a C in contemporary literature. In a somewhat sweet irony, she received a D in theater. But her intellectualism was apparent despite a mediocre academic performance. On a kitschy quiz she filled out during high school years, she answered questions in ways that showed what an active mind she possessed.[16] Under the heading "Favorite Book" she chose two. The first was the controversial white Southern author Lillian Smith's novel *Strange Fruit*, the story of an interracial romance between an upper-class white boy named

Tracy and an intelligent and beautiful Black girl named Nonnie. In it, Tracy impregnates Nonnie, and, in a bit of Shakespearean intrigue, initially plans to pay a Black man to marry her to preserve her reputation. But then at the last minute Tracy decides to admit that he loves Nonnie. Before he is able to do so, Tracy is murdered, and the proposed fiancé, Big Henry, is falsely accused of the crime and lynched. It was socially relevant and truly melodramatic. Teenaged Lorraine's other favorite novel was *River George*, African American author George Lee's 1937 semiautobiographical tale about a college-educated Tennessee sharecropper who is implicated in a murder case and has to flee to Memphis to save his own life.

Lorraine's taste for drama extended to her favorite songs: the graduation tune "Pomp and Circumstance" and the early 1940s romantic hit "Black Magic." The latter seemed to have a double meaning, both an adolescent yearning for romance and her own sense of mysticism associated with "Blackness" itself.

Likewise, Lorraine's heroes were Toussaint L'Ouverture, leader of the Haitian Revolution, and Hannibal, the North African general. Again, inklings of her deep sense of purpose matched with a romantic sensibility are evident, as are glimmers of her nascent far leftist politics and her attraction to "working people" and the peasantry. She listed her favorite author as the Nobel Prize–winning Pearl Buck, who narrated the lives of Chinese peasants, and among her favorite songs an Irish folk tune called "The Kerry Dance." Lorraine's early political inclinations, ones that departed from her parents', were shaped by the range of people she encountered. In addition to several well-known Black socialists who visited her home, Lorraine was mentored by a downstairs neighbor, Ray Hansbrough, a Black man with a strident pen and passionate political commitments, who was a member of the Communist Party and who served as the secretary of the National Negro Commission. More broadly, Lorraine came of age in the throes of the most urgent Black political debates of the day—integrationism versus internationalism, capitalism versus socialism, upward mobility or grassroots organizing—and she reveled in the ideas. The debates were at school and also at home. Future civil rights organizer James Forman, who was a year ahead of Lorraine at Englewood High School, in his 1972 memoir,

The Making of Black Revolutionaries, recalled their time together. He wrote, "I felt stimulated all the time, excited about what I read and the talks I had with fellow students. A key factor was the intense internationalism of this wartime and post war period. Half the world had united to fight fascism; the United States and the Soviet Union were allies. Our studies at school took place unfettered by the Communist bugaboo that swept in later. No topic was taboo in class."[17]

Black soldiers who were returning from World War II were emboldened in their fight against racism. The students were aware and invested in national and international debates. Lorraine and Forman (whose nickname was Rufus) were often sucked into them, sometimes on the same side and sometimes opposed. Although she was distinctly passionate about the world, she came of age in a time and place that facilitated this passion. Her growing political sophistication allowed her to understand what it meant to live in a ghetto and how ghettoization connected her to people across the globe—whether in Warsaw or India.

Unexpectedly, two months before Lorraine's sixteenth birthday, tragedy struck. Her father, Carl Hansberry, died. The loss would haunt her for the remainder of her life. He collapsed far away, in Mexico, stricken by a brain aneurysm. Carl had bitterly decided there was little hope for a racially integrated and just life in the United States, and he planned to move his family south of the border, a decision that a small but determined collection of African Americans, including Langston Hughes's father, had made in the past. Despite all his patriotism, Carl had given up the fight for racial equality in America. And he lost, far away from his family. The telegram Mrs. Hansberry sent to her children from Mexico read, "Daddy passed will be home as soon as possible with body be brave. Mother."[18]

I have no detailed record of his funeral services or the contours of Lorraine's grief. But the return to her father—honoring him, arguing with him, thinking about the aftermath of his death—is all over her work as a writer. She remained unreconciled to his death, and most of us who have lost those we love dearly can feel this in our own chests and throats. Thereafter, Lorraine also expunged all conventional American patriotism from her heart. That mythology couldn't sustain even one of its most loyal Black believers, her dead father. And certainly not his youngest child.

But she went on.

The remainder of Lorraine's high school days were far from mundane. Maybe they distracted her from grief. At least one event in school further shaped her attitude toward America and its failures. Englewood High School was integrated. The mixed student body seemed fairly amiable until the administration was forced to increase its proportion of Black students. The composition of the neighborhood had changed and overcrowding plagued the city's all Black schools. Soon, more Black youth flooded Englewood's halls. This angered Lorraine's white schoolmates. In response, in the spring of 1947, white students staged a strike. The drama that Lorraine remembered (and put into a short story) centered less on the white students and their slurs and jeers than on Black students and their response, and specifically the different *types* of Black students' responses. At her school, with its more carefully assimilated population, "well-dressed colored students, like myself, had stood amusedly around, simply staring at the mob of taunting whites, and showing not the least inclination to assert racial pride." But then another group of Black students, who heard about the white student strike, arrived. These were kids from Wendell Phillips High School. She referred to them as "The Veterans": "Carloads of them, waving baseball bats. The word had gone—into the ghetto. [. . .] And so they had come, pouring out of the bowels of the ghetto: the children of the Unqualified Oppressed; the children of the Black working class in their costumes of pegged pants and conked heads and tight anklets held up by rubber bands."[19]

They fought back. And the resistance of the working class and poor Black youth had results. The mayor met with school board members and the Chicago Commission on Human Relations, and soon thereafter a public statement was released by the Chicago school board reiterating that segregation was illegal. Police dispersed the striking students, arrested some, and made them and their parents listen to a lecture about the wrongs of their actions, which would, if persisted, result in disciplinary action against them as truants. The postwar shift toward liberal integrationism undoubtedly played a role in the willingness of the city to act finally on behalf of Black young people. But in Lorraine's fictionalized version of events, the boldness of the Wendell Phillips students was the most important force. Her literary indictment of bourgeois passivity (and of her own social class) comes in a moment in *Young, Gifted and Black* when she ventriloquized a simple shout of the Wendell Phillips students: "WE BETTER GO CAUSE THEM LITTLE CHICKENSHIT NIGGERS OUT THERE AINT ABOUT TO FIGHT."[20]

Lorraine would fictionalize this event in another unpublished short story called "The Riot." What is interesting in *that* version is that it pivots around a standoff between a Black student and a white police officer eager to brutalize the youth. In "The Riot" she changed the direction of the insult "chickenshit." A Black boy uses the term to describe the white student protestors, rather than directing it toward the assimilated Black students. In this version, Lorraine created a collective Black consciousness; together the kids resisted white attacks and police violence. She chose to create something different from what she often saw: a weak and compliant Black middle class whose elitism created a persistent tension with the rest of the Black community, notwithstanding that all of Black Chicago lived behind the veil together.

Lorraine was ashamed of the snobbery and fearfulness of Black elites. She embraced a "we" that was larger and bolder than her bourgeois origins. But most of all in the story, one feels her sense of frustration that the tension of the moment, the possibility that it might lead to a larger movement, was lost. There's a climax, a lot of talk, and finally the distraction of Christmas shopping undermines it all. She wanted to keep the fight alive.

Perhaps the loss of her father, and the losses of his brand of fighting for racial justice, made the fight of the teenagers from Wendell Phillips all the more invigorating. A different kind of fight might yield different kinds of results. But perhaps too Lorraine saw fighting of whichever sort to be part of her calling, following in her father's footsteps, because she became the person in the family who would carry forward his tradition of activism, despite her departure from his methods.

In Lorraine's senior year, she served as the president of the Forum, a debate organization of both Black and white students. Among their topics that year were the current politics and histories of Russia and Palestine, and they hosted a major debate against Austin High School with the topic "Should the federal government require arbitration of all labor disputes in basic American industries?" She was engaged with global political concerns and the particular trouble of racial injustice in the United States. She decided she wanted to become a journalist when she grew up (earlier she had expressed an interest in law). Though teenagers are fickle aspirants, Lorraine's political sophistication and passion for reading, writing, and justice made journalism an appropriate and likely career aspiration.

But she was still a kid when she graduated from Englewood High School in 1948. The comments of her peers on the pages of her yearbook suggest both her youthfulness and her inscrutability. They call her "swell" and "nice" though disorganized. One wrote, "In 1960s when we'll both be matrons I'll remember your off key singing, your junky locker, financial problems in general, maladjustments galore and most of all for your never seeming to get anywhere on time." The teasing is playful, but also suggests a lingering sense of misfittedness. One inscription, however, reads differently.

Dear Lorraine,
    These years I've known you have been the most wonderful in all my life. You don't know how I lived for each day when I could come to school each morning and behold your wonderful face. And now that we are parting I don't know how I will go on. Please hurry back to me Dear one. I would like to murder you.
    Yours always,[21]

The signature is scratched out. It appears to read "Anita," and something else is written on top, in its stead. It might be "Lynn." It might be "Lipid." This palimpsest, seventy years later, as I attempt to piece together Lorraine's story is at first tempting. I want to unearth the first layer by deduction. Which girls' names began and ended in *A*? I ask myself, going through page by page. But then I decide to leave the mystery intact. The task of the biographer is always incomplete. No matter how meticulous she takes herself to be, the biographer mustn't venture from archaeology to intrusion or wild speculation, despite the intriguing possibilities of the latter two. The word scratched out could mean a number of things: secrecy, an inside joke, a romantic reference, a lifelong attachment. I don't know. What is clear is that for some young woman at Englewood High School, Lorraine was a source of joy. And, in adolescent melodramatic form, the end of their daily life together felt disastrous. This detail added a softness to my digging, which so often for the early years of Lorraine's life seemed to yield a sense of melancholy, loneliness, and intellectual yearning, but never intimacy.

Maybe that's why she stepped off the beaten track so many times, starting in 1948. Had Lorraine been a conventional young, Black, middle-class woman, she would have gone to study at a historically Black college or university; probably the academically distinguished Fisk or to Howard University where her uncle Leo taught. But Lorraine chose to step into uncharted territory: the large, progressive, and populist University of Wisconsin at Madison, where only a smattering of Black students had enrolled since 1875. Her first major life decision, though a temporary one, would set her on an unexpected and extraordinary course.

CHAPTER TWO

From Heartland to the Water's Edge

green land. Dark land.
Land of the no winter
    My father dreamed of you
       —*Lorraine Hansberry*[1]

THE COEDS OF LANGDON MANOR were gathered together to talk about Lorraine, or rather, about the problem of her Blackness. Langdon Manor, a women's dormitory at the University of Wisconsin, Madison, was directed by Ann Miller, who was described by one of Lorraine's peers as "a thin and hypertensive chain-smoking middle aged widow."[2] In 1948, when Lorraine enrolled at the institution, the population of Langdon Manor was already diverse, including Jewish and Hawaiian students in their number. But a Black girl, of course, was a different matter entirely.

At the house meeting, Mrs. Miller told the residents that "a Negro girl from Chicago, who wanted to enroll in the university, had trouble obtaining a room in what the university administration considered 'approved housing.'"[3] Mrs. Hansberry wanted Lorraine to live in a residence hall rather than in off-campus housing, as previous Black students had been forced to do. The question at hand was whether the Langdon Manor coeds would be amenable to the presence of a Black girl. The process Mrs. Miller devised to answer it was to invite Lorraine to dinner to meet the young women residents, and following that, they would decide together whether they approved.

JoAnn Beier, one of the students, described the dinner as a rousing success: "We met Lorraine Hansberry, we ate with her, we talked with her—the entire group was won over by her warmth and charm at that first meeting. She spread her own brand of fairy godmother's dust upon us, which fell like the first light snow of a winter's evening, the kind you want to keep and save." Lorraine was stylish and smart. The women also felt rather self-congratulatory about welcoming the "first" of her kind. Lorraine defied stereotypes that her peers likely held of Black girls from Chicago's South Side. She was bourgeois and erudite. Her physical beauty—a lithe body, conventional prettiness, and a creamy and not too rich, brown skin—likely helped ease any potential worry. Lorraine was undoubtedly aware that she was being tested. Such an evaluation must have given her a feeling of, at the minimum, bitter irony. In her childhood, Lorraine was attacked by white ruffians for occupying a property her family rightly owned. Now she was called to perform with sophistication, despite her Blackness, to prove herself worthy of living with white people. Notwithstanding her charm and grace, something must have roiled within.

Later that evening, the women of Langdon Manor voted unanimously to allow Lorraine to become a resident.

Lorraine enrolled in the distinguished public research university with a declared applied arts major. She was a talented visual artist, although she later demurred on the matter, and doodled and sketched everywhere. And, consistent with that artist identity, she entered into college life passionately. One wonders what took her from a declaration that she wanted to be a journalist to art so quickly. Perhaps it was just the fickleness of youth. But maybe it was also the freedom of being away from home. She didn't have to name a "responsible" profession.

Lorraine took courses in stage design and sculpture and fully embraced becoming an artist. On Friday nights, when many of her classmates were going on dates, she turned her room into an art studio. She and her friends tacked their canvases on the walls, in lieu of easels, and experimented with oil paints. Lively and playful, Lorraine enchanted those around her with her personality and wit, according to her friend JoAnn Beier, who described her as "sly, sagacious, and [one who] used sarcasm in a most delicious way—never to harm but to amuse. She would delight in chiding, gently, humorously, and seemed to relish a giggly, off-guard response. . . . I admired her cultured lackadaisical attitude."[4]

But JoAnn could also sense a depth of feeling below the surface of Lorraine's charms. She reflected, "Later, as I came to know her better, I realized that this served as a good cover for much deeper emotions, and sometimes her eyes would take on a far-off daydream look, and I knew she was in the private world of Lorraine Hansberry. I, nor others, did not trespass. . . . I discovered that the superficial personality, frosted with sardonic wit, concealed an extremely sensitive and concerned feeling."

In Lorraine's serious and reflective moments she was contemplating so many things. Among her thoughts were questions about race and racism, war, a general concern about the state of the world, and a desire to do something about it all. It was in college that her sense that art might enable her to do something meaningful for the world emerged. At that crossroads of purpose and creativity, she began to attend and then dabble in theater. Lorraine saw a modern-dress campus performance of *Antigone* that she intensely disliked. In classes, she read and was affected by Henrik Ibsen and August Strindberg. She performed in Federico Garcia Lorca's three-act tragedy *Yerma*, a proto-feminist story about the title character's suffering due to her infertility, which was an indictment of conservative Catholic morality. In the play, Lorraine played Maria, a young wife who is pregnant yet filled with anxiety and doubt about what, according to the expectations of the day, ought to have given her joy. In contrast, in Aristophanes's *Lysistrata* she portrayed a Theban woman who very reluctantly refuses to have sex with her husband as part of a general strike the women had undertaken in order to end the Peloponnesian War. In other productions Lorraine inserted herself into the action behind the scenes.

One play, however, struck the deepest chord with Lorraine in her college years. It was the second work in the Dublin trilogy of Irish playwright Sean O'Casey: *Juno and the Paycock*. *Juno* depicts Dublin tenement life and broken intimacies in the midst of the upheavals

of the Irish Civil War. Lorraine described the effect the sound of the
production had upon her:

> I remember sitting there consumed as that wail rose and
> hummed through the tenement, through Dublin, through Ire-
> land itself, and then mingled with seas to become something
> born of the Irish wail that was all of us. The play was *Juno and
> the Paycock*, the writer Sean O'Casey—but the melody was
> one I thought might have been sung in a different meter . . . a
> melody that I had known for a very long time.[5]

O'Casey's use of the everyday music and sensibility of the Irish
brogue resonated deeply with Lorraine. It was familiar to her, not in
a genealogical sense (there is a world of difference between Ireland
and Chicago's South Side) but in the sense of also coming from a
people for whom there was poetry in everyday expression. She could
have easily said the same of Lorca, who wrote with deep fidelity to
the poetry of the everyday lives of Spanish peasantry. For whatever
reason, she wasn't nearly as affected by any of the other playwrights
as she was by O'Casey.

From O'Casey, Lorraine also got a taste of realism. He wasn't
concerned with making sure the Irish looked good or countered stereotypes. He freed her from a sense that as a Black writer one had to
constantly be worried about depicting characters who were "cred-
its to their race," as the commonplace saying went; or to put it in

contemporary terms, she didn't have to think about positive and negative representations but rather simply true ones. Furthermore, O'Casey provided a model of an artist who did not have to choose between a faithful reproduction of social realities and social commentary and the pursuit of beauty. He embraced it all.

Just because O'Casey captured young Lorraine's artistic imagination, doesn't mean she was following in his footsteps just yet. She wasn't a playwright, not even a nascent one at Wisconsin. If her journals are any indication, she leaned much more, at least as an artist, toward the exploration of beauty than toward social criticism. For example, one of her journal entries from her time at Wisconsin celebrated sunlight and the natural landscape:

> In a house where there is much beauty and color and shapes
> that are free and casual and then . . . sunlight.
> How can men exult shadow and night
> When there is for the earth, the radiance that is sunlight . . .
> sunlight wafting through blinds now in a cold city . . . just
> for a few seconds and then the long hours of darkness and
> coldness before the dreary sunshine can come again.
> Sunlight full and glorious on a plain somewhere.[7]

Her words are melancholy. They capture the cool, pale darkness of Wisconsin in every season save summer, and the unquestionable desire of any lover of sun and sea, while stuck in the cold plains, to imagine something, some*where,* else. The yearning is also a form of judgment. She asks, "How can men exult shadow and night?" when light can be found in another time and place. Her lines only narrowly avoid melodrama solely because they are unself-conscious. Even in such personal reflections Lorraine was direct about what appealed to her and what dragged down her spirits. Honesty, sometimes brutal, was a trait she admired and cultivated. One example she witnessed, and delighted in, was offered by Frank Lloyd Wright, one of the many artistic geniuses she would encounter in her youth, who delivered a lecture at Wisconsin. The campus was excited for his arrival. Wright arrived with an entourage of men with long hair, skinny ties, and caps. When the esteemed architect took the stage he insulted everything about the campus, "foremost among them, the building he was standing in for its violation of the organic principles of architecture; he attacked babbitry and the nature of education, saying that we put in so many fine plums and get out so many fine prunes, each like the one before."[8] Though the faculty laughed nervously, Lorraine and her peers loved Wright and cheered him on.

Lorraine was inspired by his complete disregard for the rules of politeness in order to say something true, and also found his ability to retreat into the hills after such disruption compelling. Lorraine was "scary," according to the Black English of her era, meaning she tended to be nervous and worried, an unexpected character trait with her political boldness. That is probably why she admired Wright's ability to cause an uproar and then depart. And she was ambitious. Here was another model for her. Wright was the greatest American architect, and he wasn't forced to perform graciousness precisely because of that greatness. His opinions were strong and he celebrated individualism. Wright wasn't so inclined to the assumption that universities were the best places to be educated. Neither was Lorraine. All this had to have been intriguing as Lorraine was figuring out who she would be, and looking closely at the work of many artists as she sought that path. That Wright scandalized the administration must have also excited Lorraine. Because although Wisconsin was a progressive place compared to many institutions, this was the McCarthy era, and Lorraine was becoming known on campus as a passionate leftist.

Tensions existed between the liberal and leftist circles at Madison on one side, and a more pervasive conservatism that characterized the university, the state of Wisconsin, and in some ways the entire nation on the other. The student population included a critical mass of World War II veterans, whose patriotism was readily apparent, as was the patriotic appreciation their presence elicited. A collective commitment to ensure the post–World War II global order was pervasive. The University of Wisconsin's commencement speaker the year Lorraine arrived, General Omar Bradley, had spent his entire address warning the students of the danger posed by the spread of

communism in Eastern Europe and Asia. Specific to their genera-
tional concerns, as with many campuses, anxiety ran high among
students about the prospect of the military draft (though most students were exempted from it) and the even more ominous prospect
of war, an anxiety that cut across political affiliations. The response
to this anxiety that Lorraine and other young leftists embraced, however, was outside the political mainstream, of which they were made
well aware. There were identity-based conflicts too. Although Wisconsin was less homogeneous than many universities, only a handful
of Black students were enrolled. And while there was a critical mass
of Jewish students, general animus against them was thinly veiled, in
the form of complaints about the large number of "New Yorkers"
on campus.

The conservatism of the era affected Lorraine's relationship with
her friend JoAnn directly. The two housemates planned to become
roommates in what was Lorraine's second year. However, when
JoAnn's parents were apprised of their decision, they were horrified
at the idea of their daughter rooming with a Black person and refused to allow it. JoAnn was too ashamed to admit her parents' racism to Lorraine, and so she had Mrs. Miller inform Lorraine that the
intended arrangement had to be shuttered. JoAnn recalled that after
the revelation, "Our friendship was never quite as deep as it had been
after that, regrettably."[9] Lorraine had had enough experiences with
racism by that time, much more harrowing ones, that she was probably neither shocked nor disrupted by JoAnn's parents and JoAnn's
cowardice. But it had to sting, as these things usually do. And it likely
fueled her quest to create a different world. Her personal life and
her scholarly reading, witnessing, and experiencing were shaping the
adult she would become.

Though Lorraine's artwork wasn't yet explicitly political, her political commitments developed and deepened in college. She became
a member of the Young Progressives of America, the student arm of
the United States Progressive Party, newly formed to support the US
presidential candidacy of former vice president Henry Wallace. Wallace had broken away from the Truman administration, in part because of Truman's aggressively anti-Communist stance. In the 1948

presidential election he faced off against Truman. The Progressive Party was treated suspiciously in many quarters because of its welcoming stance toward members of the Communist Party and their "fellow travelers." Lorraine worked on Wallace's campaign, much to the chagrin of her mother, who, like many members of civil-rights establishment organizations supported the far more viable candidate, Truman. But like many other young activist African Americans, Lorraine was drawn to Wallace because he had much stronger positions than Truman in support of civil rights and the rights of working people and the colonized world. Truman, on the other hand, made rather modest concessions to the civil rights establishment for its support. It was unsurprising that a young, critically thinking, and burgeoning intellectual and artist like Lorraine would support Wallace. It was also a sign of how in her young adulthood she stepped further outside her mother's expectations and her father's political legacy.

In the 1948 election, Wallace failed to win a single state, finishing fourth behind the Southern conservative breakaway party, the Dixiecrats. However, Lorraine was not defeated, and she continued to participate in progressive politics. She became the social chair of the Young Progressives of America chapter at Madison in the spring of 1949 and president that fall. Their chapter took public positions on matters of local, national, and international importance. On campus they opposed the plan to raise in-state tuition (which was about one hundred dollars) and spoke out against the ROTC program, Jim Crow hiring policies at the university, and the racial discrimination pervasive in student culture. They supported a national public-works subsistence wage for needy students and unemployment benefits of thirty-five dollars a week. The young protestors were also outspoken defenders of academic freedom who argued that the university must protect leftist faculty members who were increasingly targeted in the growing Cold War culture. They expressed national concerns by rejecting the Wisconsin governor's opposition to a federal rent-control policy and supported a civil rights bill. With respect to international matters, they opposed the Marshall Plan and the Atlantic Pact and supported the formal recognition of Communist China. Lorraine even took it upon herself to write a personal letter to Judge Harold Medina of the Federal Court of the Southern District of New York, who was presiding over the Foley Square Trial of eleven members of the US Communist Party who had been charged with treason under the Smith Act.

As with her presidencies of the Gadabouts and Ivyettes and the debate society in high school, Lorraine again emerged as a leader. But now she was part of a national political network, in a context in which women and African Americans were rarely at the forefront. Moreover, she was engaged in politics in a wide variety of forms. Some of these had to do with race, but most extended beyond matters having to do—to use a term of art—"with the race." Being in a predominantly white university, while in some ways isolating, also somewhat surprisingly provided a space for her to find and exercise a political voice beyond the circumscribed set of issues, that is, advocacy of civil rights within its most common frame of that period—an anticommunist liberalism—to which women of her race and class were often resigned.

In the summer between Lorraine's tenure as social chair and her presidency of the Wisconsin branch of the Young Progressives of America, she followed in her father's footsteps to Mexico. He had been dead for three years by then, but his presence continued to loom large in her life. Many of her peers, when they studied abroad, went to Europe. Years later, Lorraine would write that Europe never held any particular fascination for her, but the Americas did.

The 1949 summer art program sponsored by the University of Guadalajara was held in the bohemian enclave of Ajijic, Mexico. Ajijic had been attracting a motley assortment of European and American artists and intellectuals, some of whom settled there permanently, for close to a decade. Getting to Ajijic was difficult in those days. After arriving by plane in Guadalajara, Lorraine and her fellow students traveled by bus along a long dirt road through several small villages and a banana grove. Surrounded by the freshwater Lake Chapala, bordered by willow, mango, and eucalyptus trees, and mountains behind them, Ajijic is nestled in the southwest region of the state of Jalisco. The plaza of Ajijic faces a Franciscan church built in 1749 (the earlier Spanish church was destroyed by a hurricane). Constructed from a mosaic of uneven stones in shades of gray, with a single delicate cross at the top, the church of Ajijic is more elegant than grand. And I imagine Lorraine found it appealing even though she had little use for religion. She also probably enjoyed the congregation of locals who shopped and bartered for goods around the cobblestoned plaza. Trees provided shade, and mountains a rearguard vista. Farther afield, and in contrast to the church and a few Spanish colonial homes, dwellings made of mud and clay—huts, really—provided shelter for the Ajijiquenses.

In Ajijic, Lorraine entered a wholly different and lush landscape. She had been born and raised in a crossroads place, where commerce and capitalism together forged a city grid and its tall buildings with jealously guarded borders of status and station. In Madison she lived amidst simple brick buildings in the middle of America's flatlands. But here, spaces were organic, improvisational, blended, and older than any place she had called home. In addition to the distinctive woods, architecture, and landmarks, the terrain was blanketed by wild mushrooms and orchids. Fresh and unfamiliar produce was colorful and abundant: papaya, pineapple, mango, and beans. There was a riotous variety of animals and people. When she arrived at Ajijic, the rainy season, with downpours often sputtering through the night, was in full force. None of the familiar sounds of industry polluted the air. The instrumentation came from color, water, music, and rural farm fragrances.

The people were something else too. The US and European artists who had begun to settle there sought an escape from the worlds they knew. The scene was rustic for them, and certainly for the urbanite Lorraine, as electricity (and refrigeration) had just recently been installed. It was also beautiful, novel, and comparatively pristine. Like most Western expatriates to places that had been colonized, many of the US and European artists in Ajijic failed to fully appreciate the power relationships evidenced in the indigenous people living in mud huts and the European-descended landowners. And yet, this group of artists was less interested in imposing themselves on the place than most. Ajijic's settlers were more likely to romantically imagine that they could mystically become one with this place.

The program Lorraine enrolled in was directed by a New Yorker named Irma Jonas who had settled in Mexico some years prior. Jonas had been a teacher at the Ethical Culture school in Manhattan, but now made her living running art programs that she advertised in college campus publications and general market newspapers. That summer, Lorraine was one of a group of twenty-four young women and two young men from the States. I do not know the racial composition of the group, but I suspect that Lorraine was either the only Black woman or one of a few. With her classmates, she studied Spanish and took classes taught by the distinguished painters Carlos Merida and Ernesto "Linares" Butterlin.

Carlos Merida, though a visual artist, bore at least a conceptual resemblance to Lorraine's beloved playwright Sean O'Casey. Like O'Casey, Merida's work was rooted in the vernacular experience of his culture. A native of Guatemala, with indigenous roots, Merida was based in Mexico and had become a member of the muralist movement of which Diego Rivera was the best-known representative. Indeed, Merida began as one of Rivera's assistants, and early on mimicked Rivera's narrative and figurative paintings. By the time Lorraine met him, however, Merida had created in his work a distinctive blend of European modernism with Aztec and Mayan influences. He used traditional geometric forms in landscapes that depicted indigenous people along with precolonial motifs and patterns. Merida valued and celebrated, without sentimentality, his indigenous roots and reinterpreted their substance for the contemporary moment. For Lorraine this influence was undoubtedly significant. She must have recognized the power that existed in how Merida refused to shy away from his cosmopolitanism: he was connected with the vanguard of experimental European visual artists, and yet he also claimed the distinctiveness of his Central American identity, a claim that had politics attached to it. Implicitly he refused the assumptions of inferiority that had been applied to indigenous people since the early colonial era. Rather, indigenous culture was the source of artistic inspiration and innovation.

Her other instructor, Ernesto Butterlin, also known as Linares, or Ernesto Linares (he is listed on her transcript as E. Linares) was an abstractionist painter. He stood six foot four—spectacled and blond—and was a landowning Mexican of German parentage. Lin, as he liked to be called by friends, had been living off and on in Ajijic since the early 1940s. His busy, cluttered, and colorful canvases often featured moving bands of color and reaching hands. His personal life seemed to parallel the excitement on his canvases. He was passionate, queer, and often both stripped of clothing and ensnared in complex love triangles.

Among the many things that distinguished Ajijic from Lorraine's previous life experiences were undoubtedly both the sexual and the artistic freedom. The isolation of the village from many of the expatriates' former lives in Europe and the States likely facilitated the flourishing of a "free" community, which comprised not only painters but also dancers, writers, actors, and all manner of people who sought a life outside conventional Western norms and rules, and surrounded by beauty.

It is impossible and also unethical to project upon biographical subjects, no matter how dearly studied, the development of their intimate lives without having an explicit statement on their part, or on the part of their beloveds. And sometimes not even then. So I must say that I do not know whether Lorraine, at that point, had begun to explicitly catch hold of an identity that she would claim plainly later: lesbian. Nevertheless, it is clear that Ajijic was a place where her sense of possibility for her own life, her sense of romance and joy, was expanded and excited. That she could see all around her people living and loving in their own ways in Ajijic mattered, and it was her first real taste of that potential.

Yet, as was often the case for Lorraine, she experienced a tension too. Mexico was a place of mourning. It had to be, as the place where her father had passed away, so distant from his family. It is the place from which his body had been retrieved. Neither she nor her siblings could know what his last moments had been like. They didn't feel the quality of the air as he took his last breaths. They had no memory of the ending to preserve. Lorraine was a pilgrim. It is hard to avoid the sense that she had come, like her father, seeking answers that her home couldn't provide. A poem she wrote while in Mexico is an opaque reference to that truth:

> green land. Dark land.
> Land of the no winter
>   My father dreamed of you,

> My father
> Franciscarosa Medico
> Chapultepec
> Lovely.[10]

Lorraine's reference to the pastoral, and specifically a "dark" pastoral, is not merely descriptive. Her father's dream of a place free of the badges of servitude that marked Black Americans was not lost on Lorraine. She recalled that he was "bitter" at his death, disposed of all his patriotic faith in American entrepreneurship and democracy. Perhaps, too, in Mexico she dreamed a dream of a life even more free than Carl's hopes. As a reader of her private poem, I wondered at the paucity of words. To whom or what does "Franciscarosa Medico" refer? Is it a place or a person? At first when I read the word *Chapultepec*, I wondered, Is she thinking of the castle or the forest? Or perhaps she wrote it simply because of the delicious taste the Nahuatl word leaves on a speaker's tongue. Then later I found out her father had been in attendance at the Inter-American Conference on Problems of War and Peace in 1945. It was held in Chapultepec Castle, Mexico City. He had seen Chapultepec.

The landmark conference had included representatives from all over the Americas. Over a week and a half they worked out principles of the region, including a mutual agreement to protect the sovereignty of all member states. Carl was among the participants who fought to support Haiti's resolution against racial discrimination in the Americas. Some countries' representatives resisted, including the United States, which eventually supported a watered-down version of the resolution that passed. His country's resistance to equality on a hemispheric stage may have been the final straw that prompted Carl to move his family to Mexico, a "colored" nation. And certainly the memory of Carl, his ambition and passion, was part of what moved Lorraine to travel to the site of his aspired exile.

Lorraine took delight in words and ideas as much as sights. Her poem reveals longing and reveling. At the same time, we can't forget she was also simply a late adolescent who was having a great deal of fun in a tropical landscape. That combination of play and seriousness was at the core of her personality.

Another poem from the same summer includes the following stanzas, a mix of trifles and profundity:

> Foreign paper told me about Miss Bergman,
> apart of my soul left me
> and the others chatted on about the
>   little village
> apart of my soul
>   from the days of adoration . . .
>   (you humans are an unhappy lot, Jesus)
> and I weep
>   My Maria[11]

The lines intertwine some heartbreak of Lorraine's own life with the gossip-pages scandal of married movie star Ingrid Bergman falling in love with her director, Roberto Rossellini. Or at least that's how it seems. The sense of prohibition, forbidden love, perhaps, hit close to home, making her weep for someone she simply refers to as "My Maria." I dare not speculate as to who or what relationship that was, but at the very minimum it provides evidence of the canvas of passion that apparently was awakened in Mexico. She held on to it after the summer was done. According to JoAnn Beier,

> [Lorraine] came back utterly delighted with the remote village she had lived in with a group of art students.
> "We literally threw paint on canvas," I remember her telling.
> And she really wasn't ready to come back. She told how much she loved it and had expressed the wish that she could remain there for a lifetime.[12]

What was possible in Ajijic was not possible in Madison. And that was much more than a question of landscape. It was a question of living. She found intimate friendship at Madison. That is apparent. But hardly freedom. Years later, through the careful mining of her effects and her connections, Lorraine's future husband, Robert

Nemiroff, collected the remains of a deep connection with at least one schoolmate from Madison, a woman named Edythe Cohen. Cohen wrote Nemiroff a letter in the summer of 1968, in response to his posthumous public call for communications that anyone might have had with Lorraine. In the letter, she said:

> I have just now gotten around to the *Times Book Review* in which your request for letters etc. about Lorraine appeared. I have a dozen from her written twenty years ago. Obviously they meant something to me then or I wouldn't have saved them. Since they are 95% of a personal nature I doubt very much that they would be of any interest to you. It was very upsetting to re-read them and if it were not her husband making the request, this letter would never be written.[13]

Nemiroff replied to Cohen with sensitivity and grace: "Lorraine spoke to me so often of you and your friendship—and how much it meant to her—so that it really comes as no surprise that her letters to you are '95% of a personal nature.' She told me a great deal about those years and so I understand why the letters mean so much to you and why you have hesitated about sending them."[14]

The letters themselves are tender and self-conscious about their sophomoric times together. It is clear that both women were politically engaged, though Lorraine was more strident. Both were passionate about the theater, and both at least a bit heartbroken at having lost each other's presence. Lorraine wrote to Cohen from New York, "I do reflect quite often to these wild miscalculations of the Langdon Manor discussions. How far-fetched we all were, the sophisticated and the naïve alike."[15]

The sense of possibility, the vastness and remoteness of Ajijic on the one hand, and the "wild miscalculations," the sophomoric, the unrealistic, in the context of Langdon Manor; those two truths might very well have been the same thing. It is possible that what was unrelentingly misfitted at the University of Wisconsin, Madison, was precisely what brought Lorraine such a sense of hope in Mexico and what drove her desire to never leave it. And yet, when the program was over, she left Ajijic and returned to where she was supposed to be, Madison. But by February she was on scholastic probation. Soon thereafter she departed from Madison again, and this time permanently.

Lorraine would say later that when she left Madison, she was looking for an education of a different sort. One can take that at face value. But she was also clearly looking for a living of a different sort: something bigger than what she would find in a college town, even one as vibrant and populous as Madison. She went home and stayed with her mother for a bit in the summer of 1950 and enrolled at Chicago's Roosevelt University temporarily. She was admitted on academic probation because of her lackluster performance at Madison. That summer, Lorraine completed about half of an introductory course on German before dropping out of there too. A friend of hers at the time, Joseph Elbein, a student at the University of Chicago and a young member of the Communist Party, recalled that they spent much of the summer discussing social realism, which was undoubtedly more up Lorraine's alley than conjugating verbs or campus dances. But Chicago in the summer was only a temporary landing before her next embarkation. And this one was major. She moved to New York City.

CHAPTER THREE

The Girl Who Can Do Everything

A girl who should have been born
tomorrow instead of some yesterday.[1]

HARLEM WAS NEW YORK'S EQUIVALENT of the South Side of Chicago. But Lorraine didn't start there. She moved downtown, to Greenwich Village. And she took another stab at college, enrolling in courses in jewelry making, photography, short story writing, and the History of American Civilization at the New School for Social Research. That lasted for about "two erratic months" before she dropped out again.[2] But she stuck with New York.

Lorraine was among the thousands of pilgrims to "the Village." Many were of the same sort as those found in Ajijic, but the numbers in the city were exponentially greater. Poets and painters alike were drawn to Manhattan's downtown. Artistic movements that are now counted among the most important of the twentieth century—beat poets, abstract expressionists, folk music—were all growing there, the art blooming out of gatherings of scruffy young creators. They hung out in bars and coffee shops. They had house parties and lived in lofts, and the more politically minded among them handed out mimeographed leaflets and went to rallies. New York University and New School students blended in with dropouts. Knowledge and experimentation circulated wildly. And as with Ajijic there was a greater degree of personal freedom than most places in the US. The Village became a place that was open to gay and lesbian people and had more interracial socializing than almost anywhere else in the US.

That fall Lorraine had her first publication. She was finally an artist, but of a different sort: a writer. It was a poem in the leftist magazine *Masses and Mainstream*, titled "Flag from a Kitchenette Window." It reads:

> Southside morning
> America is crying
> In our land: the paycheck taxes to
> Somebody's government
> Black boy in a window; Algiers and Salerno
> The three-colored banner raised to some
> Anonymous freedom, we decide
> And on the memorial day hang it
> From our windows and let it beat the
> Steamy jimcrow airs[3]

The poem was a sparse indictment of American militarism and hypocritical proclamations of liberty in the face of Jim Crow: an ironic commentary on Memorial Day. It was also a work that was clearly influenced by a distinguished Chicago Black woman poet, Gwendolyn Brooks. Brooks's "kitchenette building" had been published in her 1945 book *A Street in Bronzeville,* at a time when Lorraine was still in high school. While Hansberry's poem faces outward, Brooks, always a master of the interior, attended carefully to the feelings, senses, and space inside the kitchenette apartments of Chicago. She writes:

We are things of dry hours and the involuntary plan,
Grayed in, and gray. "Dream" makes a giddy sound, not strong
Like "rent," "feeding a wife," "satisfying a man."

But could a dream send up through onion fumes
Its white and violet, fight with fried potatoes
And yesterday's garbage ripening in the hall . . .[4]

Lorraine was not a master yet. Her poem paled in comparison to Brooks's. But she tried to do something like her fellow Chicagoan yet also distinct. The daughter of the "kitchenette king," Lorraine wanted to present the lives of her father's residents, people oppressed and exploited, offset against the national lies of liberty and democracy. She was political. But she was also an aesthete. Her words were chosen with care, for their sound and their rhythm. She had begun to step into herself.

And into a raucous public. The primary gathering spot in Greenwich Village was Washington Square Park. Named after George Washington, its arch bears one of his quotations: "Let us raise a standard to which the wise and the honest can repair. The event is in the hand of God." Though they were the very opposite of a stodgy memorial to the "father of the country," these iconoclastic young people took his words fully to heart. Their honesty was a collective event, often sung out in the square accompanied by guitars, banjos, and mandolins. Lorraine found plenty of other young artists, plenty of passionate conversationalists, plenty of unsure seekers in the Village, and yet she was still one of just a smattering of Black women.

And she was a Chicagoan. Early on in her New York days she reflected on her home. Lorraine had come from the big city at the center of the country, but in contrast, Chicago must have seemed awfully small and simple. One of her diary entries from her first year in New York has a tinge of nostalgia for her home, and more than a little desire to keep capturing it artistically:

> I remember the winters that have come before in my life . . . these same colored days when I could smell the paint of hot radiators with sleep in my eyes . . . when sometimes there was the dirty feeling of being in the thick wool smelling clothes of the school morning . . . and the times they say were happy times . . . (times that were not but were) bitter bitter times for the young soul . . . always these same cold days, I thought were kind because they made others my brothers.[5]

In the same note, she goes from the bittersweet sense of connection to others in Chicago to a deep loneliness in Wisconsin:

> A grey world I did terribly love through the awful hurt . . . narrow black trees somewhere, fighting with the sky and always the greyness . . . moving lonely . . . wonderful rhythms just for me . . . others would be there; [football crowds of laughers] it is worse because I cannot hate them now . . . only they say I must not love my greyness now . . . how can they know.[6]

And then she is back to yearning:

> I want to be inside . . . on a floor . . . near a piano, near a leg
> that must press against my side or my shoulder or my breast
> so that I can feel the music in the roots of my eyes . . . and then
> let my greyness come.[7]

She was depressed but also hopeful. That was quintessentially
Lorraine. Even in the saddest moments she reached for something,
usually intimacy. She had excitement, but she yearned for closeness
and connection, something still elusive in the throngs of other seekers. Years later a friend reflected, "Many times when I watched her
unguarded moments, her thoughts were beyond the second of which
she was a part. I could see that here was an extra special kind of
human being, one who seemed ordained for something beyond the
everyday scheme of things. [. . .] Sometimes I even thought to be un-
friendly, anti-social, a girl who should have been born tomorrow
instead of some yesterday."[8] Notwithstanding her passion and playfulness, Lorraine had a melancholic disposition.

But she also had a sense of mission and perhaps was grateful that
it could distract her. But this mission also seems to have been at least
as powerful as her intimate yearnings. In 1951 Lorraine moved uptown, to Harlem, to fulfill it, and to be with her people. She attended
tenant strikes and civil rights protests. She lectured about racial and
economic justice at the famous Speakers' Corner at 135th Street and
Lenox. And she took a job. In a letter to Edythe, she wrote: "I am
living in New York now, since last November and I can't remember
what I wrote you last or how much I told you when I did write. Probably a lot of nonsense about Greenwich Village and that business.
Fact is, I have finally stopped going to school and started working.
Which means a lot of things. I work for the new Negro paper: FREE-
DOM, which in its time in history, ought to be *the* journal of Negro
liberation . . . in fact it will be."[9]

Freedom was the brainchild of the leftist actor and singer Paul
Robeson. Robeson was its publisher, and the editor of the weekly pa-
per was Louis Burnham, a Harlem native who had been active in the
American Student Movement and the Young Communist League. In

his youth, Burnham had also organized the first chapters of the American Student Union on Black college campuses and served as youth secretary of the Communist-affiliated National Negro Congress and also as the executive secretary of the Southern Negro Youth Congress. Fifteen years her senior, though still quite young, he was a key figure in the Black leftist community. He welcomed Lorraine into the *Freedom* digs. The humble office overlooked Lenox Avenue. There were two desks, one typewriter, Louis, and Lorraine, and not much else. The resources were limited. Their operations were meagerly funded by the Committee for the Negro in the Arts, which was another outgrowth of the American Communist Party. Lorraine earned a take-home pay of $31.70 a week, which, she noted wryly, kept her lean. But the lessons were abundant. Louis Burnham became a close mentor of hers and would refer to her as "the girl who could do everything." He quickly moved Lorraine from clerical to editorial and writing work. She learned as she labored.

Freedom provided its readers with incisive articles about global anticolonialist struggles and domestic activism against Jim Crow. It shared a clear feminist message with stories about women's activism and images of women to represent activist movements. The paper also included television, film, and book reviews; children's stories about Black history; for adults, fiction with political messages; and Robeson editorials. The general manager, George B. Murphy, scion of the family that founded the *Baltimore Afro-American* newspaper, who like Lorraine had gone from bourgeois to communist, worked diligently to ensure the paper's distribution. It became a home of sorts, and ground for immense growth.

At least three of her writings for *Freedom* show how Lorraine was thinking about art during that period. She chillingly dismissed Richard Wright's *The Outsider*: "He exalts brutality and nothingness; he negates the reality of our struggle for freedom and yet works energetically in behalf of our oppressors; he has lost his own dignity and destroyed his talents."[10] In her review of Howard Fast's novel *Spartacus* she questioned whether his depiction of the freedom-fighting figure of Spartacus could have been better made if he had written through the eyes of the enslaved rather than the slaveholders, whom she referred to as a degenerate class. In her review of the

Japanese film *Hiroshima*, she argued against the dismissive critiques of the film, calling them vulgar for their shortsightedness. *Hiroshima* was, she opined, both great propaganda and great art. In calling it both art and propaganda she echoed the sentiments of her uncle Leo's mentor, and her newly adopted mentor, W. E. B. Du Bois, in the 1926 essay "Criteria of Negro Art." He argued that all art is propaganda and should be intentionally so for those advocating racial justice. Likewise, her critique of Black subjects on television indicated that she was concerned with the question of representation of Blacks in media, an issue that had been taken up (controversially) by another family friend, Walter White, when he served on the Hollywood bureau of the NAACP in the 1940s.

Lorraine also wrote about international politics. In a December 1951 issue of *Freedom*, she covered Kwame Nkrumah (her uncle's former student) of the People's Party in Ghana—and his election as the first prime minister of "the Gold Coast" since the Portuguese first established it as a slave trading post in early 1500s. In this article, Lorraine connected the struggle for Ghanaian independence to the one for racial justice in the United States, saying, "The people of Ghana clearly see their struggles and victories in connection with Black folk on the rest of their continent as well as in the United States. A U.S. Negro reporter for the Pittsburgh Courier commented not long ago 'Whenever I make an interview in Accra it is a two-sided affair. I ask questions about events in the Gold Coast and they ply me with questions about the Willie McGee case, the Cicero Illinois race riot, Dr. Ralph Bunche and topics American Negroes are discussing today.'"[11] She similarly noted that Black Americans admired Ghanaian independence, a transformation that was visually marked by the transition from European business suits to traditional draped robes. She also wrote about liberation struggles in Egypt, delinquency and child labor at home, and women's activism in the case of Willie McGee, a Black man who was falsely charged with the rape of a white woman and who had been given a death sentence. In covering that case, Lorraine traveled with other activists to her father's home state of Mississippi to organize and advocate on McGee's behalf. Afterward, his electrocution haunted her pen.

Lorraine was also prepared to tell people about her unequivocal embrace of communism by 1951. She had attended a Communist Party meeting at Wisconsin in January of 1950, but it wasn't until she moved to New York that she claimed it. In a letter to Edythe, she wrote:

> You I imagine are still quite rich with the hopes of a thriving theatre in the U.S. and I . . . in my own way dream of such a theatre also, but somehow in a discussion I think I know what would happen Edythe I would recall the picketlines and demonstrations I have seen and been in; I would recall the horsemen I have seen riding down human beings in Times Square because they were protesting . . . lynching. Quite simply and quietly as I know how to say it: I am sick of poverty, lynching, stupid wars and the universal maltreatment of my people and obsessed with a rather desperate desire for a new world for me and my brothers. So dear friend, I must perhaps go to jail. Please at the next painting session you have . . . remember this "Communist!"[12]

For Lorraine, Black freedom and the prospect of a society free of capitalism were intertwined. This was partially a result of the influence of mentors like Paul Robeson, W. E. B. Du Bois, and Louis Burnham, but it was also the result of her studies. She believed that the exploitation of people, labor, and the land by the wealthy while most of the world suffered was fundamentally unjust. The only redeeming organization of society, as far as she was concerned, would be one of common wealth and common good.

Lorraine's writings for *Freedom* were political and critical, not creative. Although she didn't write poetry or fiction for *Freedom*, Burnham encouraged her creative aspirations. She once confided in him:

> I was desperately worried about having become too jaded, at twenty, to retain all the lovely things I had wanted to say in my novel when I was eighteen. It was part of his genius as a human being that he did not laugh or patronize my dilemma, but went on gently and seriously to prod me to consider the possibilities of the remaining time of my life.[13]

And she did pursue her art. In July of 1951 she had another poem published in *Masses and Mainstream*, titled "Lynchsong" in honor of Rosalee Ingram, who, along with her two sons, had been given a death sentence for killing a white man who tried to rape her.[14] Lorraine wrote:

> See the eyes of Willie McGee
> My mother told me about
> Lynchings
> My mother told me about
> The dark nights
> And dirt roads
> And torch lights
> And lynch robes . . .

As was often the case, Lorraine referenced her mother's lessons, earned in the brutal, segregated South. But also characteristically for Lorraine, she reminded readers that the phenomenon—the violence of racism—was a national rather than a regional phenomenon. And both extralegal lynch-law and Jim Crow courts, which were as common up North as down home, were unjust. The poem continues:

> White robes and
> Black robes
> And a burning
> Burning cross
>   Cross in Laurel
>   Cross in Jackson
>   Cross in Chicago
> And a
> Cross in front of the City Hall
> In:
> New York City . . .

Consistent with the messages in her poetry, Lorraine lived her life in New York as an activist. She was often on picket lines and at protests and worked on local campaigns for the American Labor Party and the People's Rights Party. Rather than dedicating herself wholly to one organization, she moved about in various leftist groups, including being both a student and an instructor at the Jefferson School of Social Science, a Communist Party–affiliated adult education center. The Jefferson School's 1952 Winter Term bulletin announcement regarding the significance of Negro History Week gives a sense of the politics and thrust of the organization. It read, in part,

> Negro History week 1952, has special significance coming in the wake of the most brutal and intensified attacks upon the Negro people, and at a time when they are moving with ever greater militancy in the struggle for full democratic rights. It comes also at the moment when hundreds of millions of oppressed colored peoples in the colonial countries are fighting as never before for their freedom. . . . The school's campaign of last term has brought fruits in a significant increase in our enrollment of Negro and Puerto Rican students, and a much higher level in our struggle against white chauvinism. . . . Let us use the month of February to consolidate our gains and to win for ourselves and all we associate with a greater understanding of the contribution and role of the Negro people in today's struggle of all people for democracy, peace and progress.[15]

At the conclusion of the message, the bulletin announced a Sunday forum on the evening of February 10, featuring Lorraine and the poet Gwendolyn Bennett, "Working Class Poets of the Negro People," in which they would read and analyze poems with musical accompaniment.

As a frequent participant in the Jefferson School's Sunday forums, Lorraine spent time with one of its instructors, W. E. B. Du Bois. Perhaps the greatest scholar of the twentieth century, Du Bois had years prior recognized her uncle Leo's talent when he was an undergraduate at Atlanta University and arranged for him to study at Harvard. Likewise, he recognized Lorraine's gifts, and, according to his wife, she became his favorite student, one whom he believed was gifted enough to teach others as well as study under his tutelage. Among the assignments she completed for him in a 1953 course on Africa was "The Belgian Congo: A Preliminary Report on Its Land, Its

History and Its Peoples," a paper that traced the politics, economics, and social arrangements of its precolonial and colonial history. After she completed the course, Lorraine held on to the copious notes on Algeria, Egypt, and French West Africa and referenced them in her future writing. Du Bois was a heroic figure in Black life, and particularly for the Black Left. For a young Black intellectual, studying with him was the very height of apprenticeship. Lorraine captured that extraordinary feeling in verse-like lines she wrote to herself on May 8, 1953, in her class notebook:

> —Imagine then what it is for me a young Negro sprung
> from all the unrest and fervent searching & anxiety
>   His back against the sunlight of May afternoons.
> Blue suit, line/d/ shirt, bow tie, pince nez,
> Goatee & moustache—Relaxing black leisurely, full and
> confident in his vast knowledge and his splendid sense
> of interpretation of history—
>   His voice coming always perfectly measured. His
> Upper lip curling now and again in appreciation of
> His wit—
> Freedom's passion, refined and organized, sits there.—[16]

Tenderly noting his idiosyncrasies alongside the enormity of his influence, she distilled Du Bois. He was freedom's passion personified. To her mind, this must have been a dramatic contrast to her own youthful restlessness. Unlike her, he was neither stormy nor chaotic but refined and organized. Her own admiration of beauty and elegance, her own aspirations toward the life of the mind, sat there in front of her.

As an intellect, Lorraine read books as Du Bois encouraged her to read them: critically and voraciously. Lorraine the artist and activist took to heart both his belief that all art must be political and a quotation of his that she wrote down: "Somehow you have got to know more than what you experience individually"—a commitment to thinking beyond one's own experience.[17] Surely she applied that lesson when she worked alongside other Communist Party activists like the Trinidad-born Claudia Jones (who was briefly roommates with Lorraine) and Alphaeus Hunton, with whom she taught at the Frederick Douglass Educational Center, "Harlem's new school for Liberation," a Marxist adult education institution housed at 124 West 124th Street that opened in March of 1952. At Frederick Douglass, Lorraine taught "public speaking for progressives" and gave presentations such as "Negro History in Poetry and Prose."[18] But she also had to listen, learn from, and attend to the concerns of her pupils, working people who shared her race but not her circumstance. That year, Lorraine also moved into various apartments in Harlem: In March, 499 West 130th Street. By July, she shared an apartment with Claudia Jones at 504 West 143rd Street, unit 6A. At the end of the year, she moved to a place in the Bronx, 820 West 180th Street, apartment 41, for a short time. Lorraine was physically and intellectually immersed in Black New York.

In Harlem, Lorraine also found a community of artists who had devoted themselves to serving their communities in both political organizing and creative production. And she grew as an artist in Harlem just as she grew as a thinker and an activist. Lorraine befriended South Carolinian actress Alice Childress, who was sixteen years her senior. Childress was a frequent contributor to *Freedom* and both an actress and a playwright. Childress brought Lorraine into the Black theater world of New York. For example, they wrote a pageant together for the Freedom Negro History Festival in 1952, which was narrated by Harry Belafonte, playwright Douglas Turner Ward, Sidney Poitier, and novelist John Oliver Killens.

Hailing from South Carolina, Alice Childress had herself come into the world of Black New York through the American Negro Theater, which was the product of the WPA-sponsored Federal Negro Theater and the Communist Party–affiliated Rose McClendon Players. A cooperative, the American Negro Theater survived for eleven years before buckling under financial pressure. By the time Lorraine came to New York, the theater was almost defunct, but what is important is that she arrived into an established theater community that included Childress and her husband, Alvin, and also Poitier, Ruby Dee, Harry Belafonte, Isabel Sanford, Helen Martin, and many more. They gave her a taste of what a Black theatrical life could be, and some of them would eventually be instrumental to Lorraine's success as a playwright.

Lorraine's unpublished experimental writing in the early 1950s reveals the ways in which she saw herself as both part of an activist community and part of an intellectual and artistic tradition, specifically a Black tradition. Black history and her milieu made their way into her imagination, and her imagination revealed her commitments. In a short story written in 1950, she riffed upon Ralph Ellison's classic 1948 essay, "Harlem Is Nowhere," in which he asserted that the world of Harlem was a sort of no-man's-land, one in which the imagination and artistic sensibilities of migrants to the North were held captive by the social discrimination of Harlem. Harlem was a landscape that didn't match up with folkways learned on plantations, according to Ellison. What and how they'd learned to navigate down home, wasn't quite right for up North. Lorraine imagined one of those migrants of whom Ellison wrote, and wrote a story about him. In the process, Lorraine troubled Ellison's focus and formulation.

Lorraine imagined a Georgia-born Black soldier returning to the United States from World War II battlefields in Europe with an eye missing. Rather than going home, he goes to Harlem, looking for something different from what he's known: "Suddenly, outside the train window there's New York. Sunshine on bridges and skyscrapers. Sunshine. Different from Georgia sunshine, different from deep inside him where he can still see other sunshine, something through the thin, unhappy trees of a German forest."[19]

Lorraine's critical response to Ellison is found in her character's voice. She has him think, in free indirect discourse: "The soldier came up out of the subway with his friend and . . . Harlem is everywhere." Then she scratched that out and wrote, "Everywhere there is— Harlem." Rather than Ellison's "Harlem is nowhere," for Lorraine's character Harlem is found everywhere and encompasses wholeness of Blackness. All the beauty of Blackness can be found in Harlem, according to her protagonist. He goes on, "I am home man . . . no stuff. I hear Dinah Washington and see Joe Louis' picture in a window."[20]

Lorraine appears to have been struggling with Ellison's sympathetic portrayal of migrants, not because of its sympathy, which she shared, but rather because of what he believed racism had made of them. Ellison wrote,

In relation to their Southern background, the cultural history of Negroes in the North reads like the legend of some tragic people out of mythology, a people that aspired to escape from its own unhappy homeland to the apparent peace of a distant mountain, but that, in migrating, made some fatal error of judgment and fell into a great chasm of mazelike passages that promise ever to lead to the mountain but end ever against a wall. Not that a Negro is worse off in the North than in the South, but that in the North he surrenders and does not replace certain important supports to his personality.[21]

For Ellison, being displaced from down home meant that the migrants' survival techniques went from heroic to tragic, or as Ellison put it, that to which "Faulkner refers as endurance" became "mere swagger."[22] Lorraine chose instead to focus not upon the limitations of Black folks' skill at navigating the white folks up North, but the everywhereness of white supremacy, even up in Harlem. To make this point clearly, her soldier is shot and killed by police:

"You"
Sharp, clipped fast . . . a white man's voice.
Danger. Hatred. Georgia hatred. Georgia woods and Georgia sun.
Why? Where did they come from.
"You there . . . put your hands up."
And then the sound in the Harlem night. Gunshot. Lynchshot.[23]

The story ends awkwardly. There is a gesture toward the ugliness of McCarthyism: a witness to the killing is warned by police that he should not go to a communist meeting. With this strange conclusion Lorraine tried to (unsuccessfully) weave together the Red Scare and the Jim Crow police state that ensured, despite the promises of the North, Georgia was everywhere.

These scribblings of Lorraine's were done before Ellison's classic novel *Invisible Man* had been published, a vast and profound text that included a powerful indictment of white communists and their patronizingly romantic view of Black people. However, Ellison had already distanced himself from the Communist Party when he wrote "Harlem Is Nowhere." At first he rejected communism, because it had lost a rigorous analysis of class relations and was trying too hard to fit into the American mainstream. Later, he moved toward political liberalism as an aesthetic ideal and virtue. Lorraine, in contrast, unflinchingly embraced the party. Perhaps that was part of her quibble with Ellison. But her troubling of his essay, at least as I read it, is less rooted in communism than it is invested in a more impassioned confrontation with white racism, a resistance to the arbiters of aesthetics who might objectively evaluate "quality" without always attending to inequality. Her point was this: white supremacy was terrible and ubiquitous. Period. There was no need to equivocate or blame its victims.

Lorraine blended the tradition of Black literature and resistance with her radical politics in these early works. However, she consistently refused to see race merely as a form of class oppression, or Black people as merely the lumpen, a sector of the proletariat of America. Racism was, to her, a monster of its own that must be confronted.

Confrontation had degrees, however. It was one thing to protest or to write protest literature and articles. It was another to step into the line of sight of the powers that be. Though Lorraine had come from a family that challenged the color line, they had done so while remaining hewn to patriotic ideals of American liberal democracy and capitalism. In the early 1950s, however, she stepped boldly onto another path. She had to know it was risky. Her mentors Du Bois and Paul Robeson were prime targets within an intellectual and political community of Black socialists and communists who were under surveillance. Being a communist wasn't strange back then. It didn't have the sting of revulsion attached to it that one often senses today. But it was, in the United States of the early 1950s, most certainly an identity that made you vulnerable to steady attack from the powerful. In 1951, Du Bois had circulated a petition protesting nuclear weapons, and in response he was arrested and indicted for being an agent of the Soviet Union. As a result of the trial, he became a pariah in many circles. At the time when Lorraine sat before him as a student, he was so stigmatized that he found himself struggling to buy groceries. And in 1952, his passport was revoked. The State Department claimed they took it because they could not authorize him to attend a peace conference in Canada, but it had the effect of limiting his connection and political influence and potentially his moving abroad.

Paul Robeson's passport had been revoked even earlier, in 1950, the year Lorraine had arrived in New York. The revocation was dramatic. Robeson, a global performer, attempted to renew his passport in order to work. Before granting him the new passport, the State Department requested that he sign an affidavit declaring that he was not a member of the Communist Party and that he was loyal to the United States. Robeson refused to do so. He was thereafter denied a passport for eight years.

As a result of Robeson being denied the right to travel abroad, Lorraine was asked to go as his representative to the Inter-American Peace Conference in Montevideo, Uruguay, in March of 1952. The conference, a communist gathering, raised concerns across the Americas. It had been originally planned for Buenos Aires, Argentina, then Brazil, and then Chile, where it was formally banned by the government. It was finally set for Uruguay. Many prospective delegates were refused visas and passports and otherwise prevented from attending. Lorraine slyly obtained a passport under the pretense that she was going to be vacationing in Europe.

The answer to the question why Lorraine was chosen as a representative for Robeson can be found in who she had shown herself to be in just under two years' time: a diligent student, a worker, a laborer for the cause of freedom, and also an artist like Robeson. She was, in a sense, his and his friend Du Bois's political daughter. She could be Robeson's proxy. As she was wont to do with meaningful events in her life, Lorraine wrote a fictional vignette about the trip. In it, a wife has been banned from travel because of her activism, but she gets her husband to travel to South America for a peace conference in her stead. In Lorraine's story, a self-possessed young woman is at the vanguard, not the proxy.

Lorraine accepted the responsibility granted by Robeson, and was one of five US delegates at the 280-delegate conference. The American delegation consisted of Angel Torres, a Puerto Rican seaman; a Mrs. Schwartz of Chicago; Mary Russak of the New York Labor Conference for Peace; and Elmer Bendiner of the National Guardian. All of them were affiliated in some way with communist peace organizations. Other delegates came from Venezuela, Argentina, Puerto Rico, Chile, and Colombia, in addition to local organizers from Uruguay.

The gathering began secretively because Uruguay, like the previous countries from which it had been canceled, also declared it illegal. The subterfuge consisted of delegates pretending they were having parties by playing loud music and dancing outdoors. Whenever they retreated indoors, they delivered conference papers. On Lorraine's first full day of the conference, she attended a women's meeting. She sat in the audience and listened to an address by a former woman deputy of the Uruguayan parliament. After the address ended there was some communication in Spanish that Lorraine didn't understand. The crowd applauded, although Lorraine didn't know what for. A woman approached her and said, in English, that Lorraine had been elected as one of the honored women who should sit on the presidium and speak. Stunned, Lorraine stepped up to deliver her report, with the help of a translator. Midway through, she was interrupted by a police officer who strode into the room. The women quickly pretended that they were having a prissy ladies' tea. Once he left, and the coast was clear, Lorraine finished her report. At its conclusion a Brazilian woman brought her a bouquet of red carnations. Lorraine was deeply moved. She thought of the women who had been jailed and terrorized in the US for their activism, she thought of her people suffering, and she was honored to be selected, the sole Black American woman at the conference, to represent them all.

As the sessions were being held indoors, local protestors took to the streets to object to the government prohibition against the conference. Dockworkers, trade unionists, and journalists demanded a repeal of the ban. A delegation appeared before the Department of State in Montevideo and won a permit to hold the conference on the condition that no nation, and by this they meant the United States, be attacked by name.

After this victory, five thousand people took to the plaza. It was nighttime, but a platform at the center of the plaza was lit by floodlights. Lorraine stepped up on the platform and played a tape of Paul Robeson's voice greeting the delegates, and the crowd cheered. Afterward, Lorraine was embraced and told repeatedly that Latin Americans stood in solidarity with Black Americans.

Lorraine found common ground there, and not just on the question of peace. She met Uruguayan activists who opposed racial discrimination and exclusion in their country. Later, in a written newspaper report of her time in Uruguay, she recounted marching in tandem with other young people of the Americas. Lorraine felt her persistent anger at police officers rise up in Uruguay as it often did in the States, but she walked with a group that was fighting back against the cops' bullying ways. And that thrilled her. Armed with a hopefulness about the possibilities of struggle, she said, "We began to walk, I shall never know where so many young people came from and of course there were police along the streets with their long swords at their sides and their arms crossed and their faces drawn into those long sober expressions peculiar to police all over the world—and these young people linked my arms with theirs and we began to walk four abreast through the streets of Montevideo."[24] They sang, and Lorraine, with a young Argentinian man on her right and a young Brazilian man on her left, felt the pulse of the future, their linked fate pumping through linked arms.

It was a stark contrast to the United States, a place where, as she described, so many young men were turned into "monsters" in service to the US military. The gathering itself wasn't huge, but it felt that way to Lorraine. Rather than the hodgepodge of protestors on corners in the Village, she was among thousands singing for freedom.

Before Lorraine left the States for South America, the Montevideo conference had been declared illegal by the US State Department. Lorraine knew that by attending she would put herself more directly in the path of surveillance and judgment from the US government. Several months after her triumphant return, in July of 1952, a representative of the State Department came to her mother's home and took Lorraine's passport away.[25] She'd sit, the following year, at Du Bois's knee at the Jefferson School of Social Science. Teacher and student were condemned by the state. And the FBI began their surveillance of her.

The record the government kept of Lorraine in the following years was one of both visibility and invisibility. They would look for everything, and see very little.

CHAPTER FOUR

Bobby

I do wish we were closer in some matters so that there
were no aspects of my problems that we could not share.
[. . .] We are really terribly different kinds of people.[1]

—Lorraine to Bobby

IN A LETTER TO HER FRIEND EDYTHE, Lorraine wrote about her life
in New York:

> See only foreign movies, no plays hardly, attend meetings al-
> most every night, sing in a chorus, eat all the foreign foods in
> N.Y., go for long walks in Harlem and talk to my people about
> everything on the streets, usher at rallies, make street corner
> speeches in Harlem and sometimes make it up to the country
> on Sundays. [. . .] Write stories and articles for all the little
> journals of the working class around. Supposed to get married
> about September.[2]

I have thought about that last sentence: "Supposed to get married." It might just be that Lorraine didn't go for conventional "feminine" frivolousness, and for that reason it sounds flip. Maybe they'd
talked about her betrothed, Robert Nemiroff—or as she called him,
Bobby—many times before, and this was just quick information. Perhaps she was afraid to tell Edythe, so she wrote like she was ripping
off a Band-Aid. Or maybe Lorraine was ambivalent.

Lorraine and Bobby met early in 1952 at a protest against racially discriminatory hiring practices at New York University. He
was a graduate student there. Bobby was just under a year older than

60

Lorraine, Jewish, and a native New Yorker. They were different from one another. But both were, as Lorraine's friend Douglas Turner Ward would describe it, on the rebound. Bobby had been briefly married before. Lorraine had been engaged to a "Harlem slickster" named Roosevelt "Rosie" Jackson. Rosie was gorgeous, a leader of the Labor Youth League, urbane, and very working class—of the milieu Lorraine admired. But in addition to all those appealing traits, Rosie was enamored of all the bourgeois trappings that Lorraine had put behind her. More devastating, Rosie became a heroin junkie, and his addict's profligacy got Lorraine evicted from her Harlem apartment. So that ended that.

When Bobby came around, different as he was from her ideal, and from her, he and Lorraine did share a great deal: they were both members of the radical left, intellectuals, and artists. Bobby would become something much more than just her husband. He was a friend until her death, a caretaker, one who encouraged and facilitated her writing, and after her death the one who ensured her legacy.

Lorraine wasn't nearly as sure about Bobby as he was about her that first year they were dating. She was honest about it. In a letter, written the day after Christmas in 1952 from her family home in Chicago, however, she declared her love for him. And her intentions:

> My Dear Bob,
>
> Once again I wrote you a very long letter—the important simple things which it said were that I have finally admitted to myself I *do* love you, you wide-eyed immature un-sophisticated revolutionary.

She claimed to have thrown away that sentimental piece in favor of "this breezy little missle [*sic*]."[3]

The letter proceeds oddly and yet sweetly into a list of assertions about her life, and his, and their relationship. About her work she said:

1. I am a writer. I am going to write.
2. I am going to become a writer.

3. Any real contribution I can make to the movement can
   only be the result of a disciplined life. I am going to
   institute discipline in my life.
4. I can paint. I am going to paint.
The END[4]

The declarations that she already is a writer, is going to write, and
will become a writer are at once, it seems, a literal fact (she had begun publishing here and there) and a statement about both her ambition and her identity. In contrast, while she asserts that she can paint
and is going to paint, she doesn't call herself a painter. It's not even
clear whether "I can paint" is a declaration of skill or simply a statement that nothing is keeping her from doing something she loves.

But her weakness on both matters and more, by her own judgment, was a lack of discipline. Lorraine was restless, seeking, searching, and interested in dozens of things. She was always doing, never
lazy or indulgent, but not disciplined. At least not yet.

Following her statement about vocations, she shared her feelings
about Bobby. She declared her love for him, "problems be damned,"
and her need for him. They would, she said, struggle together. He
is what she wanted in a man. The words are humorous, sweet, and
clinical at once. She sounds removed but convinced:

> My sincerest political opinion is that we have reached a point
> in a truly beautiful relationship—where it may become the
> fullest kind of relationship between a man and a woman. I
> want it that way (stop blushing).
> . . . That it is possible that our sharing a life together would be
> a rather beautiful thing.
> . . . Pilar was wrong—the earth doesn't "move."
> The END[5]

Lorraine moved rather matter-of-factly through the case for their
union. She said she loved him; there were problems, but she believed
in the possibility of fulfillment and beauty. And yet she concluded
with a reference to the characters in Ernest Hemingway's novel
For Whom the Bell Tolls. In the relevant scene, Hemingway's two

protagonists, Robert and Maria, have just made love for the first time. They encounter their friend Pilar, who insists upon knowing "how it was." Maria finally responds, under pressure, by saying that "the earth moved." Pilar is at once mystified and expert, declaring that the "earth moves" only three times in a person's life.

Lorraine made a joke of the fact that their intimacy wasn't one that made the earth move, at least for her. Yet she believed a life together would be a beautiful thing. She might have been honest to a fault, or felt a bit of bittersweetness about the whole thing, or was just bitingly teasing. In any case, their love affair proceeded. It was a union that in a sense represented the avant-garde of a particular time and place. They were left-wing bohemians, an interracial couple dedicated to radical social transformation who, after Lorraine moved out of Harlem, settled in Greenwich Village, made art, and attended protests.

They scheduled their wedding for earlier than Lorraine anticipated in her letter to Edythe. It was held on June 20 in Lorraine's hometown. The *Chicago Defender* reported gleefully on the marriage of a princess of the Negro elite with a photograph of a grinning and gorgeous Lorraine. But what ought to have been a joyful occasion was overcast by tragedy. In the days leading up to their wedding, Lorraine and Bobby learned that Julius and Ethel Rosenberg, two Jewish American communists who were convicted of being spies for the Soviet Union, had exhausted all their appeals and were sentenced to death. The Rosenberg case had become an important cause for the Left, a sign of how far the anticommunist hysteria would go. The answer was, so far that circumstantial evidence would condemn the parents of young children to death. President Eisenhower made a statement, along with his refusal to grant the clemency that thousands across the world begged for. He said, "I can only say that, by immeasurably increasing the chances of atomic war, the Rosenbergs may have condemned to death tens of millions of innocent people all over the world. The execution of two human beings is a grave matter. But even graver is the thought of the millions of dead whose deaths may be directly attributable to what these spies have done."[6]

On the afternoon of Saturday, June 19, Lorraine and Bobby picketed in front of the federal courthouse in Chicago for the Rosenbergs.

Julius was executed that night at 8 p.m. He died after one shock in the electric chair. Ethel was next. They electrocuted her once, twice, three times. But her heart was still beating. The executioner administered two more shocks. Smoke rose above her head and through her ears and nostrils. Five shocks, and she was finally dead.[7] Lorraine was devastated. She wrote:

> We had come to a wedding. We had come to Chicago to lose our selves in the Bridal Song. And then there were those moments when the news came. And we spoke of it quietly to one another—our voices soft under the discussion of where the cake would be placed and when the photographers would arrive. [. . .] Our voices above the champagne glasses, our eyes questioning one another between the fresh fragrant flowers in their gleaming pots on the coffee tables of the wedding house, festive flowers. The Chicago heat in the vast living room suddenly overpowering the senses, some grim terrible fire within suddenly making it more awful, more stifling—the desire to fling the glass into the flowers, to thrust one's arms into the air and run out of the house screaming at ones country men to come down out of the apartments, down from the houses, to get up from the television sets, from the dinner tables. [. . .] The bride sits a moment in a corner alone to herself—she thinks
>
> And what shall I say to my children? And how shall I explain such a thing to them?[8]

Lorraine wouldn't have children and didn't appear to want them. But she mourned the world and felt the shame of celebrating in the midst of such heartbreak. One can't help but think about the Rosenberg children, ages six and ten, orphaned by the hysterics of the Cold War. Lorraine wondered, what did the bride and groom owe them and others of their generation?

Bobby described the day succinctly, yet also poignantly: "We spent Saturday night picketing the courthouse in Chicago and we were married on Sunday . . . and they were executed Saturday night. And we had no heart for the wedding."[9]

But they retained their heart for art and politics. Lorraine resigned from *Freedom* but continued to write and organize locally with the same sense of passion. Lorraine's mother, who had written angrily the prior year that she was worried and insisted that Lorraine must come home, was likely assuaged that Lorraine was finally a married lady. Respectable.

To make a living, Lorraine occasionally worked as a waitress at the restaurant owned by Bobby's parents, for whom she felt great affection (his mother was described by the FBI as fanatical communist), and took a variety of other jobs, mostly unsatisfying. The shortest was a four-day stint at a department store. She quit because the women working the floor were ordered about with a ringing bell. And for six months she put tags on fur coats in a clothing shop. Lorraine's barely remunerative work as a member of the Left intelligentsia also continued. In 1954, she became an associate editor for the pocket-sized youth magazine *New Challenge*. A publication of the Labor Youth League, *New Challenge* featured punchy articles and eye-catching covers. Bobby also wrote for them, under the pseudonym Bob Rolfe. In standard McCarthy era fare, *New Challenge* was publicly attacked in a pamphlet released by the right-wing publication *The New Counterattack*. The authors accused *New Challenge* of corrupting American youth and referenced Lorraine by name. She was on the radar of conservatives, even as a struggling young artist in New York. But she wouldn't stop.

For Black American political life, 1954 was a watershed year, though Lorraine wasn't entirely in step with the rest of Black America. In May, the US Supreme Court decided *Brown v. Board of Education*. The decision declared mandatory public school segregation unconstitutional and provided an important impetus to the civil rights movement and its militant integrationists. Lorraine's mind was elsewhere. Several weeks before the opinion was reached, Lorraine was involved in activism to support Jacobo Árbenz de Guzmán, the democratically elected socialist president of Guatemala. But by June, Árbenz would be ousted by a US-supported coup d'etat.

Earlier in 1954, Lorraine wrote publicly about a trial, though not about *Brown*. It was in a letter to the *Reporter* magazine regarding the trial of Jomo Kenyatta. Kenyatta, an independence movement leader in Kenya, had been arrested in October of 1952 for being affiliated with the Mau Maus, a group of radical anticolonialists who advocated armed revolution. Though Kenyatta was not in fact affiliated with the Mau Maus, he was sentenced by the colonial courts to seven years at hard labor. His subsequent appeal was denied.

Lorraine's letter was a response to a previously published article that described Africans as backward and underdeveloped, and attributed the actions of the Mau Maus and Kenyatta to that condition. Lorraine asserted that attributing cultural deficiency to the Mau Mau and Africans generally was a red herring intended to distract from the primary issue, which was "stark, brutal colonialism in one of its most ruthless expressions." The previous author's failure to acknowledge the details of British repression and domination, "the mass arrests of Africans; the destruction of entire villages; executions of great numbers of persons and various other methods of 'retaliation' which have even caused Englishmen to cry for investigation from the floor of parliament," was to Lorraine a travesty.[10] She went on to defend Kenyatta's intellect and courage. In conclusion, Lorraine spoke specifically as a Black American woman who saw that the right side of the cause must be "with the courageous and heroic Black African men and women of Kenya and their great leader, Jomo Kenyatta."[11]

Lorraine claimed that a fundamental connection existed between the oppressed across the globe, and specifically between those of African descent wherever they were in the diaspora. She spoke in this moment not only as the pupil of Du Bois and of her uncle, Leo Hansberry, but also as a child of the expansive 1940s, as James Forman described it, one who had not been chastened by the repression of the Cold War. Lorraine's international concerns were not entirely unique. Black newspapers also reported on the trial of Kenyatta, though the coverage paled in comparison to the *Brown* case. The content of Lorraine's letter was a sign of her political orientation and where her primary attention lay, even as Black politics were heating up at home. Just two days before Lorraine's twenty-fourth birthday the *Brown* ruling was front page news, in all American newspapers, Black and mainstream. But she didn't have much to say about it. Of course, being a native of Chicago, Lorraine was well aware that even without segregation by law, segregation in fact could be quite violently maintained. She almost certainly anticipated the massive resistance that followed the *Brown* ruling. But still, the case signaled a sea change, a new terrain on which her generation's organizing would unfold. It would be a case that mattered for her work, though she wasn't particularly focused upon it at the time. In truth, Lorraine's politics were increasingly on the margins of the Black political mainstream. The major civil rights organizations had largely separated themselves from the radical left in the late 1940s in the fever of postwar liberalism, symbolically and literally evidenced by Du Bois's excommunication from the NAACP, an organization he cofounded and for which he was once a key figure. Lorraine's political labors as a young adult had grown entirely within the structures of the Far Left, not the civil rights mainstream middle. For example, in a 1954 rally to restore Robeson's passport, she delivered a speech that at once reflected his influence on her own work and life as an artist and also the internationalist political vision she embraced. In the speech, she made clear that she believed the US government had placed itself in opposition to the cause of freedom and liberty. This perspective encouraged her to continuously keep abreast of developments across the globe, to resist Western chauvinism, and to maintain a global set of politics.

In describing Robeson, she said,

> This man is an American citizen, his forbearers fought tyranny on three continents, so that he might draw breath as a free being. His is a sacred heritage. When you infringe on his liberty you tamper with the labor and lives of generations of freedom seekers. We charge you with this responsibility. [. . .] We demand that [. . .] he be permitted once again to travel to the capitols and villages of the world so that his presence and his art and his humanity will again refresh the peoples of other lands and remind them that there remains still in this America of ours a people of dignity and courage and decency.[12]

While still beloved by audiences, Robeson was, like his dear friend Du Bois, out of favor with the major civil rights organizations. But for Lorraine, he was still a beacon on a global stage. In the same gathering, speakers decried South African apartheid, which they accurately charged was modeled on US segregation, and the McCarran

Act, which targeted "subversives" like them. Hers was a community that insisted upon fighting against unjust exploitation and economic domination and for racial justice all over the world as well as at home. They didn't separate these concerns. Perhaps this is why it took some time for the change in US politics to come to the fore of Lorraine's concerns. Her gaze was global.

In the meantime, she had a full, though unsettling social and political life. In the summer of 1954 she took on a job at a multiracial communist summer camp called Camp Unity in upstate New York. Camp Unity, founded in 1927 and self-described as the "first proletarian summer colony," was located in Wingdale, New York. A good deal of its appeal was due to its event programming each summer. Lorraine was director of the outdoor lawn program and responsible for organizing musical and theatrical performances. Her friend Alice Childress served as the director of drama, and other friends and acquaintances were fellow employees or guests. It should have been a task for which she was perfectly suited. But Lorraine's restlessness returned. And with it came depression.

She wrote to Robert:

> My Own Dear Husband,
>   I am sitting here in this miserable little bungalow, in this miserable camp that I once loved so much, feeling cold, useless, frustrated, helpless, disillusioned, angry and tired. The week past that I spoke to you about was the height of all those things to the point where I didn't care too much a couple of times whether or not I woke mornings.[13]

She recovered in her own letter, at least in word, from such depths of sadness by focusing on the beauty around her. She meditated on the land: "hills, the trees, sunrise and sunset—the lake the moon and the stars / summer clouds—the poets have been right in these centuries darling, even in its astounding imperfection this earth of ours is magnificent."[14]

She then moved on to trifles: her frustration about the finances of the camp and that it means that some staff will be fired (and how it angered her to be asked to do the dirty work of dismissing them). In contrast to her irritation with people, nature almost seems medicinal in her account: a balm that doesn't remove her suffering but gives her some refuge. It is somewhat ironic, however, that at this place called Camp Unity that it wasn't other people but rather inanimate living things that eased her suffering, at least a little bit.

In another letter written that summer, she complained vigorously to Bobby about the disorganization of the camp and the many failures of her coworkers. Lorraine's hypercritical and impassioned complaints and her fussiness, depression, and aestheticism ebbed and flowed. An irrepressible confidence in her own intellect always stood alongside, and in dramatic contrast to, her uncanny ability to be deeply self-critical. And the depression remained. She wrote: "A couple of days I have been feeling so miserable that I didn't want to do anything but build myself a tree house and forget it. You know what I mean—there are times when you are sure that peace in symphonies, and grass and sunlight and mountains is not to be found in life—and honey that is a desperate feeling."[15]

And yet, she left the countryside. Sometime that summer she went from Unity back to the city: not to New York but to Chicago. Lorraine and Robert spent most of the summer of 1954 apart, her handful of letters my sole evidence of their partnership in those days. In September, Lorraine wrote Bobby from Chicago, addressing him playfully as "Hello Bookie," but between the lines were sadness, tension, and also a persistent depression. Her restlessness had completely overtaken her mood by then: "I am still a little nervous, smoking too much and remarkably restless and fidgety as I indicated on the telephone. I don't know what the hell is wrong *with* me. I haven't called a single friend—my mother has been urging me to, But I dread seeing people—I am not being dramatic this time, I dread it something fierce."[16]

Her words are ones of yearning, for him, but also of ambivalence. She is wanting for something they don't have, and she's not afraid to say so. But at the same time she is passionately attached to him. He is her confidant, intimate, and friend.

She writes, "I do wish we were closer in some matters so that there were no aspects of my problems that we could not share— and I get this is not the case. We are really terribly different kinds of people." In one sentence, she tells Bobby she desires him; in another, she confesses she is troubled by things in their marriage.

And then, Lorraine pivots suddenly from the difficulty in their relationship to the problems in her writing, which seemed to be an easier terrain for connecting, and an assessment of her own work ethic:

> I have re-read my play a couple times to my disgust. Had a new idea—a libretto. John Henry—"An original American folk opera" By Serge Hovey (sp) Libretto by Lorraine etc.
>
> This of course is why I don't produce a goddamned thing— I am too full of dreams! I have quietly resolved—yes I will piddle around with a Libretto after My play is finished—my novel is well under way—I mean it! And according to that schedule and God knows what else between—it should take me 3 years to get around to the research—! Of course it will take Serge 3 years to really learn anything about Negro music.
>
> And then of course there is this tendency towards distraction—Lorraine the Actress . . . Lorraine the journalist, etc.[17]

Her deep confidence is amusing and fascinating. For example, she judges how long it would take noted composer Serge Hovey to learn something or "anything" about Negro music, and yet she has an unfailing self-criticism about her own work as an artist. The vacillating, one surmises, is what made space for what would eventually be such a bold artistry, and yet one that was also sensitive and even tender.

The letter reveals another side of her personality. She was a keen and sensitive reader, one for whom books were an aid for self-recognition. And at that moment, what she was reading was especially self-referential. She wrote, "I have been re-reading 'You can't go home again' by Thomas Wolfe. There are things to be said for that boy! And some rather crushing things to be said against him, I'm afraid (with regard to the standard 3 Negroes, Jews and Woman). Anyhow it is especially fitting that I am reading it just now. I will tell you about it all frightfully profound I assure you—Don't you wish rather desperately that your wife was a little less full of horse manure?"[18]

Beyond her endearing self-deprecation, these words illuminate

Lorraine's deepest aspirations, anxieties, and emotions. The Wolfe novel is one about a celebrated writer who returns home to find that the community that he depicted in his most recent novel is unhappy with how they have been cast. They reject the writer for the way he has stripped them down and exposed their warts. He is forced to leave home again. The writer seeks his purpose in various corners of the globe and finally gives up and returns to the United States. Despite Wolfe's flatfooted treatment of others, the "Negroes, Jews and Woman," the story resonated with Lorraine. She was raised with the precept that one must never betray the race or the family. And yet, in her persistent habit of observation and dissection, she was finding things about the family worthy of examination and criticism of the sort that would of course provide useful literary fodder. She just had to work up the gumption to use it.

Of particular irritation to her was her sister's husband, Vincent Tubbs, whose politics she abhorred. She especially bristled at his criticisms of Paul Robeson's "failure to act as a good American."[19] Tubbs was a real American-type American, not unlike her father, Carl. Lorraine excitedly took him on in political debate. She reported to Robert with great exasperation that despite her brother-in-law having been a war correspondent and traveling in Africa, Europe, and Asia, he had the nerve to repeat the cliché "This is the greatest country in the world" without any historical reflection or criticism.

In her jousting with Vincent, who would eventually become the president of the Publicists Guild of America, and therefore the first Black man to head a Hollywood film union and the first Black publicist at Warner Brothers, she admitted that she had likely killed any possibility that Vincent might help her be hired at a newspaper. Yet, after their fight, she was more self-satisfied than anything. While generally frustrated that her family hadn't been discussing politics at all, Lorraine relished confronting and eviscerating Tubbs's uncritical patriotism and patriarchal posture.

And yet, her correspondence with her sister, Mamie, and Vincent throughout the 1950s was much more often tender and warm than not. She told them about her work; they encouraged her to avoid anyone who would exploit her and anything that would create too much distraction. They kept Lorraine abreast of their brother

Perry's frequent misadventures and their mother's health and well-being. Lorraine often wanted to hear from them, and she sent them clippings, hoping that they would be proud of her. In short, like most families, the relations were complicated yet loving.

That fall, Lorraine returned from Chicago to the bustle of New York life. While politics were a central part of her day-to-day living, she enjoyed a full counterculture Manhattan life. Jazz impresario Art D'Lugoff remembered those days with Lorraine fondly, particularly the way she helped him put together early shows. He said, "Lorraine wrote my first leaflets, typed them up, and took them around to the coffeehouses. I got to know her husband, Bob Nemiroff, at NYU. They became close friends of mine, and I worked with her at her in-laws' restaurant—called Potpourri, on Washington Place. . . . Lorraine and I waited and bused tables."[20]

This is a life we've seen before. Not so much that it is a cliché, but familiar enough that we can imagine it. Midcentury interracial couple, activists, bohemian, artistic—it falls apart, but something remarkable always comes of it: brilliant children or great art. That's how the story goes. What lies underneath is always more particular and complicated. Lorraine and Bobby thought together, and also separately. In either case, her genius overtook the substance of the relationship. It was its center. He worked to keep her on course, chastised her when she was distracted, pushed her. She criticized him too, but that was on matters of personality, not his music or writing.

Feminist criticism has taught us that life for men artists is usually different from life for women artists. Men artists have often had an architecture of support behind them: people labor and resources. In contrast, women artists have often snatched at time and space between a legion of responsibilities. That wasn't Lorraine's fate. While indeed she faced racism and sexism and patriarchy, Robert, as Lorraine's provider, interlocutor, and facilitator, gave her a foundation that few women artists had.

She tried to write, but didn't really get anywhere. On the other hand, Alice Childress was at work on a play that would have bearing on Lorraine's future. Childress was already a role model for Lorraine in some sense. She'd had three plays produced. The first was a one-act play she'd starred in, titled *Florence,* about the thoughts and experiences of a Black woman domestic. That was in 1949. Then, in 1950, she wrote an adaptation of Langston Hughes's short stories *Simple Speaks His Mind*, which was produced in Harlem, and, in 1952, a work titled *Gold Through the Trees*.

Trouble in Mind was Childress's new work, its title borrowed from a blues standard. The play itself was about a play within a play. In it, the characters' efforts to put up an antilynching production are hampered by tension between the Black actors and the white director. The theme of racism, particularly in the world of theater, was sharply captured. The writer John Oliver Killens described *Trouble in Mind* as follows: "In this play Childress demonstrated a talent and ability to write humor that had social impact. Even though one laughed throughout the entire presentation, there was, inescapably, the understanding that . . . one was having an undeniably emotional and profoundly intellectual experience."[21]

The play debuted off-Broadway in November of 1955. It was a tense year. Emmett Till had been murdered that August. The Montgomery bus boycott began on December 5. And on December 7, Claudia Jones, a powerful presence in the world of the New York Black Left, who had been held in detention centers and prisons off and on since 1948, was deported. Three hundred fifty people gathered at Harlem's historic Hotel Theresa to honor and thank Jones before her departure.

In *Trouble in Mind*, Childress's indictment of racism, and specifically racism in the theater world, was both timely and well received. And yet, when she was offered the opportunity to have the play produced on Broadway, Childress declined. The changes the producers sought would have muted criticism of white figures in the theater industry.

Her refusal to change the message of *Trouble in Mind* left the door open for Lorraine to become the first Black woman playwright to have her work produced on Broadway. But one wonders too, what did Lorraine take from this moment of deportation, death, and the demand to compromise? And also, what hope did she glean from the promise of resistance that had appeared in Montgomery?

She'd soon have the time and space to explore such questions.

Bobby had a job in promotions at Avon Books. But he was a

songwriter too. In early 1956, he and Burt D'Lugoff, Art's brother, came up with the idea to use the music of a song frequently sung by Black dockworkers on the Georgia Sea Islands and match it with pop love-song words. They designed their composition to fit into the current calypso craze, a fantasy-driven flurry of watered-down versions of Trinidadian music. They titled it "Cindy, Oh Cindy." The song was a hit; first for Vince Martin and then for the heartthrob Eddie Fisher. Suddenly the struggling artists Bobby and Lorraine had a great deal of royalties money.

"Pay me my money down," the lyrics of the dockworker song, were originally sung to the owners and investors. Now, in "Cindy, Oh Cindy," the money went not to laborers but at least to someone who politically cast herself with them. The money was earned through the fantasy image of Trinidad, shortly after Lorraine's Trinidadian friend Claudia Jones was deported to England (because Trinidad wouldn't accept her). It was a strange intersection of race, politics, entertainment, and consumption. But in the middle of all that, Lorraine finally had time and resources to simply write. She searched for stories to tell, tried and failed, and read, and tried.

Lorraine returned to Chicago in the summer of 1956. The letters to Robert this time, frankly, were more sad. In one from June 29, she describes tending to her sick mother and then intimates their brokenness: "Every one asks about you. I have told them nothing. It is all very difficult."[22]

Despite what is suggested—a distance and perhaps an ending, to their marriage—he was still her interlocutor. She brought ideas to him. About her hometown, which she continued to see with new eyes, she wrote: "Chicago continues [to] fascinate, frighten, charm and offend me. It is so much prettier than New York. And so proud of its provincialness. There are no shows at all running—save summer stock. People—not just Negroes—but the radio commentators; the papers, remain as aggressively ignorant as I left them eight years ago."[23]

Lorraine was out of sorts, frustrated by Chicago's lack of cosmopolitanism, frustrated by life. We shouldn't read her ever-ready hyperbole as a lack of love for the city, but more as a sense of rudderlessness and isolation. She described the vagaries of her life to

Robert, one about an encounter with two Chinese women about literature and the benefits of Maoism that made her feel a bit less alone, a bit more like her New York self.

Chatter. Politics. She was Robert's wife, whatever the state of their relationship. They were still intellectual companions. He provided the money that was necessary for her to explore her writing. Whatever the relationship had become, it is clear she was feeling even more alone than usual. The words she wrote to herself were even more revealing on that count than those to Robert. In her diary for October 19, 1956, she writes:

> Days like these are the worst again. Yesterday I rose at eight and brushed my hair and rushed out to the car before I should get a ticket. I returned and watched Robert wash and shower and shave and listen to disk jockeys at that strange hour. . . . Then I vacuumed the rug and the corner of the house where the dog hair collects in pounds between times when I am finally moved to clean. . . . And then I scrubbed, not well at all, the bathroom and the kitchen and spread paper on the floor. . . . I did not answer the telephone, except once before ten thirty, that was Joan about an apartment[24] . . . and then I read Simone in frustration again and slept.[25]

She recorded the acts and feelings of her sadness: The chicken she ate was awful. A friend who visited was dull. The dog hair collected in mounds and she couldn't keep up with the vacuuming. Reading Simone de Beauvoir's *The Second Sex* was a bittersweet respite and ritual for Lorraine. She wrote when she felt able, through the depression. Lorraine always worked on multiple pieces at once, and you get a sense from reading them of a mind that is both racing and probing. One was a story called "Arnold" that was rejected from the *New Yorker*. The editor was encouraging, writing, " 'Arnold' comes so near to being successful that I'm going to give a much more detailed version of our criticism than we can usually manage. The piece has real backbone—a sound theme and a definite point of view on the writer's part toward that theme. Your point, that pride, or self-respect to every one, and dormant perhaps, in every one, comes from living and has an eloquent sincerity."[26] At the end is a handwritten note: "And please let us see this again if you can do more with it."

In "Arnold" one can see that Lorraine was a keen observer of life. She noticed not only the small details of human beings, their tentativeness, their sense of purpose, but also how often these important details are so easily overlooked. She wrote the story in the voice of a nineteen-year-old young woman working in a restaurant called the Golden Leaf. The woman remembers a dishwasher whom she once worked with: "As I remember Arnold, I remember that certain things had become indelible in my mind about men like him. The way they walked, all of them, the walk of men without places to go. I do not only mean that they ambled slowly and vaguely along, which they did, but it was more than that, Something about the picking up and setting down of feet that implied indecision; as though the feet could not always count on the sidewalk to be there."[27] Through Lorraine's eyes, she saw another from the outside in and what it meant to be a man who couldn't meet the ideals of man.

Looking back in time, she tells the readers that dishwashing is usually a temporary job occupied by men who couldn't find other work. They would quit as soon as other jobs became available, or else if it just felt like they had been stuck too long in the "in between." For most men, dishwashing became a humiliation, but Arnold took to it. Interspersed in the piece are subtle yet profound philosophical insights about living on the margins: "I think, and it is only what I think, it is difficult to accept the lost back into the fold of ordinary men. Maybe it is because we are afraid of them. Maybe it is because next to the dead themselves, we fear the living dead the most."[28]

One night Arnold doesn't come to the diner. Weeks go by and he doesn't return. They all wonder at his absence. And then, spontaneously, he returns. His face looks different. With his meager earnings as a dishwasher, Arnold had his rotten, painful teeth removed. For weeks, he couldn't bear to have the narrator see him, toothless. Lorraine ended the story: "How can I tell it so that you will understand what all of us felt sitting at that table that night. How can I put it down, what one feels in the face of the pride of a man who comes back."[29]

Arnold is denuded, and ashamed, but returns. It seems surprising that the character Arnold came to Lorraine when she was so despondent. But he did, and that might be because even when she felt hopeless, a Melvillean glimmer of possibility persisted. In her writer's disposition one can feel Melville's words "Faith, like a jackal, feeds among the tombs, and even from these dead doubts gathers her most vital hope."[30] And if faith is anywhere, it is in the work.

A similar sense of vocation and belief is evident in a vignette Lorraine wrote in 1956, this one called "Annie." Annie is of an indeterminate age and adorned in a long-decayed fancy purple dress. It was a garment that once suggested the temptress, but now the dress is merely serviceable. Barely. But the wearer is not defeated: "The woman, however, herself is somewhat cheerful of departure and carries herself as though life were merely beginning and that tomorrow may hold forth the most delicious of prospects."[31]

In these two remarkable pieces, one finished and one just a sketch, Lorraine was moving into a synthesis. There were her politics, centered on the poor, the marginal, the oppressed and outsiders, and there was her grasping at the interior life, especially its great disappointments with which all of us have to live.

In the same period Lorraine's critical intellectual life, her politics, and her art reveal a growing synthesis. Simone de Beauvoir's *The Second Sex* was her textbook. What she found in the book she kept returning to, calling it like a girlfriend; "Simone" was both a testimony to her suffering and a shaft of light. Among de Beauvoir's readers, Lorraine says in one of her third-person moments, "There is the twenty three year old woman writer closing the book after months of study, thoughtfully and placing it in the most available spot on her 'reference' shelf, her fingers sensitive with awe . . . her mind afire at last with ideas from France once again in history *equalite, fraternite, liberte—pour le tout monde!*"[32] In the marginalia of *The Second Sex*, Lorraine poured her ideas and engaged in a conversation with de Beauvoir, one that was passionate and enduring for the remainder of her life. She was a critical though captivated reader of de Beauvoir, and as was characteristic of Lorraine, her criticism was a sign of how seriously she took the work. She disagreed with de Beauvoir's existentialism, preferring a materialist worldview. And yet she saw the book as essential. The resonances between these two women, who rejected conventional expectations and found themselves desperately alone at times as a result, were profound. De Beauvoir gave Lorraine space to articulate a feminism that did not separate out sexuality and sexual desire for other women and also the inspiration to build a feminism that did not exclude race but treated it as a necessary part of understanding race, and race as necessary for understanding gender.

Unbeknownst to the multitudes that would come to celebrate her, it gave shape to the work that would make her both famous and a first.

CHAPTER FIVE

Sappho's Poetry

May I write words more naked than flesh,
stronger than sinew, sensitive than nerve.
— *Theresa Cha, writing as Sappho*[1]

LORRAINE WROTE TO HERSELF late on Christmas night in 1955: "It
is curious how intellectual I have become about the whole thing—I
don't mean about you. I mean about me—and what I apparently am.
My unhappiness has become a steady, calm quiet sort of misery. It
is always with me and when for a moment something or other stirs
me from its immediate ravages (thank God that is still possible)—I
wonder at its absence. I suppose I am grateful that the overt hysteria
has passed."[2]

Around that time, Lorraine drafted a play called *Flowers for the
General*. The protagonist, Maxine, is a college student whose schoolmate Marcia falls in love with her. Marcia is outed as a lesbian and
attempts suicide. Maxine comforts Marcia, who in turn confronts
Maxine with the knowledge that Maxine has also loved a woman.
Maxine insists that despite her desires, she will marry her boyfriend
anyway. It is a melodramatically composed and yet realistic story. It
could have easily been true.

Critics write about Lorraine's sexuality in varying ways. Some
debate whether she should be outed as a lesbian. I believe that if
we take her work seriously, we must talk about sexuality. I take the
careful preservation of Lorraine's writings in which she explored
and expressed her sexuality seriously. Though her romantic relationships remain, for me, somewhat opaque, it is unquestionable
that her desire for women and her love of women was meaningful
as part of her politics, her intellectual life, and her aesthetics, as well

as her spirit. I could not possibly write a portrait of her as an artist without it.

"IT." Lorraine was intellectual about everything, including persistent desire and yearning. She was active too. She joined the Daughters of Bilitis. It was, as they were called back then, a homophile organization, devoted specifically to lesbians. The name came from Pierre Louys's 1894 poetry collection *The Songs of Bilitis.* Louys's verses personify one of Sappho's courtesans, "Bilitis," and Louys plied her with erotic poems. Daughters of Bilitis provided an obscure yet meaningful reference for the group. Founded in San Francisco by partners Del Martin and Phyllis Lyon, within four years the organization grew from a small group of eight women to one with chapters in five cities and dozens of members. In 1956, they began publishing the *Ladder*, a magazine with articles, fiction, and opinion pieces all related to the lives of lesbian women. As with almost all the members, Lorraine's belonging to the Daughters of Bilitis was quiet. It was dangerous to be out.

But Lorraine's belonging was also passionate, as with most of what she committed to. She wrote two letters to the *Ladder*, both signed with her married-name initials: L.H.N. In the one she wrote in 1957, she displays a moving eagerness and intensity:

> I'm glad as heck that you exist. You are obviously serious people and I feel that women, without wishing to foster any strict separatist notions, homo or hetero, indeed have a need for their own publications and organizations. Our problems, our experiences as women are profoundly unique as compared to the other half of the human race. Women, like other oppressed groups of one kind or another, have particularly had to pay a price for the intellectual impoverishment that the second class status imposed on us for centuries created and sustained. Thus, I feel that THE LADDER is a fine, elementary step in a rewarding direction.[3]

She ended the letter wanting to know how things were on the West Coast, and why there seemed to be more developed homophile organizing out there. Lorraine was an organizer, after all. "Considering

Mattachine, Bilitis, ONE, all seem to be cropping up on the West Coast rather than here [on the East Coast] where a vigorous and active gay set almost bump one another off the streets—what is it in the air out there? Pioneers still? Or a tougher circumstance which inspires battle?"[4]

Lorraine's letter to the *Ladder* several months later, in August, was less about sexuality and more about feminism. It reads less like a letter to the editor and more like a letter to Simone de Beauvoir. She wrote about how the hostility toward same-gender-loving people had the same root as the domination of women. And she believed that feminism had something to offer both. This might seem like a fairly commonplace understanding today, because we associate the liberation of women generally with the liberation of desire and human connection, but in 1957 feminism and lesbianism were not necessarily, and not frequently, understood as being at all connected. That Lorraine made them so was a sign of her holistic approach to exploring her place in the world and the world itself. She believed facing profound ethical questions of her age ought to be the province of women, not just men. In this endeavor, conventions of marriage, children, and sexuality would all necessarily be challenged according to Lorraine.

In November of 1958 Lyon and Martin traveled from California to the East Coast and during that trip they furtively met with Lorraine. In advance, they'd written her, and she invited them to come to her home. They called early, at 7 a.m. (Lorraine described herself as someone who usually woke up at 11 or 12), and despite her apparent irritation at the early morning hour, she welcomed them. They described her as "Smart, pretty, and gracious."

They recalled, "She was very nice to us but said that she 'just couldn't get more involved' with the Daughters."[5] By that time Lorraine was not officially a member of the Communist Party, although she still considered herself along the socialist-communist spectrum. But her politics were increasingly of her own critical fashioning. She was a feminist, anticolonialist, and Marxist, and her sexuality became an essential part of her thinking through human relations.

And "IT" changed her life. Her calendar attests to periods of lovely socializing. One gets the sense, however, that her depression, introversion, and relentless intellectualism sometimes got in the way. This is clear in a letter she wrote to Robert upon her first visit to Provincetown, a resort community in Massachusetts that, like Ajijic, was known to be welcoming to artists and gay and lesbian people. As usual, she was taken by the beauty of the landscape: "The setting is quite beyond anything you or anyone else (including the various and assorted writers) had described. This surely is nature more lovely and more perfect and dramatic than I have seen elsewhere in the world— it is marvelous in the original sense of the word."[6]

Yet she also unloaded anxieties and insecurities in her letter to Bobby. This, too, was characteristically Lorraine. On the one hand, she is passionate and unflinching; on the other, a bit tender and nervous. She wrote of attending an art opening with the foreign editor of the *Daily Worker*, Joseph Starborin, and his wife. It was, according to Lorraine as she expected: "smeary, sick, meaningless contemptible trash."[7] Lorraine was surprised, however, that her company didn't share her disaffection for the show. Doris Levin, a specialist in Asian antiquities and the wife of the Bauhaus-inspired jeweler Ed Wiener, curtly shut Lorraine up. Edwin Burgum, a literary critic and Marxist who taught at NYU, also disagreed with her. And it got even worse. She wrote: "I won't go into it all here but suffice it to say that the Starborins make a great differentiation between abstract painting and non-objective painting and can go on at great and mistaken length about 'more than one way to look at reality' which is the worst of all bullshit when it comes to art, yes I am angry about it because at the back of their arguments seems to lie the idea that I am a bit of a sectarian who will outgrow it all as the 'Soviets' are doing??? ME—sectarian!"

It was odd for anyone to imply that Lorraine was fixated upon divisions within the left; after all, she was an ecumenical believer in freedom. On this point, it seems Burgum did defend her. But by that time she was already upset with the man she called "so heavily intellectual as to be tiresome . . . as well as historically inaccurate on occasion."

Though insecure and disgruntled while there, Lorraine also exercised her artist's gift for keen observation. "Already the main thing Provincetown reminds me of is Ajijic (Mexico). Same people, same circumstances, scenery, art shows and cocktail parties and I have been advised about six times already by different people that 'one either likes it—or one doesn't.' "[8] Lorraine's choice to spend the rest of her visit writing and alone indicates that she didn't take to Provincetown as much as she had to Ajijic. Lorraine's playful, critical, fiercely intellectual disposition was offset by her melancholy, a simultaneous yearning for solitude and a deep loneliness. The discomfort she experienced in various places no doubt intensified those feelings.

It is telling that she wrote to Robert about her time in Provincetown. Later, some of Lorraine's friends saw Robert as "getting in the way" of her life as a lesbian. This was particularly a problem, according to a girlfriend-turned–friend, Renee Kaplan, once Lorraine became involved with Dorothy Secules, her longest relationship.[9] Lorraine sometimes brought Robert, Dorothy, Renee, and others together socially, although I am not sure how successful that was. It certainly could have been awkward to have one's husband always present in the middle of living a life as a young lesbian. And though Robert was deeply committed to ensuring Lorraine's place in the canon of great American artists—even until his dying day—their attachment couldn't have always been easy for him either after the romance had ended. Regardless, the ongoing connection was not one way. Robert was not merely holding on to Lorraine—Lorraine also held on to him—and he was, to all appearances, her best friend even when he angered and frustrated her. Theirs may not have been a romantic union, but it was a union.

From the perspective of someone who has spent years mining pages to see who Lorraine was as an artist, that Robert, his second wife, and her daughter left neatly maintained folders with her writings on lesbian themes is a gift to Lorraine and to those of us who love her that cannot be denied. Yes, the writings remained shrouded for many years. But they were maintained. His dedication to her craft extended decades beyond her life.

Among the pieces in those folders are the short stories Lorraine published in the *Ladder*, and also *ONE*, a homophile publication that featured more work about men than women. She did so under the pseudonym Emily Jones. It was her second pseudonym. According to the FBI, she also wrote articles for the socialist publication the

Daily Worker under the nom de plume John Henry, after the steel-driving Black folk hero. That reference is clear. Emily Jones is more curious. The Jones perhaps was taken from Claudia Jones. Emily is intriguing. It could be that she was thinking of the poet Emily Dickinson, especially in her loneliest of days. Or maybe it was just that, together, Emily and Jones sounded like a nondescript and unidentifiable person.

The stories she wrote as Emily Jones, published and unpublished, were about love and desire. They are part of the early Lorraine, the writer before *Raisin* made it to Broadway. Her voice in them is tender.

"The Anticipation of Eve" was published in the December 1958 issue of *ONE*. The protagonist is a young newspaperwoman named Rita, short for Marguerite. She, like Lorraine, is a Midwesterner with a French name who has moved out East. The action of the story takes place on a visit to her cousin Sel, who is also a transplant from the Midwest and recently married. Sel and Dave have an infant son. Rita feels warmly toward them, and comes to their home with the hope of revealing a secret, thinking: "It is horrible to make a beautiful thing a dreadful secret, horrible for anyone."[10] Rita believes she can divulge her secret, because Sel and Dave are unconventional, they support Negro rights, and even (here Lorraine displays her cutting wit) men having beards. "It was because of all these things and others that I had decided to tell them about my secret—whose name was Eve."[11]

But then Sel interrupts Rita's internal conversation with her plan to set Rita up with a man named Kevin. Dave attempts to dissuade her, but Sel persists: "Let's face it honey, you're twenty-six. You're beautiful and all that but you are twenty-six."[12] Sel's insistence that she be married soon sticks in Rita's throat as she realizes that, to Sel, marriage "was the beginning and end of life." Sel says further, "You can't go on living with roommates for the rest of your life Marguerite." There is a small implication that perhaps Sel's insistence is rooted in her suspicion. But Rita reflects, "I had been so careful about all the obvious things" and, moreover, "they had seen Eve only a few times and I rarely mentioned her at all. . . . I knew they had to consider my relationship with my roommate as cordial but perhaps a little unpleasant. . . . In three years Eve had remained an unimportant enigma to them."[13] Sel provokes further, implying Eve must be "loose" or in some other way shameful.

Rita loses the impulse to tell them about Eve: "Suddenly it all seemed very remote and alien; something that might after all in spite of beards and Negro equality, turn the simple good face into something hostile and painful and yes, frightened. It might be a terrible mistake."[14]

Rita removes herself from the moment with her thoughts. She recalls meeting Eve while on an interview assignment and being both disturbed and compelled by her eyes. It is a sly inversion of the biblical story of Eve in which she is the temptation rather than the tempted.

Rita then thinks about how she, not Sel, was the pretty and desired one in their hometown. But now Sel believes she has something over Rita because she has adhered to conventions of womanhood. Rita has her own union, however. She thinks of Eve's hands, one bearing the ring Rita gave her. She wears it even in public. And the gift that Eve offered Rita in return, "the little flat, gold heart, on the fragile almost invisible chain which she said could hide from the world, yet lie quite near my heart."[15]

Perhaps she should tell them, she thinks, but is interrupted by the baby, "little Davie," crying.

Rita is left alone with Dave. At first she suspects he knows: "Didn't know how or how long, but I could see he knew." But then it seems she is incorrect. Dave says, " 'This guy, this Kevin,' he waved his hand in something that could have been an unfulfilled ballet gesture, 'he's gay as a Mardi Gras parade, you know what I mean?' "[16]

Rita likens the moment to being on the battlefield, when a man can feel only relief when he sees his buddy fall instead of him. She responds in the expected way, saying that his sexuality is horrible. "And then it was clear to me why I could hate myself. I realized at first that there had been a sadness in Dave, a trouble, a disturbance, but now a voice had concurred, had spoken from everyday and in front of my very eyes I saw his lips turn town."[17] Dave's words are hateful, and Rita observes, "It was 1956 and the 'clean' were still casting out the lepers."[18]

But something else is behind Dave's words. He says he knows the guy well, he spent time with him, and that "he doesn't want to be helped."[19] The sadness and disturbance in Dave's face suggests there might be some intimacy and identification between Dave and Kevin . . . and Rita. This suggestion deepens as Dave cautions Rita not to tell Sel about Kevin.

This queer and layered moment is interrupted by Sel reentering the room with the baby. She tells Rita, "This is what being a woman is,"[20] referring to the child in her arms. It is as though Lorraine has created in her the very embodiment of what she saw Simone de Beauvoir writing against. Lorraine wrote, regarding *The Second Sex*, "The problem then is not that woman has strayed too far from 'her place' but that she has not yet attained it; that her emergence into liberty is, thus far, incomplete, primitive even. She has gained the teasing expectation of self-fulfillment without the realization of it, because she is herself yet chained to an ailing social ideology which seeks always to deny her autonomy and more—to delude her into the belief that that which in fact imprisons her the more is somehow her fulfillment,"[21] meaning the conventions of marriage, domesticity, and children.

Rita not only yearns for but also has found something else far more fulfilling. When she leaves her cousin's apartment, it is as though she at once retreats and escapes. It is night, and Rita is enchanted by the sweetness of spring air and her anticipation of her Eve is not a damnation but a resurrection. At first, she rues the noble things she did not say to Sel, then doesn't care, because

> I could think only of flowers growing lovely and wild somewhere by the highways, of every lovely melody I had ever heard. I could think only of beauty, isolated and misunderstood but beauty still, and only beauty. Someone had spoken to me of something they thought was unclean and sick and I could think only of beauty and spring nights and flowers and lovely music. [. . .] Someday perhaps I might hold out my secret in my hand and sing about it to the scornful but if not I would more than survive. By the time I reached our block I was running.[22]

It is tempting to think of Lorraine's cousin Shauneille whose name sounded close to Sel; whose husband was named Donald while Sel's was named Dave. Shauneille and Lorraine were close, had grown up together in Chicago, and both moved to New York and became play-wrights. But I cannot say this story is autobiographical, in whole or part. What I can say is that the tension she captured, between family and gender expectations and the way homophobia could crush intimacies in the most heartbreaking of ways even as romantic love made space for them, was absolutely real.

Two things stand out for me in Lorraine's Emily Jones work. One is the importance of the out-of-doors. In her most famous published work, interior domestic spaces are always important, so much so that the apartments become characters. They are sites of intimate reckoning with large social forces and also the closest of relations. But in the Emily Jones work the moments of deepest reckoning happen in the public, whether outside or in restaurants or clubs. If anything, *The Anticipation of Eve* shows that this public space motif is not a simple metaphor for the difficulty of the closet and the desire for public recognition. Rather it seems as though a freedom from a certain form of domestic constraint gives breathing room, and possibility. Her characters yearn for fresh encounters and fresh air.

The second distinctive feature of the Emily Jones fiction, for me, is found in its aesthetics. Lorraine reveled in female beauty. She poked fun at Simone de Beauvoir's hypocrisy in harshly judging women's adornment: "The writer brilliantly destroys all myths of woman's choice in becoming an ornament; and the charm of it is the photograph then on the dust jacket which presents a quite lovely brunette woman, in necklace and nail polish—Simone de Beauvoir."[23] Lorraine teasingly suggested that perhaps it was pleasure and not just constraint that shaped the Parisian philosopher's style. Likewise Lorraine was unapologetic about her own appreciation of beauty, whether natural or artifice, writing, "Nor, need we despair for the promotion of beauty anywhere. Scent, jewelry, rouges have undoubtedly assumed some cultural identification with womanhood that hopefully will henceforth be independent of an association of the centuries of slavery which has been the lot of woman."[24]

Apart from her pseudonymous fiction, Lorraine didn't spend much time writing about women's beauty. Maybe she worried that it would sound frivolous (or even too feminine) in comparison to the way many of her literary heroes wrote character descriptions.

Perhaps she worried that her attentiveness to female beauty might be too revelatory. But in truth, these lush descriptions were in line with a tradition of Black women's writing with which Lorraine was familiar, from Harlem Renaissance novelists Nella Larsen and Jessie Fauset to the Chicagoan Gwendolyn Brooks.

And yet, most of the Emily Jones fiction doesn't feature Black characters or focus upon race at all. It seems odd. Because it is not as though Lorraine thought race was superfluous when it came to her sexuality. She mentioned it in her letters to the *Ladder*. Maybe she avoided it for the same reason James Baldwin gave for not dealing with race in his 1956 queer novel *Giovanni's Room*. He said of it in an interview,

> I thought I would seal Giovanni off into a short story, but it turned into *Giovanni's Room*. I certainly could not possibly have—not at that point in my life—handled the other great weight, the "Negro problem." The sexual-moral light was a hard thing to deal with. I could not handle both propositions in the same book. There was no room for it. I might do it differently today, but then, to have a black presence in the book at that moment, and in Paris, would have been quite beyond my powers.[25]

Maybe a discussion of race would have complicated matters for Lorraine too. Or it might have been the case that she was simply trying to provide what her largely white audience was seeking. Or she was depicting a world that seemed to have not yet made space for a woman like her, not really. There was already a long history of Black lesbian artists, writers, and musicians. But the downtown scene she traveled in was overwhelmingly white.

However, race is a theme in one of the published and at least one of the unpublished Emily Jones stories. In both, the Black woman character is opaque though admired and ultimately triumphant. There is hope in these works, and a bit of resentment.

"Chanson Du Konallis," published in the *Ladder* in September 1958, begins with the sentence "She was exquisite," referring to a Black jazz chanteuse.[26] Though the protagonist, an upper-class, blond white woman named Konallia and nicknamed Konnie, observes her husband's excitement about the singer somewhat mockingly, she is also captivated:

> The cheek bones high; the full lips sensuous beyond description; and the eyes like dark slanted slashes across the face. . . . The eyes! Konnie shifted in her seat and looked quickly to the table. What a strange moment. It had happened before in life. On the street; parties; in classes in school years back; the thing of being surrounded by many people and finding another girl's or woman's eyes, commanding one, holding one's own. It was extraordinary. Pleasant, she thought. No, not pleasant. Terrifying because of the kind of pleasure it brought.[27]

Konallia Martin Whitside, the reader learns, possessed a cultivated reserve that frustrated her husband. She prided herself on maintaining control over rebellious thoughts and spontaneous action. And yet this control is wildly overstated. Underneath the surface, Konallia's fantasy about the woman is a sensuous spectacle, reminiscent of Jean Toomer's classic Harlem Renaissance work of experimental fiction, *Cane*:

> Egyptian queens . . . striding along mammoth corridors in the temples (or palaces or whatever the hell they usually strode along) graceful the way only queens could be (one was taught!) . . . in something white and tight and gathered at the hips with those long pleats hanging down to the golden sandal tops. . . . Anyhow—Egyptian queens . . . very young, very supple and very beautiful with the stiff black hair hidden under those curiously attractive head dresses. . . . No—not Cleopatra, she was Greek or something. This particular queen would be darker—like the Nile without moonlight; with high cheek bones and—full, impossibly sensuous lips—like—like her![28]

Konallia struggles with the rules of her class and caste in this moment of pleasure. She asks herself, "Who were all those dead people who were deciding things from their graves?"[29] Those past respected generations of illustrious attainment had nothing to do with her, not really, and yet she felt bound by their expectations.

Konnie's husband, Paul, invites the singer, Mirine Tige, to the table. Mirine dismisses his small talk and condescending statements about France and turns the questions and comments on Konallia, asking her if she'd liked France and complimenting her accent (as Paul did of Mirine's). Before departing to finish her singing, Mirine tells Konnie that she reminded her of someone she knew in France, by way of explaining her attentiveness. She calls meeting them pleasant, but Konnie thinks it was not pleasant, although there *was* pleasure. That is the difference between satisfaction and desire.

The story ends sadly. Her husband is sated, but Konnie expects she will have to drink to "make it easier." And curse the figures of her desire: Paris, Egyptian queens, and a girl named Lila she once knew. There is a doubleness in this story. We have to imagine that Konnie, though a WASP, shared some of Lorraine's own feelings of class and caste pressure. Lorraine was raised to "never betray the race" and to maintain middle-class respectability. Despite having scandalized her mother politically, she had mainly succeeded in being a proper bourgeois daughter. Living publicly as a lesbian would have been an entirely different matter.

And yet, Lorraine was also in a sense like Mirine. She was one of the few Black women and few political radicals in the lesbian set to which she belonged. She was different and likely faced projections of some fantastic imaginings of what her Blackness and womanhood meant. In truth, she saw herself, and other Black women, as more liberated than their white counterparts. Lorraine wrote, in an unpublished essay on Simone de Beauvoir, "We have been, even the black slave woman, paradoxically assuming perhaps the most advanced internal freedom from a knowledge of the mythical nature of male superiority inherent in our experience as chattel."[30]

The dance between steeliness and vulnerability repeats itself throughout the Emily Jones fiction, and it is a reflection of Lorraine's interior life. In her diaries and her letters she questions and judges herself, at times finds herself intolerable. She is melodramatic and even adolescent. When the writing treats queer sexuality, this personal vulnerability is fully expressed artistically. I do not think this is because her vulnerability existed wholly around her sexuality. After all, "she was scared of heights, tunnels, water, planes, elevators and hospitals."[31] She once wrote to Robert a panicked note in response to him having traveled by plane: "I can tell you know that that was a positively horrible Saturday that you all left on that damn thing—I am now convinced that they should be banned. . . . YOU ARE NEVER TO FLY AGAIN." Put plainly, she was generally a scaredy cat. But when she wrote on queer themes she was better able to access that emotional register, a tense and immediate sense of fear, than anywhere else in her work.

Lorraine's community of lesbian friends provided an important social world and undoubtedly facilitated her literary ventures in this period. One woman, however, stands out among the others. Molly Malone Cook was a Californian transplanted to the Village and five years Lorraine's senior. She worked as a photographer for the *Village Voice* and later would build a life in Provincetown with her long-term partner, the poet Mary Oliver. When they were together, Molly took photographs of Lorraine. These photos are different from all the others and tell a story in and of themselves. In them, Lorraine does not have her race-woman armor on as she usually does. Nor is she posed. She is casual, tomboyish. Her hair is mussed. Her back curved, adolescent, languorous, and playful at once. The light and wonder that we know must have often been in her eyes, because of her wicked humor and deep curiosity, I have seen only Molly capture on camera. The images are a dance of love.

In general, Molly's photographs are dynamic and social, sensitive yet lively. The subjects are clear, yet their edges are soft. Her portraits are painterly. As an artist she shared some things with Lorraine: a brilliance when it came to framing and staging the social and the intimate at once, a sensitivity to the dynamic relations between beings within the allotted space. Molly also shared Lorraine's tenderness for vistas. They both made staging look natural. They were masters of portraiture. In that vein, the plays Lorraine would later write are novel-like. They include narratives beyond what is standard for theatrical productions. Their stage directions include epigraphs and sense making, not just scene setting. They are works of art that are composed for readers and also theatrical viewers. And, unsurprising from an author who started as a visual artist, their scenes beg to be painted, hence, the magnificent stills that remain from the Broadway productions.

Both Molly and Bobby were part of Lorraine's life as she wrote *Raisin*. But only one is known publicly. As the story goes, one evening in the summer of 1957, Lorraine shared the play she was working on with Philip Rose. She and Bobby hosted him in their apartment at 337 Bleecker Street. I do not know if this was before or during or when her relationship was just beginning with Molly, but it doesn't really matter for this anecdote. She and Bobby hosted together regardless of who she was with. Bobby and Lorraine fed Rose spaghetti for dinner and banana cream pie for dessert. And they read him the draft of the play. Rose was captivated by *A Raisin in the Sun*. The trio talked into the night and the next morning. After he had returned home, Rose called Lorraine and said he wanted to get the play to Broadway. It was a life-changing moment, and like many, one she shared with Bobby. The entanglement and intimacy, the way Bobby was a lifeline to her work, was unceasing, even as she was finding her way with lovers, including with Molly, who was her kindred spirit.

Years later, Mary Oliver would describe what I believe was Molly and Lorraine's relationship, though she deliberately doesn't name Molly's lover as a matter of care and respect. Just suppose it was Lorraine. It would say something that rings so true:

> In 1958 and 1959 she traveled by car across the country to California, leisurely, through the south and back through the northern states—taking pictures. She had, around this time, an affair that struck deeply, I believe she loved totally and was loved totally. I know about it, and I am glad. I have an idea of why the relationship thrived so and yet failed, too private for discussion also too obviously a supposition. Such a happening has and deserves its privacy. I only mean that this love, and the ensuing emptiness of its ending, changed her. Of such events we are always changed—not necessarily badly but changed. Who doesn't know that, doesn't know much.[32]

The fabric—dead ancestors, living expectations, a husband, a series of political causes, all those things mattered—but so had love.

Lorraine and Molly were together and then split as she was developing *A Raisin in the Sun,* around the time it went through tryouts in various cities, the cast was composed, and money was raised to put it on Broadway. Molly, someone with a brilliant eye for composition, must have seen and to some degree influenced what others would see on stage and film: the simple poignant triangles between characters at odds yet intimately bound. Reading her joint memoir with Mary Oliver, I came across a journal passage of Molly's that I just knew had to be about Lorraine. Cook wrote sometime in the 1980s,

> Last night I turned on the TV and there she was,
> It was wild. Her voice. I couldn't replay it.
> She spoke only a few words. It was mind-boggling.
> I wonder if I shall ever be able to
> come back to listen and watch her again.
> Strange I should have fixed the VCR just a
> Moment before she came on.
> Well I never thought I would see her again—
> Knew I would never hear her voice again in
> This world. Oh I did always think I would
> See her again and hear her voice again but,
> Not in this world.[33]

But I didn't know for sure. I just felt it and hoped it. It seemed so right. After Molly and Lorraine's relationship ended, perhaps around 1958, Molly drove across the country. Then she met Mary in Edna St. Vincent Millay's home in Provincetown. They built a life. And Lorraine became famous.

After *Raisin* is also after Molly. Lorraine's life changed. My story of her love life thereafter becomes even more impressionistic, but it deserves a bit more treatment here before I turn back to Lorraine's work of writing and politics. For a while, Lorraine dated Ann Grifalconi, a public school teacher, writer, and visual artist who had been trained at Cooper Union. From some time in 1960 until her dying day, Lorraine loved Dorothy Secules, a fiercely opinionated and smart blonde who climbed the ladder from working as a receptionist at Loft Candy Company to an executive. Her eyes were bright blue;

her gaze in photographs is knowing. From her high school yearbook photo I learned that Dorothy's youthful nickname was Dick. Dorothy was there beside Lorraine at key life moments, as were other women. Lorraine wrote in her diaries of their beauty, her desires, time spent together on dates and in the most intimate, sweet moments. Though Lorraine sought out what she described as "women of accomplishment," her lovers didn't become interlocutors for Lorraine the artist. Perhaps they were inspirations for characters; probably they were. But to the extent that queerness appears in subsequent texts, and it does, it does not connect to specific women in any way that I have explicitly traced. Their company, however, brought threads of joy that appeared throughout her art and ideas.

In 1960, fresh off of the success of *A Raisin in the Sun*, Lorraine bought a building at 112 Waverly Place in Greenwich Village. Dorothy was a renter and Lorraine took the top floor. The FBI was aware of this purchase, and agents looked for Lorraine there. The notes of the FBI agent who was following her describe how he physically checked all residences on Waverly Place from McDougall to Bank Street in the last week of March and the first week of April, but didn't find her anywhere. On March 30, the agent used a pretext to ask Bobby about why he lived at 337 Bleecker Street while Lorraine lived elsewhere. Based upon his response, the agent wrote in his notes, "It is believed that the purpose for these two addresses is for business reasons inasmuch as during the above-mentioned pretext subject's husband stated that his wife was unavailable for interview. The subject's husband mentioned that this was the customary practice of his wife whenever she was engaged in writing."[34] The FBI seemed to have accepted this explanation because an interview with a mail carrier revealed that Lorraine was not receiving mail at Waverly Place but rather on Bleecker Street. It appears that thereafter the FBI stopped watching the Bleecker Street address.

In Lorraine's datebook for March 28, 1960, as the FBI were attempting to surveil her domestic situation, she wrote to herself:

Are you happy in your present living? Or are you looking for something else, or do you just want to play? You see, I must know because it is Spring . . .

Have toys—will play
I wish to light up the stars again.

The FBI's frustrated efforts to peer into her life coexisted with a marvelous though morose period of self-exploration. On April 1, 1960, she wrote two columns in her datebook titled "I like" and "I hate." They read:

I LIKE	I HATE
Mahalia Jackson's music	Being asked to speak
My husband—most of the time	Speaking
getting dressed up	Too much mail
being admired for my looks	My loneliness
Dorothy Secules eyes	My homosexuality
Dorothy Secules	Stupidity
Shakespeare	Most television programs
Having an appetite	What has happened to
Slacks	Sidney Poitier
My homosexuality	Racism
Being alone	People who defend it
Eartha Kitt's looks	Seeing my picture
Eartha Kitt	Reading my interviews
That first drink of Scotch	Jean Genet's plays
To *feel* like working	Jean Paul Sartre's writing
The little boy in "400 Blows"	Not being able to work
The way I look	Death
Certain flowers	Pain
The way Dorothy Talks	Cramps
Older Women	Being hung over
Miranda D'Corona's accent	Silly women
Charming women	As silly men
And/or intelligent women	David Suskind's pretensions
	Sneaky love affairs.[35]

The lists are mundane and profound. The great joy of her sexuality and also its difficulty courses through them. Lorraine the passionate and opinionated intellect and the aesthete are there. One also gets a sense of how trying fame could be: from the challenge of writing again after one has become a star to the desire to be out of the public gaze and also her frustrations with superficiality. But on the other hand, she delighted in being physically admired. Contradictions are a universal part of the human personality. Hers are fascinating: a vast intellect and a girlish charm, wisdom and wonder, pensive and playful, depression and exultation. These lists were two of the first publicly circulated artifacts asserting Lorraine's sexuality. They were, in a sense, irrefutable evidence of the sort that travels quickly in the digital age. Their loveliness aided their circulation. Essays and articles have been written about these lists, and there could be more. It is a testament to the delicate strength of her pen that even this exercise in simple accounting became poetry.

When I first read the lists, my eyes kept returning to the items I especially liked: Eartha Kitt (it seems Orson Welles was not the only one who found her the most exciting woman in the world) and "the little boy in '400 Blows.'" The François Truffaut film was just a year old when Lorraine was writing. It starred a troubled boy named Antoine who is treated with clinical distance and disdain by his mother and stepfather. Antoine is also mistreated at school. Anguished, he becomes a truant and a runaway. He is ultimately jailed for stealing a typewriter, and then sent to a reformatory school by his mother where he receives psychoanalytic counseling. In the facility, the children are berated and brutalized for their failures to be properly disciplined according to the rules of gender, sexuality, and decorum. A film that begins as Antoine's desire for connection becomes Antoine's quest for emancipation. In the final scene he escapes from a soccer game at the facility. He slips under a fence and runs until he reaches the ocean. The final scene is a close-up of his face as he stands in the water.

Lorraine wrote this list in the early days of her fame. Her deep ambivalence about it is palpable. In *400 Blows*, Antoine escapes to the shoreline. He also escapes from the game. Lorraine loved the little boy, and she did not.

CHAPTER SIX

Raisin

Some day the Awakening will come, when the pent-up
vigor of ten million souls shall sweep irresistibly toward the
Goal, out of the Valley of the Shadow of Death, where all
that makes life worth living—Liberty, Justice, and Right—
is marked "For White People Only."   — *W. E. B. Du Bois*[1]

IT TOOK PHILIP ROSE fifteen months to raise the money to put *A
Raisin in the Sun* on Broadway. Backers, even those who were sympathetic to his enthusiasm, didn't believe that a play featuring Black
people "emoting" would draw crowds. And, so, the *Raisin* cast and
crew did tryouts in Philadelphia and New Haven, traditional places
to test a production's future prospects on Broadway. The play was
a great success in both cities. The Chicago show, which caused Lorraine a great deal of anxiety, was also successful. *Raisin*'s extraordinary cast, including the already-established Sidney Poitier, and a
brilliant though untested young Black director, Lloyd Richards, rendered Lorraine's words with vigor and depth. With those stamps of
critic and audience approval, *A Raisin in the Sun* made it to Broadway on March 11, 1959. It was a very big deal. Broadway audiences
had never before seen the work of a Black playwright and director,
featuring a Black cast with no singing, dancing, or slapstick and a
clear social message. Here was a family living in the Chicago South
Side ghetto. Armed with a $10,000 life insurance check after the
death of the father, they hope to move out of their tiny kitchenette
apartment and into a house in a segregated white neighborhood. The
adult son, Walter Lee, dreams of becoming a businessman. His sister, Beneatha, aspires to become a doctor. The matriarch, Lena, and
her daughter-in-law are most of all hoping for a home of their own.

Despite the early misgivings of financiers and skepticism from many quarters, *A Raisin in the Sun* played at the Ethel Barrymore Theater for nineteen months before transferring to the Belasco Theatre for another eight. Lorraine would win the Drama Critics Circle Award for Best Play with this, her first stage production. She was only twenty-eight years old, yet already had an imposing presence and powerful intellect. The theater world was forced to reckon with her.

Ruby Dee, who played Ruth Younger in the play, described feeling anxious around Lorraine because of her impressive mind. And yet Lorraine was still young and hopeful and more than a little insecure. Though she had not followed the expected course for a good, bourgeois young Negro lady, Lorraine wrote to her mother, Nannie, a bit shyly, that she hoped the play would make her mother proud.

It had been a long time in the making. From her first publication, "Flag from a Kitchenette Window," with its gesture to Gwendolyn Brooks's "Kitchenette Building," she'd shown signs that the source of her father's wealth would become the substance of her art. And she'd kept rewriting versions of her childhood encounter with white mob violence when they moved out of the boundaries of the ghetto. The details of her play were different from those of Lorraine's family, but squarely within the life she knew and lived.

A Raisin in the Sun used her mentor Langston Hughes's poem "Harlem" as an epigraph and the source of its title. Hughes's poem is a meditation on deferred dreams. The consequence, he suggests, might be explosive outbursts, woundedness, depression, or as Lorraine took up, sweltering and defeated people barely clinging to parched hopes, dried up like a raisin in the sun.

But we also ought to read Lorraine's play alongside Gwendolyn Brooks. In Brooks's "Kitchenette Building," the poet asks if dreams might exist in the kitchenette apartment, despite all the constraint and the pressure. Hughes asks what happens to them when they do. Lorraine enters the interior of each of her characters, members of a family with a dead father's insurance money and the choices it brings, and she answers Brooks's question by finding all their dreams, the dreams of Black people trapped in the ghetto, and she depicts the barriers—the harrowing prospect of deferral—that Hughes anticipates. Her answer to both literary predecessors—and Lorraine was quite explicit about this in her interviews about the play—is that stepping toward something, or what she called the "affirmative" deeds of her characters, and stepping away from the limits imposed by a society bent on your destruction, was a revolutionary and liberatory move no matter what was bound to come. She had finally figured out how to answer Ellison's "Harlem Is Nowhere" fully: racism was everywhere in Black America, but so was the human constitution necessary to fight it.

A Raisin in the Sun was received with acclaim and became wildly popular, though a few of the reviews were condescending and vaguely racist. There is a photograph of Lorraine taken by Gordon Parks from the cast party at Sardi's opening week. Her eyes are glassy— probably she's had a little wine—and at once stunned and joyful. Her skin glistens, her hair is rumpled. She is elegant in a black dress (her go-to choice for formal gatherings) as she watches musicians play. Such delight was preceded by years of loss and restlessness, failure, depression, loneliness, and also persistent seeking and experimentation and reading, learning, and most of all a commitment to what she took to be right, good, and meaningful. She was young, but so much had been packed in the previous eleven years. This was not a Cinderella story.

But it would become a story of illusion, or perhaps fantasy. Maybe a more straightforward word like *misperception* is warranted. The point is that as popular as the play was and is, it was woefully misunderstood if one believes that the author's intent matters. In 1958, J. Edgar Hoover, head of the FBI, directed the special agent in New York to determine whether Lorraine's play was communist in content. The bureau collected reviews and playbills, and even sent agents to view the play. One said, "The play contains no comments of any nature about Communism as such . . . but deals essentially with negro aspirations, the problems inherent in their efforts to advance themselves, and varied attempts at arriving at solutions."[2] Though their worry regarding the message of the play was diminished once FBI agents saw it, the popularity of the play once it hit Broadway also chastened the bureau. They had planned to interview Lorraine, but decided against it. The note about this decision read, "In reconsidering an interview with subject it is to be noted that the subject and her play have received considerable notoriety almost daily in the NY press. In view of this it is felt than an interview with her would be inadvisable at this time since the possibility exists that the Bureau could be placed in an embarrassing position if it became known to the press that the Bureau was investigating the subject and/or the play."[3]

Lorraine, though unwaveringly a member of the Far Left, had written a play that wasn't overtly political, didactic, or heavy-handed. She had chosen to write characters who were true, who were oppressed, who sought freedom, and who were also shaped by the society in which they lived. Her craft had grown too nuanced to read as propaganda.

Lorraine found herself in an inversion of the quandary her mentor Langston Hughes described in the 1926 essay "The Negro Artist and the Racial Mountain." Hughes protested the demands from white Americans that Black artists produce exotic images, and from Blacks that Black writers produce respectable ones. According to him, both sets of pressures limited creativity. Lorraine was caught between one strand of Black politics that advocated for assimilationist respectability and another that consisted of Black Nationalist commitments and leftist critiques of the bourgeois. The way the mainstream interpreted *Raisin* placed it squarely within integrationist-assimilationist respectability. For example, Lorraine was quoted in an article as having said, "I told them this wasn't a 'Negro play.' It was a play about honest-to-God, believable, many-sided people who happened to be Negroes." But in her scrapbook, beside a clipping of this interview, Lorraine wrote these words: "Never said NO such thing. Miss Robertson [the interviewer] goofed—letter sent posthaste—Tune in next week."[4] Her letter of correction was never printed. The misquote was repeated and even changed to "I'm not a Negro writer—but a writer who happens to be a Negro."

James Baldwin, with whom Lorraine became friends in 1958, got to the heart of the matter, however, when he talked about the impact of *A Raisin in the Sun*, writing in reflection, "I had never in my life seen so many black people in the theater. And the reason was that never in the history of the American theater had so much of the truth of black people's lives been seen on the stage. . . . But, in *Raisin*, black people recognized the house and all the people in it."[5]

The popularity of her play with Black audiences provided a vision of what the theater could and should do for Black communities consistent with the aspirations and values of the artistic community she belonged to in New York. Ossie Davis, who would replace Poitier in the role of Walter Lee when Poitier left the production, also understood what some other Black leftists didn't:

> I have a feeling that for all she got, Lorraine never got all she deserved in regards to Raisin in the Sun—that she got success but that in her success she was cheated, both as a writer and a Negro. One of the biggest selling points about Raisin . . . was how much the Younger family was just like any other American family. Some people were ecstatic to find that "it didn't really have to be about Negroes at all!" . . . This uncritical assumption, sentimentally held by the audience, powerfully fixed in the character of the powerful mother with whom everybody could identify immediately and completely, made any other questions about the Youngers, and what living in the slums of South Side Chicago had done to them, not only irrelevant and impertinent, but also, disloyal.[6]

But this was incorrect, according to Davis. And she did right not to hit the audience over the head with the politics because, as he said, "Lorraine's play was meant to dramatize Langston's question, not answer it."[7]

Many years later, one of her harshest critics, Amiri Baraka, wrote:

> We missed the essence of the work—that Hansberry had created a family on the cutting edge of the same class and ideological struggles as existed in the movement itself and among the people. What is most telling about our ignorance is that Hansberry's play still remains overwhelmingly popular and evocative of black and white reality, and the masses of black people dug it true. . . . It is Lorraine Hansberry's play which, though it seems conservative in form and content to the radical petty bourgeoisie . . . is the accurate telling and stunning vision of the real struggle.[8]

Although much of the critique from the Black Left was unwarranted, and I think incorrect, it *was* curious that the public so easily embraced the play. Broadway aesthetics entail certain ethical commitments. Why didn't *A Raisin in the Sun* trouble them? It might have something to do with how in the play Lorraine mastered the strategic art of appeal—the use of comfortable conventions for the sake of political argument and subversion. Given that the civil rights movement protest itself was so often a highly aestheticized performance of respectable citizenship, Lorraine's play was consistent with the energy of struggle in that moment. In other words, by making a family that was conventional in some ways, Lorraine invited her audiences to identify with them as they struggled with the depth and breadth of American racism and inequality. The danger was, however, that people could stop at their comfort with the characters and never push themselves further on the question of racial injustice.

The skepticism of some members of the Black Left was heightened precisely because of the way Lorraine became a darling of the theater world. In that process, she was placed into categories that were familiar American archetypes, ones that lay in contrast to her politics as a leftist, a feminist, and a believer in global anticolonial, antiracist politics.

Oftentimes Lorraine was described in the press as a sort of ingénue. Her physical beauty and grace added to their confusion about *who* she actually was, politically speaking. Lorraine cut a striking figure long before her fame, as evinced by one FBI agent's physical description in 1956: "5'4" 105–110, Negro, Italian hair cut, no glasses, light brown, yellow shirt and black toreadors."[9] Several years later, as she became famous, it seemed journalists couldn't help but mention her appearance. *Vogue* magazine described her as a woman still dressed in the "collegiate style." The article about her in the June 1959 issue was accompanied by a full-page photograph taken by David Attie. All the images from that shoot were staged yet gorgeous. Attie captured her intellectual confidence, armor, and remarkable beauty. In some she wears a textured French-style boatneck top, chinos, thick white socks, and laced shoes and poses at her desk, or with crossed legs with a pen in hand, or leaning on her typewriter.

The other set is more serious. She poses in front of a bookshelf and behind flowers in a dark blazer and pearls, arms crossed with a knowing smile. Her hair is freshly hot-ironed and her lipstick is conservative. She is glamorous in a manner that seems at once studied and casually self-assured.

The journalist Sidney Fields described her as "slight, small, pretty with a soft voice and a skyfull of life and ideas for opera librettos and new plays." He also mentioned her penchant for self-deprecation and playfulness when speaking of her Ping-Pong game. "At the start I look devastating. At the finish everybody beats me badly."[10]

Ted Poston, another journalist, referred to her as a "tousle-headed gamin" and "the comely but strong-minded lass," and commented in a way that indicated he was both amused and taken by Lorraine:

> There'll be no rags-to-riches moving, for instance, from the third floor walk up apartment in Greenwich Village where she lives with her husband Robert Nemiroff and her happily neurotic collie, Spice. She seemed horrified at the idea the other day as she sat half curled in a living room chair, her black-sweatered arms clasped around slim legs clad in rumpled brown corduroy trousers.
>
> "I'm a writer," she said rather indignantly (an opinion endorsed by every first string drama critic in town), "and this is a workshop. We're not celebrities or anything like that.
>
> "But I am going to get the landlord to paint that hall. We're not bohemians. They can't carry us that far."[11]

While some critics couldn't get enough of her charm and beauty, others failed to see her as anything but one of the stereotypes of Black experience. It was as though the very word *Negro* conjured up images that overtook all evaluation. One wrote,

> Miss Hansberry says that her many years of living in a squalid Negro ghetto inspired her to write the play depicting the plight of a typical Negro family who much like herself is trapped by housing discrimination, forced to live in tenement jungles. . . .

Miss Lorraine Hansberry, twenty-eight-year-old authoress of the play, drew heavily upon her own background as a child and a young woman raised in the slum section of Chicago to produce this supreme effort.[12]

Of course Lorraine *was* raised on Chicago's South Side, but her upbringing was far from squalid. Other critics overemphasized her middle-class status, as though the life of the Black working class was a wholly separate realm from Lorraine's life. One wrote, "Her Chicago family was, unlike the family in the play, comfortably middle class."[13] Her middle-class background formed the basis for her dismissal by many Black leftists who ought to have known better, both because of her history of political activism and because they, like she, certainly knew that class distinctions in the Black community were often more theater than substance.

Lorraine's responses to the class-based dismissals of her work were nuanced rather than defensive. These people, thinking abstractly rather than empirically, misunderstood the position of the Black middle class and its distinction from its white counterpart. Lorraine saw this ignorance as the inevitable outcome of a segregated society. While white elites might not find themselves in the thrall of their working-class brethren, Black elites lived in the thick of the segregated ghetto. She described how her "two best friends in high school regarded themselves as much of the 'middle class' as I. Yet, one of them was the daughter of a postal clerk and the other the child of a chauffeur. Our dress habits, recreation and, in most ways, aspirations were virtually indistinguishable."[14]

Lorraine was frustrated by some critical evaluations of the play, even as she understood them. She was particularly frustrated that Walter Lee's "ends" were read without complication. They were deliberate and clearly shaped by Irish playwright Sean O'Casey, the WPA Negro in Illinois project's publication *Black Metropolis*, and Thorstein Veblen's *Theory of the Leisure Class*, which she considered an essential companion to the writings of Karl Marx. Walter Lee's yearnings were a manifestation of Veblen's theory of desire in a capitalist society, one that cut across class and caste. Her mastery of full characters, her sensitivity to speech and personality so that the characters never read as types, made the politics invisible to so many. But Lorraine intended to correct that.

In May of 1959 she wrote a letter to Bobby about a lecture she delivered at Roosevelt University. In it, she compared Arthur Miller's classic character from *Death of a Salesman*, Willy Loman, and her Walter Lee Younger and argued that Walter Lee had more heroic potential. The audience responded with a standing ovation. In an essay from the *New York Times* based on that talk, "Willie Loman, Walter Younger, and He Who Must Live," Lorraine argued that Loman, that iconic figure of American drama, was a sign of the crisis provoked by the closing of frontier. He is "left with nothing but some left over values which had forgotten how to prize industriousness over cunning; usefulness over mere acquisition, and above all humanism over success."[15] Walter Younger, though wholly American, according to Lorraine, possessed a typicality that was different because he is Black and at every turn denied. His actions might affirm life rather than be caught in the death cycle of manifest destiny and consumerism.

This was in the tradition of Black Americans, according to Lorraine, a people who she says "have dismissed the ostrich and still sing 'Went to the rock to hide my face, but the rock cried out: No hidin' place down here!'" quoting the traditional Negro spiritual "Sinnerman," which her dear friend Nina Simone would record six years later. Walter Lee's assertion that they will move into the house despite the resistance of the white neighbors does not change the basic social order, according to Lorraine. It is not revolutionary. But it nevertheless matters a great deal, because it puts him at cross-purposes with "at least certain of his culture's values" and he draws "on the strength of an incredible people who historically have simply refused to give up." He has "finally reached out in his tiny moment and caught that sweet essence which is human dignity, and it shines like the old star-touched dream that is in his eyes."[16]

Even while defending her play, she accepted that in some quarters any critical judgment of it was attacked as racist, and she found that amusing. And yet "the ultra sophisticates have hardly acquitted themselves less ludicrously, gazing coolly down their noses at those who are moved by the play and going on at length about 'melodrama' and/or 'soap opera.' "[17]

Though she said some critics got the play terribly wrong, Lorraine admitted her own failures. The problem was just that *Raisin*'s critics had failed to actually ascertain what was wrong with it. She instructed them that the real problem with *Raisin* was it lacked a central character who anchored the play. She said that while some saw that as an inventive choice, it was a consequence of her indecisiveness and the limits of her skill. I am not sure Lorraine was correct. Mastery of the ensemble form was perhaps her greatest gift. But regardless of whether one takes her position or mine, her confident reading of her own work is unusual in its sharp assessment. It often amounted to quite brilliant ways of saying "they have no idea what they're talking about."[18] In particular, and this became a recurring point of hers, she was highly critical of those who believed obscurity, total uniqueness, and inscrutability were markers of artistic sophistication. They attacked her play's simplicity and use of convention or what she called "old bones," but she believed more meaningful discussion tended to "delve into the flesh which hangs from those bones and its implications in mid century American drama and life."[19]

Then she commented that though people made comparisons between her work and that of O'Casey and Chekhov, only one critic had noticed the connection between *Raisin* and Arthur Miller's *Death of a Salesman*. (She noted this is partly because the ensemble overwhelms Walter Lee so he doesn't stand out the way Willy Loman or Hamlet do.) But she also thought people failed to see Walter as like Willy because they couldn't help but see Walter as an exotic character of the sort previously imagined in American drama in " 'Emperor Jones' or 'Porgy,' . . . the image of the simply lovable and glandular 'Negro.' "[20] That figure of emotional abandonment and joyfully tolerated poverty, according to Lorraine, acquitted white viewers of their haunting guilt about American racism.

These observations were all part of Lorraine's effort to show why so many people couldn't really understand Walter Lee, and his motivations, as distinctly American. She ended that section of the article with a joke about a critic who remarked "of his pleasure at seeking how 'our dusky brethren' could 'come up with a song and hum their troubles away.' It did not disturb the writer that there is no such implication in the entire three acts. He did not need it in the play, he had it in his head."[21] This is funny, but it is no laughing matter. Lorraine identified a problem that persistently dogs Black artists. How does one navigate racial perceptions that overlay everything, that obscure and cast such that they effectively become part of the production no matter what the artist does? For Lorraine the answer was to become a critic.

It was unusual for a playwright to function as a critic. And in her critical assessments Lorraine eviscerated many of those who diminished her characters. That was even more unusual. Shortly after the publication of the Willy Loman essay, Lorraine ran into Brooks Atkinson, who had refused to publish it in the *New York Times* precisely because it was so strange for a playwright to write her own criticism. Years later, Philip Rose recounted this meeting. It took place in a theater, shortly after Atkinson announced his retirement from the *New York Times* after thirty-five years. At the intermission Lorraine walked directly up to him and introduced herself: " 'Mr. Atkinson, my name is Lorraine Hansberry.' She reached out and held his hand as she continued to speak. 'I have just read and been saddened by your announced retirement. I have admired and respected for years your contribution and love for the theatre and its playwrights. Your leaving will be a tremendous loss for all of us.' "[22] Rose believed this encounter had quite an effect on Atkinson, because a few days later he sent a note of apology to Lorraine, explaining he had been suffering from personal problems when he declined her essay.

She was just so unusual. Lorraine was not a typical figure of the New York theater establishment because of her gender, race, and politics but also because of her relation to art as an intellectual. She pushed against all sorts of barriers and seemed to often captivate people despite their disinclinations.

By 1961, once Lorraine was firmly situated as a great playwright and audiences were waiting for more from her, her voice had grown firm and her eyes steely in her social and artistic criticism. It was as though the mischaracterization of her play had straightened her backbone and she was insistent upon making her positions widely known. Lorraine was invited to deliver the Martin Weiner Distinguished

Lecture at Brandeis University that year. In her address, she used her biting sarcasm to retaliate against some critics: "I have discerned from conversation and published thesis alike that it is only bad artists who load their statements with a point of view and that they shall be known forever more in hell as something called 'social dramatist.' "[23] In fact, she believed that label has some nefarious purposes. Certain rules that served to control the content of art created a situation in which a person who accepted all standard social and political conventions was not considered to be someone who was taking a position, but rather simply an artist. But the person who challenged dominant values was routinely reduced to being nothing more than a political extremist. She found this practice reprehensible, because whether one followed the status quo became a standard of artistic evaluation, rather than the quality of work and its composition, elaboration, or ideas. In an elegant turn, Lorraine criticized dominant ideology and the normative assumptions that went along with it a generation before postmodernists would issue the same criticisms. Further, she argued that the casting of her art, and that of many others, into narrow confines was an anti-intellectual gesture at best.

Later in the same address, when talking about Bertolt Brecht's theater of the absurd, she said, "I have heard it said even that it is the mysteries remaining in his plays which excite us rather than that stunning illumination and revelation which I had always thought to be the most special mark of his genius. It is as though we cannot bear the light."[24] She persisted in her belief that great art emerges through the imagination of an alternative social order, the kind of imagining that comes about only through shifting the frames that we assume. Hence, there was no necessary tension between art and politics, according to Lorraine. She believed, instead, that great art *required* one to say something about society.

In an address at Swarthmore College that same year, she again rejected the label "social dramatist" while also arguing that great art necessarily deals with the social. In the process, she criticized the critics who classified poetic drama (good) on one side and social drama its opposite. According to Lorraine, the social dramatist was dismissed as one who plots out the dreary course of life as it is lived: continuing all action—and all possibility of man into the little "peep-hole" proscenium of highly representational productions; imposing the unilluminated prosaic and pedestrian lives of his character on audiences who have innocently and hopefully come expecting and deserving the stimulation and release of Dionysius.[25]

Especially interesting for a writer who was so concerned with the domestic arena, Lorraine strongly criticized Walter Kerr for his ideas in the essay "How to Write a Play," because in it he asserted that the best dramas were the most intimately concerned. He believed that drama grew larger if the scope of concern was reduced and that a tangle with society made for consistently mediocre plays. Lorraine found this argument specious at best. Lorraine's Left politics are clear in this criticism of Kerr, but also her investment in the social architecture of her own play in which intimate relations are tied to the fact of racial segregation, economic exploitation, service labor, and private property. It was not either-or in her work. She knew quite well that we live and love and desire within the economic and racial regime. We are of the ether.

It was on this point, specifically as it regarded race, that Lorraine had a particular beef with the Beat writers, her fellow Greenwich Village–dwelling, counterculture artists. The Beats had offered themselves up as outsiders to the mainstream who could provide insightful interpretations of Black people, who could even be likened to Black people, according to Norman Mailer in his 1957 essay "The White Negro," which incensed Lorraine. In it Mailer described the white hipster, lover of jazz and Black style, who "absorbed the existentialist synapses of the Negro, and for practical purposes could be considered a white Negro,"[26] a man who had adopted the Black man's code of existentialist living in the face of the ravages of capitalism and violence, finding like Black people that "the only life-giving answer is to accept the terms of death, to live with death as immediate danger, to divorce oneself from society, to exist without roots, to set out on that uncharted journey into the rebellious imperatives of the self."[27] Of these hipsters, Lorraine said at Brandeis,

"They have made a crummy revolt; a revolt that has not added up to a hill of beans. I am ashamed and offended by their revolt because they have had artists in their number and they have produced no art of consequence and they have proven no refuge for true revolutionaries. I accuse them of having betrayed Bohemia and its only justification."[28]

And specifically, with respect to race, she found them no more righteous, responsible, or thoughtful than the rest of white America. In an essay titled "Thoughts on Genet, Mailer, and the New Paternalism," published in the *Village Voice* on June 1, 1961, she decried their romantic racism and traced the roots of it to Mailer. He and his ilk had also dismissed her work. She wrote, "Nelson Algren agrees in print with Jonas Mekas that 'A Raisin in the Sun' is, of all things, a play about 'insurance money' and/or 'real estate.' This particular absurdity, it is true, is rendered a little less frightening only by the knowledge that there are people who sincerely believe that 'Othello' is a play about a handkerchief."[29]

Despite the sense of personal affront, the bulk of Lorraine's problems with the Beats didn't have to do with her ego but their arrogance. In the essay, she focused the bulk of her attention on Jean Genet's play *The Blacks*, a play within a play about the inversion of racial stereotypes and filled with Black subjects. Mailer, in his accounting of the play (and Genet admitted this), noted that it was, among other things, a conversation among white men about themselves. Lorraine said that that was *all* it was. And it certainly had nothing to do with Black life and thought. Genet's projection of white desire upon Black people might have been liberatory for the hipster, but was, according to Lorraine, simply racist: "He fabricated his own mythology concerning certain 'universals' about 20 million 'outsiders' and rejoiced because his philosophy fit his premise. . . . The new paternalists really think, it seems, that their utterances of the oldest racial clichés are somehow, a demonstration of their liberation from the hanky panky of liberalism and God knows what else."[30]

She then catalogued some things that hipsters truly failed to understand about Black perceptions of white Americans, including how Black Americans generally thought white people, especially white women, were dirty and inherently cruel; thus revealing the silliness of their argument that Black people were either nihilists or desired whiteness. Black aspiration, Lorraine instructed them, did not pivot around love or desperation regarding whiteness.

Lorraine speculated that perhaps Black writers had aided the misperceptions of Black feelings that these paternalists had run with: "We [Negro writers] may have carried the skin-lightener hair straightener references too far for a climate where context is not yet digested. Pride of race is not alien to Negroes. The Lord only knows that what must be half our institutions seem to function on the basis of nothing else."[31] She was bold and courageous in her criticism of the Beats. She was also ahead of her time. She attacked the racial essentialism that the Beats so heavily trafficked in. She wrote, "Of course oppression makes people better than their oppressors, but that is not a condition sealed in the loins by genetic mysteries. The new paternalists have mistaken that oppression for the Negro."[32]

Lorraine's friends were thrilled by this piece that put the Beats in their place. Langston Hughes wrote her, playfully and admiringly, "*Wonderful* piece of yours on 'The New Paternalism' in the 'Voice.' I could read you all night long—and *stay* awake! I hope you will write books as well as plays—and lots more articles and commentaries in lots more places. I sure do!"[33] He recognized the power of her critical chops, ones that arguably equaled her creative ones.

Others, mostly white critics, accused her of being too angry and of alienating her allies. Some Black ones did too. Baraka responded to her in a letter in which he suggested that her bourgeois background made her hopelessly alien from real Black struggle, though ironically he made that charge in defense of white critics. He wrote, "I read your 'exchange' with Norman Mailer with a great deal of interest . . . and I thought you might be willing to take Mr. Mailer's suggestion seriously that the two of you along with Jimmy Baldwin . . . along with W. E. B. DuBois, and either Max Lerner or Roy Wilkins to go at it at some kind of forum."[34] Apparently she rejected his suggestion, because his next letter read, "I am extremely disappointed that you don't think your differences with Norman Mailer are significant. Or, more baldly, how you can think that the differences which make for your such antithetical conclusions to Mr. Mailer's socially as well as aesthetically can be of such little import to yourself as you say. I suppose it is as they say, i.e. talk is cheap."[35]

Then he really went for the jugular, at least it was the jugular for someone with Lorraine's politics, which were much like his own (although at that point Jones was not as Far Left nor as deeply entrenched in Black life). He called her out of touch with the Black masses: "To my mind, the position you have made for yourself (or which the society has marked for you) is significant, if only because it represents the thinking of a great many Americans . . . black as well as white. Your writing comes out of and speaks of the American middle-class. . . . The critics . . . were joyful about Raisin for that reason. . . . The forum was designed, or is being designed, to at least straighten people out about the nature of your differences . . . not only with Mr. Mailer but with W. E. B. Dubois, Max Lerner and Jimmy Baldwin."[36]

Jones attempted to cast her out of the countercultural Left because of her middle-class origins and the success of her play. He also concluded she was at odds with two of the most beloved people in her life, Du Bois and Jimmy. It was a mean-spirited jab, but there was nevertheless some insight in the midst of it. Although he miscast Lorraine, her politics, her values, he was correct in some regard about how so many critics saw *Raisin*, and how that allowed them to celebrate it. Their misunderstanding of the play haunted her from the beginning. It seems to be the case that she resisted ever running the risk of writing in a way that her politics might be misunderstood again. She had written a masterpiece, but its meaning had been excruciatingly submerged by the admiration of so many. When Amiri Baraka reflected on his youthful dismissal of the play (back when he was named LeRoi Jones) he said, "We thought Hansberry's play was 'middle class' in that its focus seemed to be on 'moving into white folks neighborhoods' when most blacks were just trying to pay their rent in ghetto shacks. But it should be placed in context."[37] It was pretty common for Black communists and socialists to critique their less radical peers who were assimilationists in a fashion that often verged on vitriol. For example, even *Freedom*, which was rather ecumenical in terms of Black activism, if at times deeply frustrated with the civil rights establishment when it failed to support the Black Left, published an absolutely demeaning review of Ralph Ellison's *Invisible Man*. And Lorraine, as noted earlier, hadn't been too kind to Richard Wright in its pages. Lorraine became, in a sense, a victim of her own tradition and deeds.

Over the next decades some members of the Black Left would continue to reject Lorraine as a symbol of assimilationist politics, none more virulently than Harold Cruse in his book *The Crisis of the Negro Intellectual*. He described *A Raisin in the Sun* as being filled with middle-class sensibilities poured into working-class figures; a sort of class-based blackface. Even though she presented the noble working class in line with a socialist-realist doctrine, according to Cruse she couldn't get past the blinders that came from her own bourgeois roots. He questioned the entire premise: How would they get an insurance check? he asked. He was incorrect in his doubtfulness. In fact, the insurance check was an important reflection of Black working-class economic behavior in midcentury Chicago. For Black Chicagoans, life insurance provided an important old age provision, especially for the millions excluded from Social Security benefits because they, like Mrs. Younger, worked as domestics. In the 1950s, at least a half-dozen insurance companies were crucial institutions in Bronzeville, the majority-Black Chicago neighborhood. The largest was Supreme Liberty and Life, owned by a Hansberry family associate and which provided life insurance to thousands of working-class Black Chicagoans.

Cruse also questioned the daughter Beneatha's attendance at college, asking who would have paid for it. I imagine that Lorraine imagined Beneatha as a student at the University of Illinois's Navy Pier campus, which had a two-year program that served first-generation college students who, upon successful completion of the program, could go on to the University of Illinois at Urbana-Champaign. A significant number of Black female students were there in the early 1950s, and they had a Negro heritage club that studied African history and culture of the sort Beneatha was fascinated by. Many of the students at the Navy Pier campus studied the biological sciences, because the university had recently purchased a medical school, a dental school, and a school of nursing in the city, and therefore had the faculty and resources to support that branch of academic study. So Beneatha's path did in fact make sense. Lorraine's attention to detail was painstaking yet wholly neglected by some of her most aggressive critics.

Lorraine spent years trying to correct the misunderstandings of *Raisin* in various ways, including rewrites of the play and a more explicit elaboration of politics in her later artistic work. Her letters to the editor, essays, and other written corrections of the misunderstanding of the play reflected a practice she adopted about everything. She obsessively and insistently wrote down her complaints about how she was mischaracterized and misconstrued, and how often critics generally misunderstood art and politics.

A glimmer of the source of her urgency can be found in a letter she wrote to the *New York Post* in 1959. She praises Billie Holiday's biographer, William Dufty, for an article he'd written about the recently deceased singer. There is a sense of yearning and admiration in the letter. She wrote,

> There is a bold and ungarnished, yet sweet humanity in the writing which is undoubtedly the right, the incredibly right kind of tribute to what was apparently her true greatness as an artist and human being. I never knew her. William Dufty makes it possible. I am, from his account of her life, much moved. I mention greatness above because of the way it haunts Mr. Dufty's testimony, in the things he selects to remember: her appraisal of Louis, her pronouncements of the world race question, and what the Spanish speaking people call her on the street.[38]

One gets the feeling that Lorraine was already contemplating what it meant to be understood well and remembered fully. She wanted the same for herself.

A Raisin in the Sun was such a rousing success on Broadway that there was soon buzz about it becoming a film. Lorraine was hesitant at first about doing a movie. She was fearful of the "glossy little paws of Hollywood."[39] But she gave in because of the much larger audience that could see the film, asking herself, "How could a writer who literally took pride in what some intended as an epithet, the label of 'popular writer' not see it. The popular writer in me did see it."[40]

In writing the screenplay, Lorraine took the Youngers out of the kitchenette and into the landscape of Chicago. She displayed the racism the Youngers faced day in and day out: scenes between Lena Younger and her employer, Lena going to the grocery store in her neighborhood and seeing the poor quality of produce, and then traveling out to white neighborhoods to shop, where there was better food but where she was mistreated. Lorraine also included a scene in which Walter Lee, George Murchison, and Joseph Asagai listen to a street-corner Black nationalist. Additionally, she wanted the film to begin with a view of the South Side of Chicago in all its ghetto realism. Though the film crew shot three hours of footage with these additional scenes, all the overtly political revisions ended on the cutting-room floor.

In one of her journal lists of likes and hates, the producer of the film, David Susskind, took a hit. So did the politically moderate Sidney Poitier. Privately she felt less warmly about the film than the *Times* article she wrote about it suggested. But the movie was, notwithstanding her ambivalence, enormously successful. Lorraine was nominated by the Screen Actors Guild Awards for the best screenplay of the year and won an award at Cannes. Perhaps it was the time. Perhaps it was the fame. There was only so much she could do with *Raisin*. But in her deeds in the following years, there would be no more mistaking her politics at all.

Lorraine's artistic desires sharpened. In a prospectus she wrote on December 13, 1962, for what she imagined would be a theater devoted to Black drama (she called it the John Brown Community Theatre), she envisioned an institution that rejected the rules of markets and money and was wholly devoted to Black Americans. She described it as

> a theatre dedicated to, and propagated by, the aspirations and culture of the Afro-American people of the United States.
> . . . a theater wherein the cultural heritage of that people, which owes to their African ancestry, will find expression and growth.

> . . . a theater which, at the same time, will readily,
> freely and with the spirit of creativity of all mankind,
> also utilize all and any forces of the Western heritage of
> that same people in its arts.[41]

Lorraine wanted hers to be a theater neither bound by commercialism nor the snobbery or self-congratulatory postures of the avant-garde or arts establishment.

Lorraine believed in art, and she also believed in struggle. She dreamed about what her people might do, and what she might do, constantly. Though she had yearned for fame, it was a bitter pill. Perhaps this is why as she encountered fame, her melancholy and her need for meaningful community grew deeper. As she stepped into celebrity, she found friends who shared her yearnings and dreams. Though they never quite filled the void, they illuminated and loved one another. They dreamed and created together.

CHAPTER SEVEN

The Trinity

We had that respect for each other which is perhaps only
felt by people on the same side of the barricades, listening to
the accumulating hooves of horses and the heads of tanks.
— *James Baldwin about Lorraine*[1]

We never talked about men or clothes or other such
inconsequential things when we got together. It was always
Marx, Lenin and revolution—real girls' talk.
Nina Simone about Lorraine[2]

ON MAY 12, 1959, Studs Terkel interviewed the newly famous Lorraine
at her mother's apartment for his radio program. Lorraine described
her time with the writer and working-class hero in a letter to Bobby:
"Studs came out and did a tape last night and stayed for hours—
because we liked him very much. He is a very wonderful and very
interesting man and we got to drinking and eating and talking with
Mamie and Carl and Perry and Vince up front and it was really good.
. . . I asked if he had met Beauvoir when she was here and he said
yes and that she is a wonderful woman who strictly knows what the
hell she is about."[3]

In the midst of the interview Terkel asked Lorraine what she
thought about the scene of contemporary young Black writers. She
responded by saying there wasn't much happening. Not much at all
except for a young exile who had come back, along with some other
writers, from places like Paris and Rome. From what she'd read of
this young man, she said he was "undoubtedly one of the most talented American writers walking around. . . . If he can wed his particular gifts, which are just way beyond most of us trying to write on

many levels—with material of substance, we have the potential of a great American writer."[4]

He was James Arthur Baldwin. Jimmy, as she called him.

The friendship that grew between Lorraine and Jimmy is storied. It was both an intellectual and a soulful partnership. Less often described, but no less significant, was her relationship with the singer Nina Simone. The three of them formed a sort of trinity. Geniuses, they produced enduring work at the cusp of the great social transformations of the mid-twentieth century. All three were, according to early twenty-first-century terminology, queer, though only Jimmy's sexuality was publicly known. They struggled together at the crossroads of social, familial, and parental legacies with the tide of revolutionary action and deed. Jimmy and Nina are still everywhere in the public eye and popular culture. Their archives are widely shared. Books about their lives are numerous. Everyday people know their faces and voices. Lorraine remains in their shadows, but she was key to them and they to her.

Jimmy first saw Lorraine in 1958 at the Actors Studio, in Manhattan. She was there to see a theatrical workshop production of his novel *Giovanni's Room*. She sat in the bleachers. But when the lights came up and luminaries of American theater expressed how much they disliked the play, little and unknown Lorraine argued with them intensely. Jimmy was grateful. "She seemed to speak for me; and afterward she talked to me with a gentleness and generosity never to be forgotten. A small, shy, determined person, with that strength dictated by absolutely impersonal ambition: she was not trying to 'make it'—she was trying to keep the faith."[5]

Lorraine's advocacy for Jimmy's play was likely born of a number of feelings. The kinship of queerness, though silent, was undoubtedly one element. This work, she knew, was important. And then she shared his persistent questioning of the rules of patriarchy and religion. After all, the character most like her in *Raisin* is famously slapped in the face for questioning the existence of God. There was also the matter of Lorraine's constant racial solidarity. She took up for Black folks, as it were, and often felt herself to be at battle against the racism they experienced at the hands of white critics who frequently pointed fingers at them without introspection. She'd also already seen the potential in Jimmy. And Lorraine never hesitated as a critic, despite her youth, to make assessments of promise and possibility. Not only that, she also hoped to steer his promise.

Jimmy wasn't completely correct in his assessment of her, however. Lorraine *did* want fame, she wrote as much in her diaries. But he was right, she wanted to produce meaningful art far more than fame, and wasn't willing to compromise.

Lorraine and Jimmy met again when *A Raisin in the Sun* was in tryouts in New Haven and he came to see it. That was when their friendship really began. About a month before their reencounter he'd had a dream "in which he was joined by a beautiful, very young black woman who, after performing a song and cakewalk with him, seemed to merge with him 'her breasts digging against my shoulder-blades.' "[6] Jimmy prophesied Lorraine.

Jimmy would refer to her as Sweet Lorraine. Sometimes her mother did, too, in letters. "Sweet" is a lesser-known archetype of Black American culture. White Americans generally know sassiness and chops-busting Sapphire. They do not know sweet. Sweet is not, as it might seem if one attends only to the mainstream rules of American gendering, a diminishing word. Among Black Americans it describes a welcoming and caring disposition and a way of being cherished. Those women who are called sweet can be and often are steely and strong. This was how Jimmy saw Lorraine. Plus he was passionate about music. And I believe she called to mind the pop standard "Sweet Lorraine," probably the Nat King Cole version, in which he sings about her beauty, her brilliance, and leading her "down the aisle."

Jimmy wasn't going to marry Lorraine. But he did lead her down an aisle of sorts. And she did the same for him. He was already famous when they met. His semiautobiographical novel *Go Tell It on the Mountain* had been published in 1953 and *Giovanni's Room* in 1956. The latter had stirred up quite a bit of controversy because it portrayed a tender and tragic love affair between two men. Lorraine was six years his junior and new to fame. And yet he treated her as an intellectual peer, a confidant, and at times a friend whom he implored for help. In the spring of 1959 he wrote her a letter asking for assistance with his play *The Amen Corner*. Jimmy wrote,

> Out here on a sand bar, working and taking walks by the ocean, which seems to be my particular brand of therapy . . . back at the end of the month. This is a begging letter. I wish you'd make a point of giving Lloyd Richards the script of Amen as soon as possible. . . . I think I'd like to try to explain to him that my reluctance—or something—about handing him the script had only to do with a certain, treacherous shyness, and with my reservations about my script.[7]

He was vulnerable and playful at once. "Begging," that simple word, has a particular Black vernacular ring. It is often issued as a complaint about somebody who asks for too much. He wrote this word, and writing was of such importance for the two of them, and it cued their common ground, the soulfulness in these highbrow thinkers. Both Lorraine and Jimmy tended toward the speech affectations that public figures routinely adopted in those days. They enunciated and sounded almost haughty in public. Yet the rhythm of everyday Black speech is there in their private communication. She answered on her birthday, May 19, teasing him:

> Jimmie Dear—Got your "begging" note yesterday. Been out of form myself for a week. Here is Lloyd's address. . . . Have fun on your sand bar and work very hard. I shall try to get the manuscript to Lloyd—though I ordinarily see him seldom. Haven't read it myself yet—haven't even read a newspaper since I last saw you. Love, Lorraine.[8]

It wasn't the only time Jimmy would ask her to help him with his nervousness about writing. But most of the time their interaction was simply that of a raucously good friendship. As the writer Gene Smith described, "She and James Baldwin were great friends, although at times a passerby might believe that they were about to slug it out at a party or at his place or hers. They yelled at each other, ranted and raved, drank. They also laughed."[9]

Jimmy would, in several places, try to describe their bond. There were other figures, like Medgar Evers or Martin Luther King Jr. or Malcolm X, about whom he also wrote retrospectively, and loved, but that was always quite different from his memories of Lorraine. It might have had to do with her gender. When he wrote about the assassinations of these other friends, men, he tried and charged the nation. He also autopsied it, exposed its festering innards. But about Lorraine he wrote intimately, though he also insisted upon her genius, power, and righteousness. In describing her as "Sweet Lorraine," Jimmy said:

> That's the way I always felt about her, and so I won't apologize for calling her that now. She understood it: in that far too brief a time when we walked and talked and laughed and drank together, sometimes in the streets and bars and restaurants of the Village, sometimes at her house, gracelessly fleeing the houses of others; and sometimes seeming, for anyone who didn't know us, to be having a knock-down-drag-out battle. We spent a lot of time arguing about history and tremendously related subjects in her Bleecker Street, and later Waverly Place, flats. And often, just when I was certain that she was about to throw me out as being altogether too rowdy a type, she would stand up, her hands on her hips (for these down-home sessions she always wore slacks), and pick up my empty glass as though she intended to throw it at me. Then she would walk into the kitchen, saying, with a haughty toss of her head, "Really, Jimmy. You ain't right, child!" With which stern putdown she would hand me another drink and launch into a brilliant analysis of just why I wasn't "right." I would often stagger down her stairs as the sun came up, usually in the middle of a paragraph and always in the middle of a laugh. That marvelous laugh. That marvelous face. I loved her, she was my sister and my comrade.[10]

Full of drink and mirth, he left her place enchanted by her marvelous face and laugh. And they shared something profound: loneliness. He wrote, "Her going did not so much make me lonely as make me realize how lonely we were. We had that respect for each other which is perhaps only felt by people on the same side of the barricades, listening to the accumulating hooves of horses and the heads of tanks."[11]

Their retreat into "down home" talk, the echo of the South in both of these second-generation migrants in apartments and bars in the Village, was essential. It beat back loneliness of a personal sort, which both of them carried everywhere. It also must have been a relief to cast off the burdens of being in the public eye. And yet, when they were in the public eye, together, they could function like a marvelous tag team, their ideas bouncing back and forth, rapid-fire. They both participated in a roundtable titled "Liberalism and the Negro," hosted by *Commentary* magazine, a publication that vaulted the literati of the 1950s and 1960s into the sphere of public intellectualism. This discussion consisted of a group of writers: Langston Hughes (Lorraine's mentor and Jimmy's sometime nemesis), Alfred Kazin, Nat Hentoff, Emile Capouya, and Lorraine and Jimmy. At one point, Jimmy responded to a question from Hentoff, who wondered whether Black writers had sufficiently questioned the value of assimilation.

> BALDWIN: I feel that there's been far too little.
> HENTOFF: In other words, equal for what?
> BALDWIN: Equal for what, yes. You know, there's always been a very great question in my mind of why in the world—after all I'm living in this society and I've had a good look at it—what makes you think I want to be accepted?[12]

Then Lorraine jumped in:

> HANSBERRY: Into this.
> BALDWIN: Into this.
> HANSBERRY: Maybe something else.
> BALDWIN: It's not a matter of acceptance or tolerance. We've got to sit down and rebuild this house.
> HANSBERRY: Yes, quickly.

BALDWIN: Very quickly, and we have to do it together. . . .
You know, in order to be a writer you have
to demand the impossible, and I know I'm
demanding the impossible. It has to be—
But I also know it has to be done. You see
what I mean?

In the same discussion, they echoed each other another time, this time with Jimmy responding to Lorraine's calls. In considering the failures of Southern white writers Carson McCullers and William Faulkner when it came to racial matters, Lorraine said:

William Faulkner has never in his life sat in on a discussion in a Negro home where there were all Negroes. It is physically impossible. He has never heard the nuances of hatred, of total contempt from his most devoted servant and his most beloved friend, although she means every word when she's talking to him and will tell him profoundly intimate things. But he has never heard the truth of it. . . . The employer doesn't go to the maid's house. You see, people get this confused. They think that the alienation is equal on both sides. It isn't. We've been washing everybody's underwear for 300 years. We know when you're not clean.[13]

And then Jimmy said Lorraine's point was very important, and remarked that Carson McCullers's treatment of Black people "doesn't reveal anything about the truth of Negro life, but a great deal about the state of mind of the white Southern woman who wrote it."[14]

This call and response between Jimmy and Lorraine would also move throughout their written work. At the beginning, it was in the way they both struggled with the legacy of Richard Wright. He was the great Black literary father. Wright had taken an early interest in Jimmy as a young writer, but Jimmy turned on his mentor and attacked Wright's *Native Son*. He considered Wright a nihilist who diminished the full humanity of Black people. Lorraine agreed, although she thought the way Jimmy upbraided Wright gave fodder to racist white people (despite her own rather aggressive criticisms of Wright in *Freedom*). With *A Raisin in the Sun*, Lorraine made her criticisms of Wright's messages more oblique than Jimmy's. Like *Native Son*, *Raisin* begins with the sound of an alarm clock, alerting the viewer or reader that one is waking up in the ghetto. In *Native Son*, the protagonist Bigger's first duty is to kill a rat that has entered their cramped apartment. Lorraine rejected Wright's analogy between rats and Black people. When Lena Younger has chosen the new house, her daughter-in-law Ruth refers to their soon-to-be departed kitchenette apartment as a rattrap. The description gives Lena pause, and she responds by telling Ruth a story about Walter Lee's and her dreams. The message is they are not rats; they are human. The most dramatic rat reference of the play comes after Walter Lee has been swindled out of their money, including that which would send his sister, Beneatha, to college. Beneatha refers to Walter Lee not as a man but rather a "toothless rat." Lena Younger angrily lectures Beneatha. She tells her, when you measure a man, measure him right, meaning she must have sensitivity to his experience when evaluating him. Yet again, through the voice of Lena Younger, Lorraine says: we are not simply what circumstance has made of us, we are more.[15]

Lorraine also worked on a novel, *All the Dark and Beautiful Warriors*, which was a response to *Native Son*. Her character Son (that is, not somebody's nigger but somebody's child) is an answer to Wright's Bigger Thomas. Son was not rendered in naturalist form (Lorraine despised literary naturalism) and a mere product of his environment like Bigger. Son attempted to shape it. As she was wont to do, she reinterpreted her literary father, and Jimmy's, to suit the world as she saw it.

Jimmy preferred literary patricide. He wrote of Wright's best-selling novel *Native Son*:

> Below the surface of this novel there lies, as it seems to me, a continuation, a complement of that monstrous legend it was written to destroy. Bigger is Uncle Tom's descendant, flesh of his flesh, so exactly opposite a portrait that, when the books are placed together, it seems that the contemporary Negro novelist and the dead New England woman are locked together in a deadly, timeless battle. . . . Bigger's tragedy is not that he is

cold or black or hungry, not even that he is American, black; but that he has accepted a theology that denies him life, that he admits the possibility of his being sub-human.[16]

Jimmy's criticism, ironically, was not unlike that of those who called Lorraine a social dramatist for having an explicit set of politics. Jimmy called *Native Son* "a protest novel." The difference was, Wright denied the humanity of the oppressed. Recognizing the full humanity of Black folks was, to Jimmy's mind and to Lorraine's, necessary in the fight for freedom. Jimmy believed they had to tell the truth about the dangers of Wright-like thinking regardless of how white audiences might take it.

That said, Lorraine's and Jimmy's politics were different. He wasn't ever going to call himself a Marxist, communist, or nationalist. He was just committed to honesty, ideology be damned. Lorraine was insistently though creatively ideological. Lorraine leaned more toward social theorist, and Jimmy was to his core a critic, truth teller, and doer. And Jimmy didn't refer to himself as gay, he just happened to "fall in love with a boy" a number of times, whereas Lorraine, though closeted, embraced the words *lesbian* and *homosexual* to define herself.

However, the spirit of their work was always mutually sympathetic. Jimmy called *A Raisin in the Sun* a play in which Lorraine served as a witness to Black America. He did too. In perhaps his most famous book, the 1963 epistolary text *The Fire Next Time*, he answered Walter Lee's climactic action. In *Raisin*, standing before his son, Walter Lee insists upon moving into the white neighborhood and rejects the offer of a lot of cash in exchange for maintaining segregation and abdicating his dignity. In *The Fire Next Time*, Baldwin testifies to his nephew about his late father. Jimmy wants his nephew to see how his father (like their father before him) had been crushed by the forces of white supremacy in his life. He issues an appeal to his nephew's generation to make use of their righteous anger rather than be distorted by it. Jimmy, a former child preacher, preaches to the Walter Lees of the world and to the others. He makes plain the wages of white supremacy.

In the second essay of the slim book, Jimmy echoes Beneatha, the character in *Raisin* whom Lorraine based upon herself. Beneatha, headstrong and sophomoric, questions Christianity and the existence of God. Mrs. Younger responds by slapping her across the face. As long as she is in Lena Younger's house, Beneatha learns, she is required to believe. Jimmy, too, questions American Christianity and the way in which it inures people, Black and white, to a vile order. Instead, he says, Americans ought to move beyond the status quo of their fears, beliefs, and oppressions. That was precisely what the young Beneatha, sometimes in a silly way, was trying to do. And what Lorraine and Jimmy tried to do in their lives also.

The literary dialogue between Lorraine and Jimmy continued in their other work. James Baldwin's play *Blues for Mr. Charlie*, which was completed in 1964, and Lorraine Hansberry's *Les Blancs*, which she worked on for years, were a sort of call and response. They both referenced "white folks" in the title. "Mr. Charlie" was a general term for a white man, and *Les Blancs* (The Whites) was Lorraine's play on Jean Genet's *The Blacks*. Lorraine's play takes place in a fictional African country at the dawn of its independence movement, and Jimmy's is set in the heat of the Southern freedom movement. They both explore interracial intimacy, even love, and how it coexisted with violence and racial domination. They both confronted the question of whether violent resistance to white supremacy was a necessary course for Black people to take. In Jimmy's play, a white man is put on trial for the murder of a Black man. This is the second Black man he has murdered (the first being the husband of a Black woman he loved). The killer is found not guilty, and the play concludes with a protest march joined by the only white man who has cast his lot with the Negroes in town. Though the people are despondent, their protest is the resolution and hope of the play. In contrast, Lorraine's play puts the colonizers on trial, as it were, and issues them a death sentence for the cause of emancipation, even those for whom the Africans feel affection. Madame Nielsen, a British transplant who understands the African cause, is killed in crossfire at the conclusion.

Lorraine was not only more ideologically driven than Jimmy. She was also more militant. But they weren't really at odds in these literary conversations. As though theirs was a dialectical union, they looked at the matters from different angles: it was a waltz or, better yet, like the twist, rocking back and forth and side to side. Jimmy tended to focus upon what Americans must do in order to confront white supremacy inside oneself. He sought an exorcism and challenged Americans to become otherwise. Lorraine tended to focus upon social relations and the injustice of the political order and what that suggested about who people must be for one another. Neither of these descriptions is absolute, but they mostly hold. Lorraine was an ensemble thinker; Jimmy was a soul-centered one.

In 1963, Jimmy wrote to Lorraine in a bit of a tizzy about his novel *Another Country*:

> My dear Lorraine: a very particular favor but please don't do it if you don't want to. Some people can be read to and others can't, so I'll understand.
>
> But I am finally really reaching the end of this monstrous opus of mine. And I am so weary and have already received such dire warnings as to my probable fate when it is published—and even I can see that it's not a very pretty novel—that my mind and soul might be somewhat steadied if I could read a couple chapters from it—from the beginning, from the end. I pick on you. I'm afraid, because I respect you as a writer and value you as a friend and because, as a Negro, you can call me if I have—as I certainly pray I have not—falsified my grim interracial drama—which is also something more than that.[17]

He proposed that the group reading include Lorraine and whomever she might want to bring, his brother, and "the girl to whom the book is dedicated, Mary Painter." Mary was a dear friend of Jimmy's, a white American economist, famous for working on the Marshall Plan, who lived in Paris. He continued in his appeal to Lorraine, "This note is probably more symptomatic of panic, that panic which always attacks me near the end of any long endeavor, than of anything else."[18]

I do not know if Lorraine heard him read from *Another Country*, but I know she heard him. They both were at once fearful and truly courageous. Like Lorraine, Jimmy was afraid of heights, bridges, elevators, and planes. They both were afraid that their writing might

not be good. Published in 1962, *Another Country* was, characteristic of Baldwin, a courageous book. It treated the counterculture
of Greenwich Village that they both often occupied. Its protagonist,
Rufus Scott, is a jazz musician who has a romantic relationship with
a Southern white woman. As the novel progresses, their relationship
grows violent, and ultimately Rufus commits suicide. In the aftermath of his suicide, the novel follows the people who surrounded
Rufus. His friend Vivaldo, who is white, has a romance with Rufus's
sister, then also has an affair with Eric, who had been Rufus's lover.
These are just two of a series of partnerings among the grief-stricken
and conflict- and guilt-ridden group trying to make sense of the death
of Rufus.

Another Country was controversial. Between the interracial and
same-gender sexuality and the partner sharing, the novel alarmed the
public. Jimmy finished it while living in Istanbul, perhaps because it
was one of those works that was easier to get into without the pu-
ritanical American landscape surrounding him. And even though it
was a Village novel, and the Village had become a recognized center
of the cultural vanguard, in depicting it, Jimmy nevertheless pushed
readers to the very edge of America's willingness to see itself.

An intellectual friendship can take many forms. It can consist of
long conversations into the night about books, arguments, and art.
Intellectual partners read together and write together. They also, and
this is really my point, can swim in each other's imaginations. Neither one imitating the other, but after bathing in the other's words
they return back to the shore, to the work, shaped by the beloved's
waters. That is what I see, what was so special, about these friends.

Lorraine responded to *Another Country* with *The Sign in Sidney
Brustein's Window*. Her play also treated the Village counterculture,
queer sexuality, interracial intimacy, and a suicide. But in her play,
it is a white woman in love with a Black man who commits suicide, rather than a Black man in love with a white woman. Though
Lorraine received mixed reviews for her play, it is, according to my
own critical judgment, a more effective work of art than Baldwin's
novel. Lorraine worshiped at the altar of clarity and organization in
her writing. She didn't care for obscurity or cluttered story lines and
found Jimmy's fiction, generally speaking, not nearly as good as his

essays, which she considered among the best in the history of American writing. But the point is that the consistent thread between these two works of theirs—how the politics of race, gender, and sexuality are always at work, even in the closest of relationships—placed each of them well ahead of their time. Neither saw the struggle for freedom as limited to fights for laws and full citizenship. Freedom dreams led to complex questions about humanity and existence, about who we are and might become. They asked and tried to answer them. Their explorations took them both beyond the United States, though Jimmy was far more traveled than Lorraine ever would be, and beyond their time period. For example, they shared a criticism of the queer writer André Gide that suggested their layered approaches to ideas of freedom. Baldwin, in his essay "Male Prison," and Lorraine, in her notes about Gide's life, both argued that while Gide's sexuality was transgressive, his indecent commitment to patriarchy and disdain for his wife were persistent. Neither felt warmly toward Gide for this reason. Though they were both most passionately focused on the question of race, it was a question that was never posed in isolation from other structures of difference and domination such as gender, class, and sexuality. And neither of them subjected race to monolithic interpretations. Jimmy and Lorraine understood that people, in all their messiness, had complex architectures inside and among them.

Jimmy was six years Lorraine's senior, and Nina Simone was three years her junior. At their ages, these differences mattered, though they didn't impede. While Jimmy spoke of Lorraine as a girl and also a peer, Lorraine is generally talked about as Nina's elder and teacher. This is largely because of the way Nina recounted their relationship. Nina, who with her rendition of the Gershwin tune "I Loves You Porgy" became famous merely a year before Lorraine did, described Lorraine as the person who politicized her. Case in point: on the evening of Nina Simone's debut at Carnegie Hall, May 21, 1961, Lorraine called her not to congratulate her but to discuss Martin Luther King Jr.'s arrest in Birmingham and what Nina ought to do for the movement.[19]

Two months later, Nina, who hadn't been explicitly political beforehand, was at a civil rights fund-raising meeting with Lorraine and Student Nonviolent Coordinating Committee (SNCC) officers at the apartment of the actor Theodore Bikel.[20] Lorraine had brought Nina into the movement, but they became really close in 1962, when they found they lived near each other in their vacation homes in Upstate New York. Nina described Lorraine's influence on her: "It would take a special kind of friend really to pull me into the ideas of the Black Movement and force me to accept that I had to take politics seriously. That special friend was Lorraine Hansberry."[21] Nina said Lorraine took her out of herself and pushed her to see the bigger picture. She frequently visited Lorraine in the Hudson Valley. In September of 1962, Nina gave birth to her daughter, Lisa. Lorraine was named Lisa's godmother and gave the baby "a beautiful silver Tiffany hairbrush and comb for her christening present."[22] This was characteristically Lorraine. She was gracious and cosmopolitan. She was also an aesthete, but didn't care for trivialities. Nina wrote, "Although Lorraine was a girlfriend—a friend of my own, rather than one I shared with Andy [her husband]—we never talked about men or clothes or other such inconsequential things when we got together. It was always Marx, Lenin and revolution—real girls' talk."[23]

The time Nina and Lorraine shared wasn't just political kinship; it also provided Nina with a refuge from Andy Stroud, her abusive husband. The poet Nikki Giovanni said about Nina and Lorraine's relationship, "What is important is that she loved her and she was loved in return. She never had to watch her back. With Andy, she watches her back."[24] Like Lorraine had with Jimmy, she and Nina shared an intimate retreat from the loneliness. But it was also a fertile ground for their imaginations and interior lives.

Nina described her further: "Lorraine was definitely an intellectual, and saw civil rights as only one part of the wider racial and class struggle. . . . Lorraine was truly dedicated; although she loved beautiful things she denied them to herself because they would distract her from the struggle, which was her life. She wore no makeup except lipstick and had only five dresses. "I'm pretty the way I am," she'd say "I don't need lots of clothes."[25]

This restraint, the effort to discipline herself, seems to have been at once a reflection of Lorraine's values and also perhaps a bit of ascetic self-punishment for her voracious yearning for beauty.

I do not know whether Nina and Lorraine discussed sexuality. Nina was tortured by her own. She felt deep shame over her desire for women, and Andy's rage about it made things even worse. Andy and Nina's partnership was not like Lorraine and Bobby's. It remained romantic. They were never friends, nor interlocutors. Andy drove Nina to work to the point of exhaustion, while Bobby encouraged and facilitated. And yet in a sense, Nina and Lorraine probably both felt trapped. Bobby was Lorraine's protection from a profoundly homophobic society. And though Lorraine embraced her sexuality, sometimes begrudgingly, it was unquestionably difficult to do so. But the stuff of Nina and Lorraine's intimacy in that respect is not in my hands, and cannot be read through their works the way it can with Jimmy and Lorraine's intimate relationship. It is clear, however, there was shared passion. I imagine that their special affection for the name Simone entertained both of them. Lorraine loved Simone de Beauvoir, and Nina took her stage name (first intended to hide her bar singing from her religious mother) from the actress Simone Signoret, a favorite of Nina's who would eventually translate *A Raisin in the Sun* into French.

Nina's husband, Andy, recalled, "Lorraine carried her over into high gear, put her on fire." Neither Nina nor Lorraine was interested in accommodation or respectable liberal politics. They believed the fight for freedom was for all intents and purposes a war. Nina was definitely as militant as Lorraine.

When they were in New York City, Lorraine would go to the Village Gate to hear Nina play piano and sing. As a girl in North Carolina, Nina had trained as a classical pianist. She was a prodigy. However, when she came up North with the intention of attending the Curtis Institute in Philadelphia, she was rejected. Devastated, she made a living playing piano and eventually singing in an Atlantic City nightclub. There she'd crafted a creolized sound of her own. Nina blended classical, jazz, pop, and blues tunes and cultivated a distinct genre- and gender-bending back-of-the-throat vocal sound. Lorraine heard the South in Nina's voice like she did in those of her parents. Yet Nina was also the sound of her generation. Lorraine witnessed in Nina an artist who had no hesitation when it came to borrowing and blending from every tradition at her disposal. She did so both to craft her original artistic voice and to make something unapologetically Black. Nina was a model of extreme discipline, one who composed music in her head nonstop. But Nina's discipline wasn't about restraint and closing off the imagination or the ranging and raging desires, aesthetics, and interests. It was a discipline that allowed for creative expansion. Her discipline was vivid and on fire rather than punishing. For Lorraine, who had often castigated herself for having too many ideas and running in too many directions at once, Nina had to be inspiring. She proved that expansiveness didn't have to mean failure. Even Nina's rendition of "I Loves You Porgy," from a show that Lorraine despised for its stereotypical rendition of African Americans, must have made Lorraine rethink her sense of the world. Nina changed some of the lyrics because she refused to sing a parody of Black English, and she reinterpreted it as a truly powerful and plaintive love song. She was an example of how creative one could be with the archive of art they had at their fingertips as Americans and as modern people, and how it all could be put into the service of freedom dreams.

In addition to going to meetings and fund-raising for the Southern freedom movement, Lorraine inspired Nina to compose and perform political music, including "Brown Baby," "Mississippi Goddam," and the haunting "Pirate Jenny," which she recorded in 1964. "Pirate Jenny" was written by Bertolt Brecht for *The Three-Penny Opera*, a political "play with music" with a strong criticism of capitalism. It became one of Nina's "show tunes." She'd famously said about the 1963 "Mississippi Goddam," "This is a show tune but the show hadn't been written for it. Yet."[26] When it came to "Pirate Jenny," however, the show had been written and performed many times. In the original opera, it is sung by a character named Low-Dive Jenny, a hotel maid. She is treated with derision. Jenny sings her fantasy about a pirate ship coming to burn down the town. However, when Nina sang Brecht's song, it took on an entirely different feeling.

As she cleans, Jenny plots an overthrow that teems with the fury of a thousand slave revolts. She is pirating the Middle Passage and claiming her freedom. On this ship, "the Black freighter," Black people are not cargo but its vengeful captains.

Lorraine also used Brecht as a source for her revolutionary

imaginings. However, hers were not about the moment of upheaval but rather its aftermath. Hers was a less passionate and more theoretical Brechtian exploration than Nina's. In her short story "What Use Are Flowers?" Lorraine takes up Brecht's play *Mother Courage and Her Children*. Brecht wrote *Mother Courage* in the midst of the rise of Nazism but set it during the Thirty Years' War of the seventeenth century. It stars a woman who attempts to profit financially from the war, and yet all her children are killed because of it. Brecht's criticism of war profiteering attacks both fascism and capitalism. Lorraine's first version of her riff on *Mother Courage* also took place in Germany and was titled *Gedachtnis*. It opened with children fighting because one has eaten a rat that they all want, and it had a folksy old wise man as its protagonist. Later she changes the folksy old wise man into a stuffy professor.

In all the versions of Lorraine's Brechtian story it is not the children but the mothers who are now gone. In this postapocalyptic world, the children have gone feral. They have no language and fight over scraps until they are found by the professor who tries to teach them civilization. He gives them language and cooking and building skills. He teaches them ethics, and in the poignant conclusion, moves them beyond a sense that the only purposes in life are utilitarian, by imparting the beauty of a flower. In the midst of all this, however, he imposes the rules of gender upon them. He teaches them that the girl, Lily, is "different" from the others and must be protected. He separates and categorizes and creates hierarchies among the boys and everything else in their midst. Lorraine raises the fear that the same mess might be made all over again, even if the revolution succeeds, if we aren't careful. While Nina used Brecht to imagine Black revolt, and specifically a feminist Black revolt, Lorraine used him to expose patriarchy as something ideological, not natural.

Both Nina and Lorraine interspersed feminist messages throughout their movement-inspired art, putting them well ahead of their time since the mainstream feminist movement hadn't yet begun. In another show-tune-style song, "Go Limp," Nina hilariously mocked the sexual anxieties of the mothers of young women who were joining the Southern freedom movement. Liberalism on race, the song showed, was not the same as a belief in sexual freedom or gender liberation.

Likewise, in Lorraine's final play, *The Sign in Sidney Brustein's Window*, she reveals the sexism of Sidney, who wants his wife, Iris, to look like a wild country girl. He is always undoing her tightly bunned hair and treating her like a fantasy. Sidney mocks the bourgeois sexual and racial conservatism of Iris's sister Mavis, yet remains oblivious to his own sexism for most of the play. Lorraine and Nina's ideas merged both at the level of formal experimentation, borrowing and reinterpreting and experimenting, and in their attentiveness to particular events and scenes. Just as Lorraine wrote complex characters, Nina did too, with stories embedded in songs. Theirs was a jazz practice, pursued with a sense of broad purpose combined with a penchant for drink and brooding.

Lorraine, Nina, and Jimmy were lonely, even though they had each other. They lived in a profoundly unjust society; they saw their people suffering North and South, and grew to understand that suffering in a global sense, felt by "their people" of so many sorts. Each carried the responsibility of the artist, as well as the passion, often in solitude. Strangeness is a feature of genius. It isolates even as it is acclaimed. Hence Lorraine's famous quip: "The thing that makes you exceptional, if you are at all, is inevitably that which must also make you lonely."[27]

This thing of being beloved and having true friends, and yet also experiencing profound loneliness, is important to recognize. It isn't unusual. Jimmy wrote, "You think your pain and your heartbreak are unprecedented in the history of the world, but then you read. It was books that taught me that the things that tormented me most were the very things that connected me with all the people who were alive, who had ever been alive."[28] The grounds for friendship can be common wounds. And certainly, along with the art and the politics and the commitment, that was part of it. Nina sang her a song that day called "Blackbird" about loneliness, pain, and sorrow, about feeling unwanted and misunderstood. Lorraine echoed that feeling in a note to Nina titled "Alone, the Saturday evening before Easter 1962—7 pm":

> I would give my soul to be with someone whom I really and truly longed to please. That would be paradise. But there are no such . . .

Thus, I am alone. Very. Tonight. Seven o'clock. Spice, scotch and me. I shall wash my hair. No one will call—save some one whom I do not wish to see. . . .

But worst of all, I am ashamed of being alone. Or is it my loneliness that I am ashamed of? I have closed the shutters so that no one can see. Me. Alone. Sitting at the typewriter on Easter eve; drinking; brooding; alone.[29]

She could not imagine things getting better.

Beloved but alone. The three—Lorraine, Jimmy, Nina—were apart more often than they were together, always somewhere with some long list of demands placed upon each one. Eventually that demand for Lorraine was her health. She wanted a more vital life, one that might have been possible were their lives not so far-flung. She imagined a company of friends with whom she would spend evenings, dancing and laughing. Soon after achieving it, she no longer desired fame; she just wanted a close community of people: "For money and fame I would make the exchange. But that has always been so; only now I could pay the devil his wage."[30]

They paid mightily for love, love of the people. James Baldwin died in 1987. Nina Simone, in 2003. Both were widely criticized after the 1960s for their declines. Illness and grief contorted their post-movement lives, but so did truth telling. The admiration couldn't go on forever. Celebration waned the more Nina and Jimmy knew and said about the world. They made people uncomfortable with their vulnerabilities and rage. Their loneliness deepened. Lorraine haunted. Unexpectedly but appropriately, in the twenty-first century, after death, Jimmy and Nina were reborn as icons on posters and pillows and in books upon books. Lorraine has yet to be.

CHAPTER EIGHT

Of the Faith of Our Fathers

The man that I remember was an educated soul, though I think now, looking back, that it was as much a matter of the physical bearing of my father as his command of information and of thought that left that impression upon me, [. . .] a man who always seemed to be doing something brilliant and/or unusual to such an extent that to be doing something brilliant and/or unusual was the way I assumed fathers behaved. [. . .] And he carried his head in such a way that I was quite certain that there was nothing he was afraid of.

           —Lorraine, on her father, Carl Hansberry[1]

I had inclined to be contemptuous of my father for the conditions of his life, for the conditions of our lives. When his life had ended I began to wonder about that life and also, in a new way, to be apprehensive about my own.

           —Jimmy, on his father, David Baldwin[2]

JIMMY'S FIRST BOOK, the semiautobiographical novel *Go Tell It on the Mountain*, was published in 1953. In it, the protagonist struggles with the grip of his brutal Pentecostal minister father and the hypocrisies of a church that expects his fidelity. Later, his most widely read nonfiction work, *The Fire Next Time*, is devoted in half to a letter of tenderness to his nephew, and caution, through the narration of Baldwin's brother, his nephew's father. In those books, and his later work, Baldwin repeatedly found himself wrestling with the shadow and weight of his father. It very well might have been this fixation, along with the passions and the loneliness, that allowed Jimmy and Lorraine to forge so deep a bond.

Inheritances haunt.

In her personal and political life, Lorraine both rejected and shouldered the expectations that went along with being her father's child. He was brilliant, respectable, and patriotic. She was brilliant, restless, and radical. He remained with her long after his death. One of the things I have learned about death is this: no matter how grief stricken you are, no matter how much you miss them, yearning for their laughs or hands or eyes, your relationship to the dead continues long after their bodies are gone. Memory is not simply a way of holding on, it is a reencounter. Their visits continue as long as you do. Over time, you hopefully understand more about the past and more about the absent person made present. This was the way of Lorraine and Jimmy. But unlike most, they put their visitations on the page.

A Raisin in the Sun, after all, is about what a South Side Chicago family will do with their late patriarch's $10,000 life insurance check. But it was also about so much more for Lorraine personally. Her father was known as the "kitchenette king," but what she depicted was the life of the tenants, not the owners. And that said a great deal about where her allegiances lay, politically speaking.

And so it was mortifying when, just a few months after her play hit Broadway, the notorious Mayor Daley of Chicago charged Lorraine and her family with building-code violations on the properties they owned on the South Side. The truth is that code violations were the norm rather than the exception in Chicago's South Side, and Daley, well known for his animus toward Black people, likely relished the opportunity to embarrass the Hansberrys, especially the newly famous Lorraine. For Lorraine, the idea that she might be involved in providing substandard housing to Black Chicagoans was horrifying. The *New York World-Telegram* article of June 6, 1959, about the situation bore the heading "Slum Play Author Sued as Slumlord."[3] She responded to a request for an interview from the *New York Post* about the situation by saying,

> When I first heard about the story, I didn't know what they were talking about. I called Chicago and learned that my

name had been placed on a piece of property when it was purchased some years ago. I wasn't told about it and I have no legal or equitable title to that building. [. . .] Of all the things in
the world I could have been hit with, this was the most painful. [. . .] I'm not a slum landlord. I've never derived a cent
from that building—whoever owns it. Parenthetically, I might
say I haven't drawn a cent from the family since I came east
nine years ago.[4]

Lorraine revealed more than she likely realized. She had aban-
doned the monetary part of her inheritance and with that a set of pri-
orities too. Though Lorraine was not so interested in making money,
she also knew that wasn't her father's only driver. As she revisited his
legacy again and again in her work, she explored what he taught, and
which aspects of those lessons she admired and which she rejected.
Case in point: while *A Raisin in the Sun* is certainly not about her
family's circumstance, it is filled with references to her family and
home. For example, the $10,000 check is a symbol that comes from
her childhood. In 1936, that is the amount the Hansberrys put into
the Hansberry Foundation, which was established to fight cases of
racial discrimination.

The tragic turn of *Raisin* is of course when Lena Younger gives
her restless son, Walter Lee, the $10,000. He fails to follow instruc-
tions about how much to set aside, and instead invests the bulk of it
in a liquor store venture that is actually a con. Truman K. Gibson Jr.
wrote somewhat salaciously that Carl Hansberry was once swindled
in a manner akin to Walter Lee. He said that two men came to Carl
with a get-rich-quick oil investment and drilling project in Centralia,
Illinois. Carl fell for the racket and lost a great deal of money. Fortu-
nately, Carl hadn't invested all his life savings.[5] I don't know whether
this is true or idle gossip. But it gets to a core tension of the play and
of Lorraine's politics. She saw the drive of capitalist acquisition and
accumulation as something that was deeply American, and also perverse. When Walter Lee tells his mother that business is the meaning
of life, she says sorrowfully that she remembers when they believed
that the meaning of life was freedom.

In Lorraine's literary world, mother wisdom is trustworthy

though subtle, and paternal inheritances are thorny and overpowering. In addition to responding to Richard Wright, *A Raisin in the Sun* played on Theodore Ward's 1937 play, *A Big White Fog*, a production of the Negro Unit of the Chicago Federal Theater Project. *A Big White Fog* also took place in a kitchenette. Its villain, Danny Rogers, sought to get rich by creating kitchenette apartments, a not too thinly veiled jab at Carl Hansberry. It was also a domestic drama in which the characters displayed conflicting paths to escaping the exclusions and poverty of post–Great Migration Chicago. But in Lorraine's play, unlike Ward's, the father is dead, and women have a stake in the dreaming. Ward's play ends with a simplistically happy communist ending (and a rejection of Marcus Garvey's Back to Africa message). Lorraine's play ends with ambiguity.

Although Lorraine wrote a play without Ward's crude Marxism, and also without Richard Wright's naturalist social determinism, she did embrace Richard Wright's famous call for Black writers to focus on quotidian Black existence and regional specificity. In the landmark treatise on Black Chicago that emerged from the Works Progress Administration's Negro in Illinois study, *Black Metropolis*, the authors described how, in Chicago, "the Negro community recognized the favored position of the waiter, butler and chauffeur. . . . They had close contacts with the wealthy whites and were able to acquire the manners, polish and social graces attendant to upper class behavior."[6] This was Walter Lee. Proximity to white elites created a restless yearning for that kind of wealth and leisure. The conventional Marxist idea, that susceptibility to false consciousness is maximized in the remove from proletarianism, is also evident in Lorraine's work. It is present in Lena Younger's remembrance of Walter Sr.'s description that a man was made to work with his hands. Walter appears to have been left, metaphorically, empty-handed. But he claims his inheritance not when he steals money but by rejecting it. In refusing the money a white man, Linder, offers them to not move into the white neighborhood, Walter Lee honors his father's legacy and creates a legacy for his son.

Walter Lee is not the only one who has desires regarding the paternal inheritance. Beneatha does too. She wants to go to school. Lena and Ruth, both domestic workers in other people's homes, want a home of their own. These are all hopes for something better as the fruits of the father's labor. Beneatha also seeks a collective inheritance. It drives her interest in Africa and anticolonialism and her fascination with one of her suitors, Joseph Asagai, an African student who is committed to independence. The other is the bourgeois George Murchison. Asagai and Murchison represent divergent paths of the Black and educated: one might become an intellectual and one might become bourgeois in attitude and status. While George Murchison completely rejects Africa, and says that there is no heritage of value in Africa, Beneatha's enthusiasm for the continent is sophomoric. However, when Walter Lee gets into it—jumping on the table, dancing with Beneatha, proclaiming Jomo Kenyatta as his man, referencing Ethiopia, and Shaka Zulu—the scene transforms from comedic to politically significant. Walter Lee is not a scholar or bourgeois. He enters into a trance of sorts, a reverie in which his political agency is real, in which money might not be the most important thing, in which he can connect joyfully with the sister he resents. Lorraine wanted theatergoers to think about the questions: To whom do Black American people belong? In which of the father's many mansions?

She believed of all the characters, Asagai had the best answer. Lorraine said of him: "My favorite character is the African suitor. I think he's a true intellectual. He is so confident in his perception of the world that he has no need for any façade. I was aware that the Broadway stage had never seen an African who didn't have his shoes hanging around his neck and a bone through his nose. The only Africans I've known have been students and he was a composite."[7]

Although it is well established that Beneatha was based upon Lorraine, perhaps Asagai was too. He is a twin of hers of sorts, also imagining a yet unseen future, one freed from yokes. And he has Lorraine's intellect. Indeed, frequently male characters in Lorraine's work say words she would say or have ideas she would have. One wonders why this is. Why give the men her voice and often the biggest ideas? Some critics have suggested that despite her feminism, Lorraine couldn't quite fully embrace a feminist vision. She often began projects with women characters at the center of her work, and then turned those central characters into men. She rarely mentioned the women writers who shaped her ideas, though it is clear several did. Patriarchy puts men at the center. Lorraine depicted that truth and sometimes succumbed to it. But that didn't mean Lorraine wasn't a thoroughgoing feminist. Yes, Beneatha is a bit silly, but she is also intellectually courageous. Even though Asagai is a captivating and brilliant suitor, she isn't ready to live an ostensible fairy tale and become his wife. Then there is Lena Younger. She could have easily been cast as a servile Mammy figure. But she is the head of the family. She is a woman with hopes and dreams and sensitivity. She is flawed, courageous, and filled with integrity. And she possesses her own sort of militancy, not unlike Lorraine's mother who sat with a pistol on her lap to protect the family from a white mob.

And Ruth. Ruth's quiet place in the play has led to her critical neglect. There are two important points about Ruth. Ruth learns she is pregnant and intends to have an abortion. But she doesn't articulate whether that plan is a result of their poverty or her deteriorating relationship with her husband. Lena is horrified and tells Walter Lee. His assertion that Ruth wouldn't do that and Lena's response that a woman will do anything to save her family that's already here don't give us a clear answer. The silence of Ruth's interior is meaningful. So much is there that we do not see while everyone is fighting over what to do with the inheritance.

Ruth's voice is strongest when she insists that despite the loss of their money, they *will* move. She says, "It is my time." She proclaims she will work with her baby strapped to her back for that house. For Ruth a home is freedom.

Lorraine began working on *Les Blancs* in 1960. It was also a play that at its root confronted the question of what to do with one's inheritances. The play takes place in a fictional African country as the people overthrow colonial authority. In this play, as with *Raisin*, the father has just died. There are three sons: Tshembe, who returns from England, where he has a white wife and a child, for his father's funeral; Abioseh, who is studying for the priesthood; and the youngest, Eric, or as his mother named him, Ngedi. Eric is different from the other two. He is not their father's biological son but the child of a British settler and rapist. He is also the only one who was at their father's bedside at his death.

Much of the play consists of Tshembe verbally jousting with a white American visitor named Charlie who stands in for the white liberals who often irritated Lorraine. Charlie wants to equivocate and preach nonviolence but refuses to acknowledge the full responsibility of colonialism and white supremacy. Even as Tshembe has a biting criticism of colonial power, he and his two brothers have to confront what precisely he and they intend to do and how they will respond to the prospect of revolution. How will they honor their father and claim their motherland?

Abioseh, to Tshembe's dismay, believes that the church and "civilization" will convince the settlers to respect them and grant them rights. Tshembe believes Abioseh has cast aside his own inheritance and placed his faith in the colonial one. In contrast Tshembe is skeptical of Eric in another way. Eric, it is implied, is in a romantic relationship with a European man, Willy DeKoven. Tshembe finds Eric with a case of makeup given to him by Willy, and shouts at the youngest brother, "A woman's cosmetics! So, Eric, if you cannot quite be a white man you have decided to become a white woman? (Cruelly knocking the pith helmet from the boy's head) And toys like this! What else does he give you to make you his playtime little white hunter?"[8]

Later, however, Eric is the only one of the three who has no hesitation about joining the freedom fighters. He says, standing before his brothers, that it is time "to drive the invaders into the sea. And that I shall carry the spear and shield of our father."

A tense exchange follows:

> TSHEMBE: You are half European. Which part of yourself
> will you drive into the sea!
> ERIC: I am African enough not to mock when my
> people call!
> TSHEMBE: And what will you do when your doctor
> calls, Eric? It takes more than a spear to
> make a man.
> ERIC: What does it take, Tshembe? You teach me! What
> does it take to be a man? A white wife and son.

Tshembe wrests their father's sword from Eric's hands. And Abioseh asks Eric why he hates "them," meaning the white settlers. Tshembe implies that Eric's intimacy with Willy is a sign of his debasement at white hands. As though he is their charge, Tshembe and Abioseh each claim that they will take Eric back home with them in order to save him. Eric interjects, "No. I am staying here—where I belong! . . . They call me by the name my mother gave me."[9]

"They," the independence fighters, recognize Eric's inheritance. And that is enough.

All three brothers are called to question their intimate connection to whiteness, a connection that is also part of the inheritance of colonialism, of slavery, of what it meant to be Black in the modern world. Tshembe wonders whether to stay and fight or return to his wife and child in England. Abioseh chooses to betray the revolutionaries, though he says he does it for the greater good of Africa and Africans. Eric, the one whose manhood is questioned, is the one who leads in courage. He is also the one who has a lover who understands the violence of colonialism.

The fictional Eric in various ways was like Lorraine's beloved friend Jimmy. Like Jimmy, he is the one in his family who was not his father's biological child. He is the one who according to Tshembe has failed to be a man. And yet he is the one who holds most closely to his father's inheritance and his mother's words—the name she gave him. His drinking and his love life are thinly veiled references to Jimmy's struggles, as is his beautiful moral imagination.

In *A Raisin in the Sun*, Joseph Asagai says that he believes in the religion of doing what is necessary in the world. It is a glorious formulation. The revolutionary moment has its exigencies. This is what Lorraine believed too. She played the idea out in *Les Blancs*. The revolutionary moment required a casting off of the mother country and the patriarchal authority of colonialism. The figure of Madame Nielsen is introduced to make this point. She is one of the settlers, an elderly European woman now blind, who has known the brothers all their lives and who holds special affection for Tshembe. Madame Nielsen knows the end is near. She touches Tshembe's face and hair, no longer able to see him. It is an intimate moment but an uncanny one. She knows him, but also doesn't. He is transforming under her hands.

At the conclusion of the play, Tshembe, encouraged by Madame Nielsen, agrees to join the resistance. Abioseh, in contrast, has betrayed the resistance. Someone has died as a result. Siding with freedom over blood, Tshembe shoots his brother. A battle breaks out and Madame Nielsen dies in the crossfire. The white mother figure, the mother country, is dead.

In her early notes, Lorraine played with structuring the play primarily around women characters. Candace, the name of Ethiopian queens, was one she favored in her notes on *Les Blancs* and in other work. But in the later versions of the play near the time of her death, which Bobby pieced together to publish posthumously, the women are minor or silent. It is odd. The play is Lorraine's voice. But she doesn't ventriloquize women, only men. Maybe it was a way of noting that revolution and the establishment of nation states have for the entire course of modern history overwhelmingly been seen as the work of men. Maybe it was because Lorraine wanted to do things that were usually reserved for men—write about politics, write grand plays, lecture on street corners, and the like—that she more often cast the heroic in male archetypes. But with Eric she shows us how she believed in troubling gender. Valor, courage, and truth were not limited to the idealized masculine man. And, as she instructed, the bastard child might be the one best suited to avenge the disinherited.

There are three Black sons in *Les Blancs* and three white daughters in *The Sign in Sidney Brustein's Window*. Notwithstanding the shift in identities, the father's legacy is again at the core of this play. It began as a work about a woman named Jenny Reed. But by the time of its completion, Lorraine put women in the minor key. It became, at least nominally, a play about a man named Sidney Brustein, a disenchanted and unfocused former radical who jumps from one failed venture to another. Over the course of the play he finds himself enchanted by a political candidate who he believes will finally buck the system, only to find that like so many others, he has been co-opted by the powers that be.

The play struggled when it went up on Broadway. The reviews

were mixed. Audiences were disturbed she hadn't written a "Negro play." Some called it a "Jewish play" instead. But it was really a play about the world Lorraine occupied in her young adult years. Lorraine wrote about *Sidney* for the *New York Times*, and as usual she was her own best critic:

> Being 34 years old at this writing means that I am of the generation that grew up in the swirl and dash of the Sartre-Camus debate of the postwar years. The silhouette of the Western intellectual poised in hesitation before the flames of involvement was an accurate symbolism of some of my closest friends, some of whom crossed each other leaping in and out, for instance, of the communist party. Others searched, as agonizingly, for some ultimate justification of their lives in the abstractions flowing out of London or Paris. Still others were contorted into seeking a meaningful repudiation of all justifications of anything and had, accordingly, turned to Zen, action painting or even just Jack Kerouac.[10]

Lorraine believed that the artistic and political grounds on which they had grown left her generation ill prepared for responding to the struggles for racial emancipation in Algeria, Birmingham, and Cuba. To put these three places together showed a great deal about her thinking. Racism wasn't, according to Lorraine, principally about sitting at lunch counters, it was about dispossession, exploitation, and raw power.

But why did she make this point in a play that featured a Jewish Greenwich Village intellectual? That "chukka booted Bergman film-loving non-cold water flat living, New School lecture-attending, Washington Square concert going, middle class" figure didn't immediately seem to have anything to do with Algeria, Birmingham, and Cuba.[11] But like so much of her work, in an interior place and particular life, she raised large questions about alienation and politics and power. It is a portrait of the counterculture milieu, not really of Sidney, and the way he and the people around him were ill equipped yet trying to figure things out at a crossroads moment in history.

To that end, the most interesting figures in the play are the secondary characters. They ask Lorraine's persistent question: How are we our father's children? How ought we be?

Sidney's wife is named Iris. She is a frustrated actress who frequents psychoanalysts and has begun to chafe at Sidney's romantic idea of her as a backwoods country girl. Her sister Mavis is a bourgeois housewife, prim and conventional, and also stuck in a loveless marriage. The third sister, Gloria, is in love with Alton, a Black communist. Though Alton believes Gloria is an international model, she is in fact a prostitute.

Sidney relishes Iris's shame-filled story about her patrilineage:

> Papa was so crude and stupid. . . . You know, I never heard my father make an abstract thought in his life, and, well, he had plenty of time to think, if you know what I mean. Didn't work that steady. And each of us, I think we've sort of grown up wanting some part of Papa that we thought was missing in him. I wanted somebody who could, well, think. Mavis wanted somebody steady and ordinary. And Gloria, well, you know—rich men.[12]

Later, Sidney is confused because Mavis describes their father as a dreamer and a backwoods poet, the type of man she wishes she had married. When Sidney confronts Iris about the sisters' differing accounts of their father, Iris says she was just trying to live up to Sidney's fantasy. Eventually Iris rejects Sidney's fantasy and paternalism. She doesn't need a second father.

The weight of the father in the sisters' minds is bound up with their decisions to choose men who were vastly different from him. It is an unspoken aversion. Mavis has chosen someone rich and urban; Iris, a neurotic Greenwich Villager who is Jewish. And Gloria has doubly stepped away from what was expected.

When Mavis learns that Gloria is dating a Black man, she is horrified. Even though Gloria is a prostitute, Mavis believes she can "do better." She says, "Well now listen, there are other men in the world! The last time I looked around me there were still some white men left in this world. Some fine ordinary upstanding plain decent very white men who were still looking to marry very white women."[13]

Sidney's upstairs neighbor walks in. He is a playwright. Mavis suggests Gloria might like him instead:

> MAVIS: Well he's sort of cute. [. . .] Is he married?
> SIDNEY: [. . .] David's got an alternative lifestyle.
> (*MAVIS considers but doesn't get it.*)
> David's gay. (*She still doesn't.*) Queer.
> IRIS: Homosexual. (*MAVIS draws back.*)
> SIDNEY: Utterly.[14]

When Gloria's actual boyfriend comes in, because of his light skin Mavis mistakes him for a white man, and also suggests him for Gloria. It is a moment from a Shakespearean comedy, a series of mistaken identities and misread surfaces. But the play soon turns into a modern version of a tragedy. Alton discovers that Gloria is a prostitute after he has proposed to her. He comes to Sidney angry that he wasn't warned. Sidney tries to convince Alton that if he loves her it shouldn't matter. But it does because of Alton's tortured understanding of his inheritance. He screams,

> THE WHITE MAN DONE WRAPPED HIS TRASH IN TINSEL AND GIVE IT TO THE NIGGER AGAIN, HUH, SIDNEY?! . . . Don't you understand, man? Like I am SPAWNED from commodities— and their purchasers! Don't you *know* this? How do you think I got the color I am? I got this color from my grandmother being used as a commodity, man! The buying and the selling in this country began with *me*, Jesus help me![15]

Alton describes his father's life as a Pullman porter who "wiped up spit and semen, carried drinks and white man's secrets for thirty years," and that of his mother, who was a domestic. He describes the shame of being given the table scraps from her employer, scraps they were forced to eat to survive: "And then one night he had some kind of fit, and he just reached out and knocked all that stuff—the jelly and the piece of ham, the broken lamp and the sweater for me—he just knocked it all on the floor and stood there screaming with the tears running down his face: 'I ain't going to have the white man's leavings in my house, no mo'! I AIN'T GOING TO HAVE HIS THROW-AWAY . . . NO MO'!"[16]

Though a Marxist and a Black man, rather than finding solidarity with Gloria having been used as a commodity, Alton cannot bear proximity to such status. It threatens his aspirational manhood. He leaves Gloria. Lorraine's depiction, though sensitive, is an indictment of the hypocrisy rooted in patriarchy. Alton, like Sidney, fails to recognize the woman he loves.

Later Gloria and David speak. She is bereft. He is wry at first: "Isn't it the great tradition for writers and whores to share the world's truths?"[17] Gloria is offended, but after David apologizes, they have a profound conversation. Gloria speaks her bitterness about Alton: "I was going to marry that vanilla dinge! Do you know what some of the other girls do—they go off and sleep with a colored boy—and I mean *any* colored boy so long as he is black—because they figure that is the one bastard who can't look down on them five seconds after it's over! And I was going to *marry* one!"[18]

"One," the categorical definition, the thing that places you here or there, of value or not, a condition that is applied, inherited, or immutable. Lorraine pressed at that. She pressed at it according to race, she pressed at it when she had Alton and Walter Lee throw about the word *faggot* as though with the slur they could recuperate their insecure manhood. She pressed at it in Gloria's vision of Alton and in his vision of her. For Gloria, being a "one" not by birth but by the Madonna-whore binary endemic to patriarchy put her at the mercy of the derision and violence of others.

Lorraine has Gloria testify about the terror of her trade. She reveals her "predilection for psychos and vice cops." She says, "This last one . . . I think he was trying to kill me."[19] Gloria has been abused by johns and attempted suicide three times. Her shame is overwhelming. It goes back to the father. She asks, "Whaddaya do if your own father calls you a tramp   on his deathbed . . . huh? Whaddaya do?" David responds by stating, "Trying to live with your father's values can kill you. Ask me, I know." Gloria retorts, "No, Sweetie, living *without* your father's values can kill you. Ask *me*, I know."[20]

Of many, this is perhaps the most profound reckoning in the play. To honor the father and to betray his wishes are both potential minefields. Patriarchy confounds and captures. The moment is disrupted when, after Sidney leaves the room, David has a proposition for Gloria. He tells her about "a beautiful burnished golden boy . . . sitting on a chair upstairs. He is from one of the oldest, finest families in New England. He is exquisite. But great damage has been done to him—" Gloria interrupts:

> GLORIA: (For this girl there are no surprises left) He
> requires . . . the presence of a woman. . . .
> Not just any girl, but someone young enough,
> fresh enough, in certain light, to make him
> think it is somebody of his own class.[21]

Their intimacy instantly rots. Gloria realizes that for David she is a potential object, a "one" whose usefulness is that with her presence she might allow the golden boy to maintain the fiction that he has not betrayed the rules of men of his class and station. The golden boy lives in what Jimmy termed a "male prison." In Gloria's character, Lorraine imagined the effect of the patriarchal prison on a woman deemed unworthy of marriage yet worthy of purchase. What could have been a profound connection between Gloria and David, a pained yet shared confrontation with broken inheritances, is ruptured by the hold of yet another inheritance. Gloria, devastated, attempts suicide again. And succeeds.

Lorraine had been raised with the mandate that she never was to betray the family or the race. She maintained loyalty to the race in an expansive and experimental way with her art and her politics. She took these responsibilities very seriously. But she also understood that obligations were never innocent. The burden of honoring the father could also destroy. The shame of failing in that endeavor could too. Hers was a legacy not only of possibility but also, potentially, of terrible shame. She lived and worked with that cross to bear.

CHAPTER NINE

American Radical

A really serious intention . . . in so glamorous a frame.
—*James Baldwin of Lorraine Hansberry*[1]

WHEN I WAS A CHILD, *radical* was a compliment my parents gave to people whom they considered smart and politically righteous. It was a mid-twentieth-century leftist term of art. But even before that, the word had a long history as praise. As far back as the early nineteenth century, it meant something grander than reform. It referred to a belief that a thorough transformation was necessary to correct injustice. Hence, its etymology "at the root." That, according to radicals, is where the change must occur. These days, *radical*, at least in the mass-mediated public sphere, has mostly negative connotations. It is associated with violent fundamentalisms or irrational passions, while moderation is associated with decency. For Lorraine, however, American radicalism was both a passion and a commitment. It was, in fact, a requirement for human decency.

In the years between the production of *A Raisin in the Sun* and 1965, Lorraine's politics cohered. She sustained an overarching belief in socialism, but her focus became the liberation of Black people from colonialism abroad and Jim Crow at home, both South and North. Her internationalism and her rejection of both imperialism and capitalism still put her at odds with the most prominent mainstream civil rights organizations of the day and their postwar liberal politics: patriotism with respect to US interests abroad and advocacy of integration with a modest welfare-state model.

Lorraine wrote an article for the January 17, 1960, *New York Times* supplement prepared by the Urban League, a moderate civil rights organization. In that work, as in so many others, she made the point that we ought to look away from elites and to the grassroots to understand Black America. The piece, "Stanley Gleason and the Lights That Need Not Die," told the story of a young Black man, barely out of his teens. She argued that society had failed Stanley. His elementary school teacher had not believed him when he told her he had an outside toilet in New York City. In middle school, he had been assaulted by a police officer. And as a reminder of the international scope of the problem, Lorraine wrote about how Stanley witnessed the racist depictions of Africans in the Museum of Natural History. In that building, Black people were a hair above primates. She wrote,

> It was after the museum that Stanley developed his way of walking. It is a gait made up of the alternation of one tautly bent knee and one dragged foot which culminate to give him a bouncy propulsion through life. There is pungent irony in the fact that it resembles nothing quite so much as a limp. Stanley intends to connote something else by the way he walks which, though he would never articulate it in that way, has an organic relationship to the lie on the walls of a mighty museum.[2]

Lorraine saw in his stride an unarticulated knowledge that he came from survivors, people who made it through the Middle Passage and slavery. The bop in Stanley's walk, a performance of the disabling that race does and a defiant aesthetic mastery despite it, was and is quintessentially Black style. Lorraine interpreted its meaning in light of world history, contemporary economics, and the growing movement. The spirit of those who sought freedom, those who were Black, was beautiful.

Lorraine was part of a group of US-based artists and intellectuals who, though often in community with their less radical counterparts, were unflinching in their social critique. Even her anticolonialism was deeply connected to her criticisms of the United States and its role as a global power. And yet this didn't disrupt her celebrity and influence. In that period, fame and national prominence for African Americans was rare enough that it was not unusual for a playwright to be involved in cultural diplomacy. She was invited by the State Department to meetings of various sorts, which it appears she frequently turned down. Maybe they didn't care about her radical politics because she didn't seem so powerful. Maybe they hoped she might be swayed to the political center by proximity to power. I don't know. However, Lorraine agreed to participate in then Senator John F. Kennedy's 1960 African "airlift."

That summer, fifteen former African colonies became independent. Kennedy, as a matter of Cold War diplomacy, considered establishing relationships with these newly independent nations to be in the best interests of the United States. He said as much explicitly:

> I believe that if we meet our responsibilities, if we extend the hand of friendship, if we live up to the ideals of our own revolution, then the course of the African revolution in the next decade will be toward democracy and freedom and not toward communism and what could be a far more serious kind of colonialism. For it was the American Revolution, not the Russian revolution, which began man's struggle in Africa for national independence and individual liberty. When the African National Congress in Rhodesia called for reform and justice, it threatened a Boston Tea Party, not a Bolshevik bomb plot. African Leader Tom Mboya invokes the American Dream, not the Communist Manifesto.[3]

Airlift Africa was one of Kennedy's strategies. It brought nearly three hundred young Africans to study at universities and high schools in the United States and Canada. Both Malcolm X and Lorraine Hansberry served as orientation leaders. Malcolm was recognized as an important international voice with respect to African independence, and had been invited to meet with representatives of the newly independent nations at the United Nations that summer. Kennedy, probably with some reluctance, undoubtedly saw it in his best interest for Malcolm to be included, though he was under FBI surveillance and the US government considered him a threat. Lorraine was probably an easier choice, although she had been on the radar of the FBI for as long as Malcolm had and was at least as militant. But given how *A Raisin in the Sun* had been interpreted by the public as a celebration of the American dream, perhaps the soon-to-be-elected president imagined that she would symbolize the great promise of liberal democracy for the young Africans.

But Lorraine saw herself as a representative of the struggle for Black freedom, not American capitalism. It was the death of Patrice Lumumba a few months after the African airlift that made that fact crystal clear to anyone paying attention.

Patrice Lumumba did not come to the States like the young Africans on the Airlift Africa planes. He was born in the Belgian Congo in July of 1925 and attended missionary schools. He began his professional life as a public servant in the colonial government. While working as a postal worker he began to be politicized and organized a postal workers' labor union. At first he aligned himself with the Belgian Liberal Party, but later, when he moved to the capital, Leopold-ville, he involved himself in the independence movement. When the brilliant and charismatic Lumumba attended the All African People's Conference in Accra in 1958, he emerged as a Pan-Africanist leader with international influence. He became the most prominent leader in the Congo at the Luluabourg Congress in April 1959. Attendees decided to set aside tribal differences and build a unified liberated Congo, and Lumumba spoke to that vision. Almost concurrent with the declaration of independence, Lumumba was elected president in May of 1960. Less than a year later, in January, he was assassinated. Both the Belgian and the United States governments were implicated in his death. They considered him dangerous. Lumumba had developed a favorable relationship with the Soviet Union, although he didn't intend to make the Congo a communist country. For the sin of African sovereignty, the two nations' leadership decided Lumumba deserved a death sentence. This enraged Lorraine.

Lorraine was inspired and fascinated by Patrice Lumumba. She had studied the history of the Congo in depth with Du Bois. And Lumumba was, in a sense, a living version of the character she created in Joseph Asagai: a pragmatic freedom fighter who believed in the religion of doing what was necessary in the world.

Patrice Lumumba was killed on January 17, 1961, but word didn't get out until February 16. In response, rebellions took place all over the world. In Chicago, Nigerian students protested at the Belgian consulate. In New York, Black people, mostly American and some international, protested at the UN. They carried signs that read "Congo Yes, Yankee No!" Police responded aggressively by dragging protestors out. The protestors fought back.

Ralph Bunche, one of the most well-known African American leaders and at that time the undersecretary of the UN, referred to the protestors as "misguided misfits."

Both Lorraine and Jimmy responded to Bunche with ire in the *New York Times*. Lorraine's letter followed Jimmy's. She wrote,

> Mr. Baldwin's gift for putting down the truth in his celebrated ringing essay style prompts me to remark that I too was profoundly offended by the effort to link the Lumumba demonstrations at the United Nations with Mecca or Moscow inspiration. [. . .] We may assume that Mr. Lumumba was not murdered by the black and white servants of Belgium because he was "pro-Soviet" but because he was, unlike the Kasavubu-Tshombe-Mobutu collection, truly independent which, as we seem to forget in the United States, was at the first and remains at the last an intolerable aspect in colonials in the eyes of imperialists.[4]

Bunche pissed her off. Frequently. He had no mandate from Black America to issue such an apology. And so, Lorraine said she hastened "to publicly apologize to Mme. Pauline Lumumba and the Congolese people for our Dr. Bunche."[5]

Even rage-filled, Lorraine maintained her sharp wit. And she made clear that though she'd aided the president a few months prior, her allegiance lay with Africans and not with the US government. She was not a Bunche-type Negro.

In a longer version of the letter, she wrote further, "Lest some be falsely persuaded by the tidings that the city's 'Negro leaders' deplored the nationalist demonstrations at the United Nations, we should all be reminded that 'Negro Leaders' in such instances, are held to be any and all commentators who tell the white community exactly what the white community has made it clear it wishes to hear.

It is an old and beloved if mutually dangerous custom in our land since plantation days."[6]

Whether domestic or internationally focused, Lorraine emphasized Black independence from white (European or American) political control. She continuously rejected the Western nations' panic around the potential influence of Islam or communism as both condescension and an effort at control. In this way, she was something of a Black nationalist, not as a matter of separatism but as an ethic of self-determination.

Lorraine belonged to a political community that agreed with her. Julian Mayfield wrote to her on April 5, 1961,

> I wanted to dispatch [a note] to you with one word "Wow" after the Times letter only to find Ossie had beaten me to the punch. What is the world coming to when us "respectable" folk start criticizing Roy Wilkins and Ralph Bunch [*sic*]! Seriously, that last sentence must have caused Mr. Charlie some consternation—and somebody had to say it. . . .
>
> Ossie and I have been thinking that a few of us ought to get together one afternoon to knock around some of the problems that are bound to face us in the near future: Africa, Sit ins, Passive resistance, etc.[7]

These artists stayed radical even as organizations like the NAACP and Southern Christian Leadership Conference (SCLC) tried to cautiously negotiate between the government and the people. Her artist community reached out with bold freedom dreams to organizing students down south and other like-minded people overseas. This is an important historical detail. The traditional narrative of Black radicalism in the US usually jumps from the 1930s to the late 1960s, but in fact there was a steady thread, a small but persistent network across the intervening decades. Lorraine and her people were a part of it.

Several weeks later, on May 20, Julian wrote a letter inviting Lorraine for a visit, because he and his wife, Ana Livia Cordero, were planning to move to Ghana soon, "despite what Isaacs said in the New Yorker about those Africans not being our natural brothers."[8] Julian joked, but it was serious. They believed Africans were their brothers, not in a romantic sense but in the shared commitment to a global struggle against white supremacy and for Black freedom.

As was her habit, Lorraine crafted fictional characters who allowed her to explore her political concerns about Lumumba specifically and African independence generally. In *Les Blancs*, two of the characters' names, Tshembe and Abioseh Matoseh, were plays on that of Lumumba's primary political opponent, Moise Tshombe, who was supported by the US government.

In a fictional vignette that she wrote around 1960, titled "Metamorphasis [*sic*]," she used her imagination and experience to explore the emergence of African independence and its leaders, like Lumumba. The story is written in the third person but from the perspective of a white businessman named Harry. Harry travels to meet "Rochester," a former employee of his, at the airport in Washington, DC. He reveals that he called the young African student he employed "Rochester" though it was not his name. And it was a cruel joke, a nod to the stereotypical shucking and jiving Black character who appeared on the Jack Benny TV show. The student's real name was Bandele Matoseh.

Harry says Rochester has moved up in the world, though the reader is left unsure how. As he travels, Harry contemplates the intense concern in Washington about African independence. He "let his mind puzzle again on some of the attention that was being given of late to the African zigs; well, he surmised, that was Washington for you. Got itself into a positive heat every time Khrushchev yawned!"[9] But then he wonders at his own interest in seeing Rochester. Perhaps it is also undignified for him to travel to see his former custodian. At the airport his misgivings grow. The airport is filled with homegrown Black people.

> His mind jumped suddenly . . . to the newsreels of the Negroes at the U.N. the day the red Congo boy, Patrice Lumumba-balaba or what ever his name was was killed. All those screaming, fighting local colored people. They had confused him mightily: surely they didn't identify: he had always thought they only wanted not to identify. Those newsreels had upset him; suggesting as they did some passions he had not known

to exist. Oh it was a shameful day for the country all right. Put any ten of them on a boat bound for Africa and they'd turn it around in mid ocean, he was certain.[10]

Harry mistakenly and strangely thinks perhaps some royalty from the Netherlands is arriving when the crowd surges in excitement. At the denouement of the story, a shiny black limousine arrives, drums are playing, and out of the limo emerges his custodian of fifteen years prior, now called Mr. Prime Minister.

Though Bandele Matoseh had become the prime minister of an independent Black nation, Lorraine made him a man who had once served as a custodian in the States. Of course part of the point was how Harry had underestimated his employee. But it was also a sign of what kind of representative she imagined he would be, the kind of representative the people could and should have. He was of the people, or in the terms of her day, of "the Black masses."

There had been a long history of Black Americans seeing their destinies linked to other colonized and Jim-Crowed people around the world. Lorraine, however, not only identified with Africans on the continent and in the diaspora in an abstract way, she also connected US imperialism abroad with racial injustice at home. She believed in undoing the domination and undue influence of the United States upon Black people, at home and abroad.

Lorraine also continued to follow politics in Latin America, perhaps because she had been so affected by her experiences in Mexico and Uruguay. In February of 1961 the FBI reported that Lorraine's name appeared in *Excelsior*, a prominent Mexico City newspaper, in support of David Alfaro Siqueiros on his sixty-sixth birthday, urging his release from prison. The Marxist painter had been arrested in 1960 for openly criticizing the conservative Mexican president and supporting striking factory workers and teachers. Lorraine was joined by other prominent thinkers and artists, including Du Bois, Alexander Calder, Jacob Lawrence, Georgia O'Keeffe, and the architect Eliot Noyes. Then in October of 1962, Lorraine asserted her support for the Cuban Revolution during a rally to abolish the House Un-American Activities Committee. In this speech, Lorraine criticized the Cold War fiction that the United States was a beacon for freedom and democracy by virtue of the country's intrusion into the self-determination of other nations. With respect to Cuba, she said:

> I think my government is wrong. I would like to see them turn back our ships from the Caribbean. The Cuban people, to my mind, and I speak only for myself, have chosen their destiny, and I cannot believe that it is the place of the descendants of those who did not ask the monarchists of the eighteenth century for permission to make the United States a republic, to interfere with the twentieth century choice of another sovereign people.[11]

Indeed, she went a step further and accused her country of absolute hypocrisy on the matter of freedom. They should not only turn back their ships to Cuba but also focus upon the sins of the United States at home. She argued that the US government must "empty the legislative and judicial chambers of the victims of political persecution so we know why that lamp is burning out there in the Brooklyn waters. And while they are at it, go on and help fulfill the American dream and empty the Southern jails of the genuine heroes," who were, to Lorraine, the young people of the student movement.[12] The troops, she said, ought not be sent to Cuba but to the South to finish the reconstruction that had been halted in 1877 in an indecent and unjust political compromise.

It was significant that at this rally, which focused on the Red Scare, she centered the lives of Black Americans. The anticommunist hysteria had often targeted white Americans who worked for racial justice. Lorraine understood that a belief in racial equality was a great deal of what the US government found threatening about radical left-wingers.

Though she was a radical in essays and letters, it was challenging for Lorraine to bring her radicalism to the American public in her art. She'd tried and failed to add content and context to the film version of *A Raisin in the Sun*. Then she was commissioned to write the first television miniseries about slavery, titled *The Drinking*

Gourd. In it, she confronted the evils of slavery directly. But it was far from a simplistic demonization of white Southerners. That approach might have been easier for network executives to digest. Rather, Lorraine was sympathetic to poor whites. She showed how class and social stratification among whites sustained slavery and maintained investment in it, even though poor whites were more victimized by economic exploitation than they were beneficiaries of whiteness. The radicalism of the screenplay lay in her exposure of the evils of capitalism that were at the heart of slavery. She also displayed the complex intellectual lives of the enslaved. It is a beautiful script. Had it been aired, it would have preceded *Roots* by more than ten years and, arguably, it would have challenged Americans about race even more than the landmark *Roots* did. But after the network executives read Lorraine's screenplay, it was left to languish in a drawer.

Lorraine continued to write however, multiple works with many drafts. And she threw herself into political organizing. She communicated with the young members of SNCC and arranged fund-raisers for them. She lent her voice to other causes also. At the Negro History Week program of the Liberation Committee for Africa, February 10, 1963, Lorraine served as a speaker, along with Carlos Gonçalves of the National Front for the Liberation of Angola and Oyil Chakamoi of Uganda. Gonçalves spoke about Portuguese colonial domination; Chakamoi spoke of Pan-African solidarity and the particular needs of African students in the United States. Lorraine expressed her admiration for young Africans taking steps toward liberation. And she yet again decried the "present and insufferable idea of the 'exceptional Negro.' Fair and equal treatment for Ralph Bunche, Jackie Robinson and Harry Belafonte is not nearly enough. Tea parties at the White House for the few will not make up for 300 years of wrong to the many. The boat must be rocked for the good of all."[13] Lorraine much preferred the overall-wearing fieldworkers who were pursuing a grassroots model of freedom deep in the Mississippi Delta.

And though she disagreed politically with the Nation of Islam, Lorraine refused to distance herself from them like so many respectable bourgeois Black people did. While Jimmy thought their racial absolutism was a problem, he too felt a bond with the Nation. Lorraine was less bothered by their response to whiteness, but considered it strange that they romanticized Islam as a Black religion, given how sub-Saharan Africans had been enslaved and colonized by Arab invaders before Europeans. And yet she saw value in the boldness of the Nation of Islam and in Black Americans maintaining a variety of political visions, including nationalist ones. In a March 22, 1963, letter to Daniel Thompson, a professor at Howard University and an editor of the *Journal of Negro Education*, Lorraine responded to questions he'd asked for their annual civil rights yearbook. In it she explicated her thoughts on the landscape of Black politics. She did not see the problem of racial inequality through the lens of individual experiences of discrimination but rather a universal condition of oppression. On this and other counts she found traditional civil rights organizations lacking. Regarding the NAACP she wrote:

> I am not sure that our people will ever have enough money to fight ALL the court cases it would take to begin to re-state what is already on the books. I think it is probably an outmoded organization. Hostile power in this country does not appear to be in the least responsible to legalisms. The celebrated Supreme Court decision of several years ago seems to have virtually invalidated its implications by the sheer fact of the nature of Negro life as a reality today. I mean I cannot see that it changed anything.[14]

Lorraine knew something about this, had known it since she was ten when her family won their lawsuit and the ghetto stayed as segregated as ever. As a result of that, and her diligent study of race as an adult, Lorraine's hope lay in direct-action protest rather than courts or the appeals of Black elites to white elites. She believed African Americans ought to

> attract the attention of the rest of the world to our plight and thereby use international sensitivity on the matter as a weapon in behalf of our otherwise mostly powerful people. This to me, is the real value of things like the Montgomery struggle and

the subsequent student movements: they make it possible for the Negro question to be forced upon the conscience of a nation which is otherwise delighted to have any number of priority questions that it must always deal with first.[15]

Lorraine was not simply a person who felt fidelity with oppressed people across the globe; she believed that the liberation of African Americans was also a cause for international concern. And though she advocated direct action, she also sustained a belief that art and intellectual work mattered in this struggle. There was no either-or for her or for her friends. In the same letter to Thompson, she used Jimmy as an example of this. Like her, Jimmy was involved with SNCC. In fact, he was even more directly involved. Though Lorraine wrote letters, raised money, and dedicated her time to organizing in the North, Jimmy traveled down south and put his body on the line with the young people. Lorraine said of his art that it held the urgency of the political moment, that "in his essays, . . . [he] has taken the politeness out of discussions of the brutalizing experience of the black man in this country and put it down as it is. I think Mr. Baldwin has left the apologists, black or white, nowhere to go but toward the truth."[16]

The contrast between the artist who serves as a witness for justice and the use of prominent artists or other Black people as respectable representatives was significant for Lorraine. She hated the American habit of exceptionalizing certain Black people and the way such practices were used to neglect or even justify the mistreatment of others. She wrote, "I feel that the old games of giving Ralph Bunche an award (or Lorraine Hansberry for that matter) for doing something that a Negro has not been allowed to do before is today intolerable. Leontyne Price is a very great artist—but the fact of her presence in the Metropolitan alters the condition of the masses of Negroes not in the least; neither will a Negro stuck here and there in the cabinet eventually."[17]

Lorraine ultimately shared her vision for a national Black political vision, one that certainly had to be inspired by what she saw on the international stage. She believed the answer would be a "mass organization" of Black people that could be organized to boycott or vote collectively or, as imagined in her good friend Douglas Turner Ward's future play, engage in a Day of Absence and put a wrench in the works of American industry. She saw the Southern freedom movement as the root of such possibility. For her it was not a reform movement, at least not the student movement, but rather a revolutionary one. Lorraine wrote:

> I don't think there is much of another direction. Julian Mayfield has said that whether we like the world or not we are going to have to deal with the fact that the condition of our people dictates what can only be called revolutionary attitudes. It is no longer acceptable to allow racists to define Negro manhood; and it will have to come to pass that they can no longer define his weaponry. I look forward to the day, therefore, when a centralized Negro organization will direct me not to pay taxes in protest of this segregated society: it will be a privilege to go to jail.[18]

Yet again, Lorraine emphasized self-determination for Black people. She was neither interested in status nor seeing Black folks manipulated by elites, whether said elites be Black or white. She wanted to be led by the people. It is this unflinching posture that makes Lorraine and Jimmy's famous 1963 meeting with Attorney General Robert F. Kennedy so fascinating. Of course she was an elegant and poised role model, an achiever and an exception. But she'd also proven herself to be unwavering and even confrontational in ways that did not leave much room for working with elites and powerful politicians. Perhaps because RFK hadn't paid attention to her strident positions and firm convictions, or he underestimated her, Lorraine wholly surprised the attorney general.

The day has been written about in numerous books and essays. The story is as follows: In response to the unrest in Birmingham, the attorney general called James Baldwin and other prominent Black people, and a few liberal white people, to meet with him quietly. He hoped to quell the Black people of my hometown, Birmingham, which was best described, for lack of a more appropriate metaphor, as a powder keg. The meeting took place on May 24, 1963, at a Kennedy-owned apartment at 24 Central Park South in Manhattan. In addition to RFK and his aide, Burke Marshall, present at the meeting were Jimmy and his brother David; Harry Belafonte; famous Black psychologist Kenneth Clark; Edwin Berry of the Chicago Urban League; Clarence Jones, an advisor to Martin Luther King Jr.; the singer, actor, and activist Lena Horne; the actor Rip Torn; June Shagaloff of the NAACP; and Southern freedom movement organizer Jerome Smith. Smith had founded the New Orleans chapter of the Congress of Racial Equality (CORE) and had initially come to New York so that doctors could attend to the jaw and head damage he'd sustained from beatings at the hands of Southern cops.

The energy of that time in history is important to understand. That year, Baldwin was touring the South and said, "There is, I should think, no Negro living in America who has not felt, briefly or for long periods, simple, naked, unanswerable hatred; who has not wanted to smash any white face he may encounter . . . to break the bodies of all white people and bring them low, as low as that dusk in which he himself has been and is being trampled."[19] Lorraine also felt this rage. Though the meeting began quietly, things heated up when Jerome asked about the government's real role in Birmingham. He implied that they were insincere with respect to protecting the civil rights of African Americans. Having faced the violence of the white South with no assistance from the federal government, Jerome had an empirical basis for this feeling. Jimmy recalled that "Bobby— and here I am not telescoping but exercising restraint—had turned away from Jerome, as though to say, 'I'll talk to all of you, who are civilized. But who is he?' "[20]

And then she unleashed. Recalled Baldwin, "Lorraine said (in memory she is standing, but I know she was sitting—she towered, that child, from a sitting position). 'You have a great many very accomplished people in this room, Mr. Attorney General, but the only man you should be listening to is that man [Jerome Smith] over there. That is the voice,' she added after a moment during which Bobby sat absolutely still staring at her, 'of twenty-two million people.' "[21]

For Jimmy, Lorraine became a representative of a special sort, of

Black womanhood, of freedom fighting, of her people writ large. He watched her face, saw her insistence that Bobby Kennedy hear her. He wrote,

> Her face changed and changed, the way Sojourner Truth's face must have changed and changed, or to the truth, the way I have watched my mother's face change when speaking to someone who could not hear. Who yet, and you know it, will be compelled to hear one day. . . .
>
> "We would like," said Lorraine, "from you, a moral commitment."
>
> He did not turn from her as he had turned away from Jerome. He looked insulted—seemed to feel that he had been wasting his time.[22]

Lorraine stood up and Jerome continued. Jerome talked about the "perpetual demolition" faced when Black men tried to protect their families' homes and lives. Lorraine interjected, and though it might seem like a contradiction, it was her way of getting to the root. "That is all true," she said, "but I am not worried about black men—who have done splendidly, it seems to me, all things considered." Jimmy remembered a pregnant pause, and her words "But I am very worried . . . about the state of the civilization which produced that photograph of the white cop standing on that Negro woman's neck in Birmingham." She smiled a cutting smile at the attorney general, turned, and walked out. Most of the others followed.

Jimmy wrote more than once about this meeting. In each account, Lorraine was magnificent. But just as she was at once towering and childlike, she was both mighty and vulnerable. This struck him deeply. He returned to it in the way Thelonious Monk would go back to a song he wanted to turn over in his head, to see it for all its beauty and majesty. That was how Jimmy saw Lorraine. And remembered her. After the meeting was over, he wrote,

> I had forgotten that I was scheduled to be interviewed by Dr. Kenneth Clark, and we were late. We were hurried into the car. We passed Lorraine, who did not see us. She was walking

toward Fifth Avenue—her face twisted, her hands clasped before her belly, eyes darker than any eyes I had ever seen before—walking in an absolutely private place.

I knew I could not call her.

Our car drove on; we passed her.

And then, we heard the thunder.[23]

Years later, in recollection, her posture was ominous, but it followed a moment that would become legendary. Small but overtaking a room, hers was a presence much greater than her remarkable attractiveness, stylishness, and poise. It was a presence beyond the expectations of her role, her place, her celebrity. She gave public voice to her belief that the Black working class were at the center of the struggle for liberation, and that she must be an amplifier not a figurehead. That was something for which Robert Kennedy was not prepared.

Though RFK was reported to have considered the meeting a great waste of time, less than one month later, his brother President Kennedy, at RFK's urging, gave his landmark civil rights address during which he proposed the legislation that would be known as the Civil Rights Act of 1964. In the address, JFK spoke of civil rights as not just a legal issue but also, as Lorraine said, a *moral* one. He asserted that the Congress must pursue equal access to education, public accommodations, and employment.

On Lorraine's end, after the meeting she returned to her home in the Hudson Valley and held a rally and fund-raiser for the Southern freedom movement five days later. The performer Judy Collins began the event by singing folk songs, and Jerome Smith was an invited speaker. Lorraine wasn't simply making a point in directing RFK's attention to him. She held Jerome in high regard. As a child of nine or ten, he'd first challenged segregation on a public bus in New Orleans after having seen his father, a seaman, do the same. When the white passengers responded angrily, he was protected by an elderly Black woman who fussed at him in front of the angry whites but privately praised his courage once they disembarked. He recollected, "She hugged me and said: 'Never stop doing what you're doing. Never stop taking that sign down.' Then she cried, and said a prayer. That was the jump-off point for me."[24]

Jerome had participated in two freedom rides, one from Montgomery to Jackson and another from New Orleans to McComb, Mississippi. In McComb, he and his fellow freedom riders were beaten with brass knuckles, sticks, and fists by an angry white mob that shouted their plans to kill the niggers. The freedom riders hid out outside McComb in a juke joint. And it was there in McComb that Jerome had first spoken to Burke Marshall, RFK's assistant attorney general, on the phone two years before their meeting in Manhattan on Central Park West. Jerome remembered, "He called and said he wanted us to stop protesting. We were in pretty bad shape, so he said, 'You need to go to the hospital.' I said: 'You deal with this just like you would if President Kennedy was down here. We're not stopping. We're going back.' "[25] His words echoed the fictional voice Lorraine gave Nannie Hansberry when she defended their right to take space in their home: "We are not moving." Jerome, however, wasn't one of the representative few who could "break barriers." He was a person who gave voice to the many unknown people who, as he said, "paid a tremendous price. He said freedom fighting had always been "about our collective strength. To face those monsters every day with no cameras rolling, plain ordinary people had to extend their hand and help you get your job done."[26] This was what Lorraine meant when she said to RFK, and to Burke Marshall, that Jerome spoke for "twenty-two million Negroes." This is also what she wanted the well-intentioned audience in the Hudson Valley to understand.

When Lorraine took the stage at the fund-raising rally, she told the crowd about the meeting she and Jerome had had with the attorney general five days prior. She described the tension in the room, and how Jerome had made clear to Robert Kennedy that "the passion and the absence of patience of a sorely oppressed, native American people is beyond anything that we can sit around and be polite about any more." She described her own words too; how she told the attorney general that he ought to reconsider his impatience and frustration because, despite the room being full of Black celebrities, "we are not remotely interested in the all-insulting concept of the exceptional Negro, we are not remotely interested in any tea at the White House. . . . What we are interested in is making perfectly clear that between the Negro intelligentsia, the Negro middle class, and the Negro this and that, that we are one people and as far as we are concerned, we are represented by the Negroes of the streets of Birmingham."[27]

The salience of her point is perhaps lost today. The Black folks on the streets of Birmingham are now talked about as heroes. But back then they were considered out of control, pushing too fast and hard. They raced beyond the authority of Martin Luther King Jr.'s Southern Christian Leadership Conference. They had their own local leaders, and they were not uniformly committed to nonviolent resistance. Even the *children* of Birmingham were ready to fight. Those were Lorraine's heroes. That day, as a result of Lorraine's organizing, the people of Croton raised $5,000 for the movement. With part of the proceeds, CORE bought a station wagon for civil rights organizers in the Mississippi Delta.

In 1964, when Jimmy was unable to complete an assignment for SNCC to write for a fund-raising photo-essay book titled *The Movement*, Lorraine filled in for him. In the pages, filled with images of protest and of daily life, both North and South, she wove a story that was about the Southern freedom movement. In it, she connected the Southern domestic struggle for racial justice with the global one—including references to the Northern US and the colonized world. Lorraine wrote about the condition of the white poor of the South, and how racism had poisoned them against allying themselves with Black people. She wrote, "The New South slams up against the Old, but the coming of industry in the Southland has not changed the problems of many of its people—white or black—for the better. This is why, for a long time, one of the South's chief exports has been people. Their destination: the ghettos of the North."[28]

Lorraine brought the lessons of others of her teachers to bear, quoting Du Bois and Langston Hughes but also the young organizer and architect of Mississippi Freedom Summer, Bob Moses. In one of the most powerful assertions of the text, she states simply and subversively, "The laws which enforce segregation do not presume the inferiority of a people; they assume an inherent equalness. It is the logic of the lawmakers that if a society does not erect artificial barriers between the people at every point of contact, the people might fraternize and give their attention to the genuine, shared problems of the community."[29]

This was almost the exact opposite of the logic presented in the legal case that ushered in the modern civil rights movement. In *Brown v. Board of Education*, the court spoke of the psychological damage and sense of inferiority created by segregation. Lorraine made clear that inferiority was constructed rather than actually believed. Hers was a subtle yet profound point. If people accepted the idea that racism was merely ignorance or misperception, white innocence could be preserved. If instead it was a system bent on the oppression of Black people, and the deliberate destruction of natural ties among members of the human community, then the whole damn nation was guilty.

Though the acronym SNCC stood for the Student Nonviolent Coordinating Committee, its members had varying positions on nonviolent resistance. For some, it was a philosophical or theological commitment. For others, it was a tactic. And many SNCC members had, like Lorraine, an interest in and commitment to international struggles. They were not simply an offshoot of King's SCLC, though they began under the umbrella of that organization. SNCC's broader and more complex set of politics allowed Lorraine, when writing on their behalf, to ask pointed questions of a sort that wouldn't be posed by SCLC or King for several more years. After seeing images of the 16th Street Baptist Church bombing she wrote, "Twenty million people began to ask with a new urgency: IS nonviolence the way?" This question is followed with an image of MLK with the words "The responsibility for an answer lies heavy on the hearts and shoulders of the men who lead."[30] What follows in her writing is a challenge to King. There are lyrics from a Revolutionary War–era song sitting above images of Black boys bearing weapons. And then two quotations, one from Boston abolitionist Theodore Parker and the other from Robert Williams, a man who became famous in the Southern freedom movement for advocating Black self-defense. The Parker quotation includes the following sentences:

> I was born in the little town where the fight and the bloodshed
> of the Revolution began. My grandfather fired the first shot
> in the Revolution. The blood that flowed there was kindred

to this which courses in my veins today. . . . With these things before me . . . when a fugitive, pursued by kidnappers, came to my house, what could I do but defend her to the last? . . . I should not dare to violate the eternal law of God![31]

Lorraine's answer to the question about self-defense was only thinly veiled. While she said that she supported and applauded Dr. King, she was clear that she did not believe his approach was enough. Black people must, according to Lorraine, be granted full citizenship and access to political participation. Absent that, Black revolt was not just possible but completely justifiable. In speeches she repeated this formulation in various ways. In one, she said,

> I think the daily press lulls the white community falsely in dismissing the rising temper of the ghetto and what will surely come of it. The nation presumes upon the citizenship of the Negro but is oblivious to the fact that it must confer citizenship before it can expect reciprocity. Until twenty million black people are completely interwoven into the fabric of our society, you see, they are under no obligation to behave as if they were. What I am saying is that whether we like the word or not, the condition of our people dictates what can only be called revolutionary attitudes.[32]

This talk was delivered almost exactly a year before Malcolm X gave his famous "by any means necessary" speech at the opening rally for his new institution, the Organization of African American Unity. Lorraine anticipated his precise sentiment by saying,

> I think then that Negroes must concern themselves with every single means of struggle: legal, illegal, passive, active, violent and non-violent. That they must harass, debate, petition, give money to court struggles, sit in, lie-down, strike, boycott, sing hymns, pray on steps, and shoot from their windows when the racists come cruising through their communities. The acceptance of our present condition is the only form of extremism which discredits us before our children.[33]

Both Lorraine and Malcolm had likely read Jean-Paul Sartre's formulation in his play *Dirty Hands* that the class struggle should be pursued "by any means necessary." But in the context of the United States, and with respect to Black people, a nation that has a long history of violent hysteria in response to their self-defense, whether in the context of slave rebellions or Black Muslims or Alabama communists, this assertion had an extraordinary intensity and would be made only by the truly courageous.

Lorraine tried to take this message to a broad public. She confronted the way that a press that claimed itself impartial tended to castigate Black protest when it went beyond the narrow bounds that the white public deemed acceptable. When the *New York Times* published a piece criticizing the Congress of Racial Equality's New York "Stall In," during which they disrupted traffic, Lorraine responded strongly. She described her own realization that such tactics were not only useful but necessary. Unfortunately, the *Times* rejected the letter. But, thankfully, it has been preserved as a testimony to her courage and power. In it she tells the story of her father's patriotism, his belief in the American way, and his years of devotion to fighting in what was deemed the respectable way. Of his experience, she said, "The cost, in emotional turmoil, time, and money, which led to my father's early death as a permanently mad exile in a foreign country when he saw that after such sacrificial efforts the Negroes of Chicago were as ghetto-locked and segregated as ever, does not seem to figure in their calculations."[34] The "right way" hadn't yielded the necessary change. And so, she said, "we must now lie down in the streets, tie up traffic, do whatever we can—take to the hills with guns if necessary—and fight back. False people remark these days on our 'bitterness.' Why, of course, we are bitter."[35]

In a different piece that *was* published, in the Sunday *Times*, Lorraine situated her political commitments in light of her generation and how she had come of age. It was as though she saw that the moment had thrust upon them an unanticipated urgency and responsibility. One response was the creation of an organization that was called Association of Artists for Freedom (AAF), which was formed in 1963 to "speak to the conscience of the American people," according to one source announcing its creation. Its founding members were James Baldwin, Ossie Davis, Ruby Dee, and John Oliver Killens. In their first campaign, in the winter of 1963, they called for people to make contributions to civil rights organizations and to make the Christmas season a "time of national shame and mourning" rather than an orgy of Christmas shopping.[36]

The following summer, on June 15, the AAF held a forum called "The Black Revolution and the White Backlash." On the program were six Black artist-activist-intellectuals: Paule Marshall, John Oliver Killens, LeRoi Jones, Ossie Davis, Ruby Dee, and Lorraine. There were three white writers too: *New York Post* columnist James Wechsler, producer David Susskind, and journalist Charles Silberman.

There were about 1,500 people in attendance, and the crowd was multiracial though mostly white. The press regarding the event described it as, frankly, something of a mess. The radicalism of the Black speakers agitated the white ones. Susskind was quoted as saying, "I have never heard such carefully couched calls for violence in a long time. I find it dangerous, irresponsible, ineffective talk."[37] Wechsler said that "time and again the thought was advanced that everything that has occurred so far in the freedom struggle has been virtually unimportant, largely because of the corrupt influences of white liberals who stealthily dominate existing Negro groups, pervert their aims, and dilute their deeds." He took particular offense at the calls for Black-led or all-Black organizations, saying, "I disagree that the white liberal has the role of water boy in the Freedom Movement." He argued that "separatism in connection with racial problems would be disastrous," and added, "I find it embarrassing and weird that I am here tonight to argue that the message of Martin Luther King still has some meaning."

The white panelists were both shocked and enraged at the militancy of their Black counterparts. The Barbadian American writer Paule Marshall responded by saying, "What has been going on right here proves poignantly how impossible it is to conduct a dialogue with a white man." She then called for "a nationwide freedom organization far more militant than any that exists today." The crowd roared their applause. Times were changing.

When it was Lorraine's turn, she took the audience on a journey.

She began with a joke: "How do you talk about 300 years in four minutes?" The crowd laughed. And then she said, "Was it ever so apparent we need this dialogue?"[38]

Lorraine told the audience about her letter to the *Times* regarding the CORE Stall In. And then she placed it in a larger context. This radicalism, she made clear, was not new and it was necessary.

> It isn't as if we got up today and said, you know, "what can we do to irritate America?" . . . It's because that since 1619, Negroes have tried every method of communication, of transformation of their situation from petition to the vote, everything. We've tried it all. There isn't anything that hasn't been exhausted. Isn't it rather remarkable that we can talk about a people who were publishing newspapers while they were still in slavery in 1827, you see? We've been doing everything, writing editorials, Mr. Wechsler, for a long time, you know.[39]

And then she repeated the charge Nina Simone made in her 1963 song "Mississippi Goddam": "You keep saying go slow, go slow, but that's just the trouble."[40] Not only did Lorraine find the idea that Black people were impatient both unbearable and absurd, she essentially said that the people who on the one hand said they supported equality yet cawed at Black people's insistence on the other hand were unbearable and absurd. They were *the* problem. The solution, Lorraine said, was "to find some way with these dialogues to show and to encourage the white liberal to stop being a liberal and become an American radical."[45] The radical could understand that the basic organization of American society had to be transformed in order for racial justice to ever become a possibility.

Lorraine's criticism of liberals was not mere chafing at their condescension or bias. She made very clear that she saw the structure of empire: exploitation and stratification at home and abroad made racism inextricable from the American project as it stood. Fighting a war against the sovereignty of the Vietnamese people and having an FBI that refused to protect Southern organizers were connected pieces of what America actually was. As far as Lorraine was concerned, liberals who claimed to believe in racial justice and yet also embraced American exceptionalism and empire held irreconcilable commitments.

Lorraine rejected the American *project* but not America. She saw her embrace of radical politics as a commitment to it, to what it could be. She said, "It isn't a question of patriotism and loyalty. My brother fought for this country, my grandfather before that and so on and that's all a lot of nonsense when we criticize. The point is that we have a different viewpoint because, you know, we've been kicked in the face so often and the vantage point of Negroes is entirely different and these are some of the things we're trying to say."[46]

The *New York Times* and *New York Post* reported on the tension-filled program, drawing out two representative quotations: Charles Silberman's "The black radical seems to be long on talks and short on specifics" and Lorraine's "We have to find some way to persuade the white liberal to stop being a liberal and become an American radical."[47]

Six days later, on June 21, 1964, the station wagon that CORE bought with the proceeds from Lorraine's Croton rally sat by the side of a Mississippi road. The three young men who had been driving it the night before were going from town to town, working on voter registration in the Delta. They had been pulled over in Nashoba County. They were abducted, taken into the darkness, and each one was shot in the head at close range. Their bodies, those of two Jewish New Yorkers, Andrew Goodman and Michael "Mickey" Schwerner, and James Chaney, a Black man from Meridian, were thrown into an earthen dam and left to decay. It was a tragedy that would shake the nation.

Three and a half weeks later, on July 16, a white police lieutenant killed another James—James Powell, a Black teenager in Harlem. He died in front of his friends. Three hundred Harlem schoolchildren marched to the police station to demand answers. Harlemites and cops battled for six days. At the end, there was another dead Harlemite, 118 who were injured, and 465 arrests. Lorraine and her peers had seen what was around the corner, because they knew what their people were tired of enduring, what they too were tired of enduring. The powder keg exploded while the government and polite society were busy repeating, "Go slow."

The story of the civil rights movement is usually told in the shape of a mountain. The apex is 1965, with a steep decline caused by the turn to radicalism and Black Power. That chronology is too neat. So are the politics. The question of Black independence and autonomy coursed through the entirety of the movement. It was a recurring theme. Tensions between liberal reform politics and more radical ones recurred too. By 1964, Lorraine had spent five years being scolded for her criticisms of self-proclaimed allies in the cause of racial justice. But it was as though in 1964 everything she had been saying became blindingly clear. A radical vision was necessary.

CHAPTER TEN

The View from Chitterling Heights

What if age and ill health don't produce serenity at all?[1]
—*Edward Said*

ALTON AND WALLY, two of Sidney Brustein's friends, mock his romanticism. Alton tells Sidney, who likes to wax poetic about nature, that Sidney admires the wrong parts of the work of Henry David Thoreau. Wally chimes in,

> How's about the rest of Thoreau, Nature Boy? Poor old Henry tried his damndest to stay in the woods, but the world wouldn't let him—it never does. What about that, Sidney? What about the Thoreau who came back and called the first public meeting to defend John Brown? What about the Thoreau who was locked up in jail when that holy of holies, Ralph Waldo Emerson came strolling by and asked (playing it), "Well, Henry, what are you doing in there?" And Thoreau, who was in "in there" for protesting slavery and the Mexican War, looked out at him and said, . . . "The question is, Ralph, what are you doing . . . out thay-ah?"[2]

I wonder if Lorraine asked herself the same question. In 1961, she purchased a home in the Hudson Valley in a village called Croton-on-Hudson. And in her final years, she was often in that pastoral place rather than in the thick of uprisings. She called it, and I imagine she laughed whenever she said it, "Chitterling Heights": a Black woman's oasis, named after an African American delicacy of pig offings, upstate.

175

What was she doing out there? Away from the Village artist activists, and even farther away from the Deep South, which held her greatest hopes.

The Hudson Valley, where Croton is located, is well known as a school and subject of American landscape paintings. The paintings are stunning and remarkably accurate. The landscape is, for lack of a more distinctive word, breathtaking. Nineteenth-century artists, a first generation of counterculture in the valley, gave way to communists and trade unionists who settled in Croton in the early twentieth century. Like Thoreau sitting at the edge of Walden Pond in Concord, up there in the midst of natural beauty the Lefties could turn away from industry, capitalism, and exploitation and imagine another kind of social relation. Eventually the Mount Airy section of Croton-on-Hudson became so popular with leftist New Yorkers that it was known colloquially as Red Hill. Numerous well-known radicals settled there: writers John Reed, Louise Bryant, Edna St. Vincent Millay, and Max Eastman; dancer Isadora Duncan; actress Gloria Swanson; *Daily Worker* editor Bob Linor and his artist wife, Lydia; William Gropper; Louis Waldman, a socialist expelled from his seat in the New York State Assembly; and Alexander Bittelman, one of the famous defendants in the federal prosecution of Communists under the Smith Act in the 1950s.

Lorraine probably settled in the area because of so many like-minded people. It was an oasis of sorts. But it wasn't completely free of the ills of everywhere. The region also had a history of racism and anti-Semitism directed toward the few Black people and largely Jewish radicals who visited. And yet, though she was certainly a rarity in many ways, and she was away from "the struggle," Lorraine fell in love with Croton. Her dogs Chaka and Spice ambled, ran, and panted. She began to learn the names of flora and fauna. And though she could not swim and was afraid of the water, she enjoyed the lakes and the trees.

The dance between retreat and revolution, like Henry David Thoreau's dance between the pond and the jail, was made especially complicated by Lorraine's illness. Croton wasn't just her Walden; it was her convalescent home.

A month before Jimmy described seeing Lorraine leave the Bobby

Kennedy meeting clutching her stomach; she'd had a seizure. In a letter to her friend Evelyn Goldwasser, Lorraine described how that spring was filled with ailments. First, she had collapsed. Doctors told her that the cause was anemia from bleeding ulcers, and she was placed in the hospital for ten days. In that time she did not improve, and so she was given blood transfusions and an abdominal operation. Lorraine didn't know anything more specific than that. In August, she fell seriously ill again and went to Boston to see gastric specialists, who told her that her enzymes were, in her words, "literally chewing me up." She wrote, "Therefore I might die, and as a matter of fact, given the nature of the operation to correct it I might *also* die on the table, etc., and all that sort of thing. Well they operated again and I didn't die and it *was* successful and I will be well again."[3]

At the time of her writing, Lorraine had been home in Croton for three days, but she was going to have to return to Boston for another surgery in October. She felt terrible, but "grateful for being alive—mostly."[4]

As she wrote to Evie, Lorraine was in bed, watching the March on Washington and "being melancholy about all those who didn't live to see 'America Awaken' and all (or, in some cases, stay out of the booby hatches—or who ulcerated a bit in the process—)." She had to be thinking of her father, of course, for whom the occasion likely would have seemed to be a sign that his noble efforts at racial inclusion hadn't been all in vain. But he was long gone. Lorraine was angry. Not just about death but also about the life she was living. She said,

> I will and have suffered and for the first time know why some can decide living isn't quite worth all this.
>
> On the other hand—I have been surrounded by all the devotion one could wish and the skill of science and am allowed by the grace of fortune to recover in this stunning setting which is my present home.[5]

There she was, a small Black woman in the mountains, in a beautiful home up a narrow incline, far away from the urban landscapes that had shaped her life. She took to that natural world, but kept looking back out into the thick of things. Beauty helped. But it wasn't enough.

The night before the March on Washington, her teacher and friend W. E. B. Du Bois died. That undoubtedly was also on her mind and added to the distress of the moment. Lorraine would spend the next two-and-a-half years dying of cancer, though she was unaware of what was wrong with her for most of that time. But, as her letter attests, she experienced the terror of a body gone awry. Bobby, who remained her caretaker and confidant, kept the seriousness of her illness from her. Doctors back then believed it helped patients to have a little hope. Even when she struggled, Bobby also kept encouraging her to write.

Though still ill, Lorraine made her way to Carnegie Hall in February of 1964 for a program to remember and honor Du Bois. Ossie Davis led the gathering. AME bishop Stephen Gill Spottswood gave the invocation. Tributes were offered by scholars Arna Bontemps and Arthur Spingarn. Bontemps talked about Du Bois's scholarship and personal history. Spingarn, who was more liberal than radical, focused on their sixty-year friendship, though he and Du Bois were worlds apart ideologically. He described Du Bois as one of the great figures of the twentieth century who foresaw independent Black nations. Eslanda Goode Robeson, Paul's wife and an activist in her own right, said that Du Bois was a great statesman and an inspirational leader who had a keen political insight. Historian John Hope Franklin gave the main address, commenting on the news media's failure to note the death of such an important man. Further, he asserted that the vision that made the March on Washington possible began with Du Bois's early twentieth century drive for first-class citizenship. Langston Hughes, Ralph Bunche, Daisy Bates, William Patterson, and Whitney Young also spoke.

Lorraine read a message of thanks from Du Bois's wife, Shirley Graham Du Bois, and then delivered her own remarks:

> I do not remember when I first heard the name Du Bois. For some Negroes it comes into consciousness so early, so persistently that it is like the spirituals or blues or discussions of

oppression, he was a fact of our culture. People spoke of him as they did the church or the nation. He was an institution in our lives, a bulwark of our culture. I believe that his personality and thought have colored generations of Negro intellectuals, far greater, I think than some of those intellectuals know. And without a doubt, his ideas have influenced a multitude who do not even know his name.[6]

Not only did Du Bois have a huge influence, but, according to Lorraine, he also left the rest of them with a responsibility:

> His legacy is, in my mind, explicit. I think that it is a legacy which insists that American Negroes do not follow their oppressors and the accomplices of their oppressors—anywhere at all. That we look out of the world through our own eyes and have the fibre not to call enemy friend or friend enemy, [. . .] never *never* again must the Negro people pay the price that they have paid for allowing their oppressors to say who is or is not a fit leader of our cause.[7]

Lorraine's words cut through the palliative that often attends death. In those moments, mourners are told that our differences are supposed to be muted. Great figures are often made into flat paper dolls of themselves, less challenging, less difficult. Lorraine said no to that. Her caution was subtle yet pointed to the mainstream of the civil rights movement. To honor Du Bois could mean sustaining his Pan-Africanist and socialist vision, or it could mean leaving him behind, along with others who were concerned with a global struggle, in order to pursue assimilation into the fabric of American empire. Lorraine clearly thought the latter would be a terrible sin. Du Bois's greatness, according to his spiritual and political daughter, was inextricably tied to his radical courage, his truth telling, his calling out of white supremacy, his willingness to risk and to be cast aside. He died an exile, like her father, because he could not bear the stink of this unrepentantly racist nation to which he devoted his remarkable gifts for decades. She would not let anyone in that room forget it.

Sylvester Leaks, a renaissance man—dancer, actor, public intellectual, and sartorial splendor—who also served as the editor of the Nation of Islam's newspaper, *Muhammad Speaks*, wrote to Lorraine in response to her comments at Du Bois's memorial, and he penned a feature in the paper that highlighted her words. His admiration for Lorraine was deep. In his article, Leaks called her statement brilliant and timely, and said he believed "Dr. Du Bois would have given his gracious approval with alacrity I am sure. For brevity, clarity of thought, and courage of convictions, they are simply matchless in this era of overkill and silence. Perhaps, most of all, the most important thing about your remarks is that they penetrate the concentric layers of falsehood, hypocrisy, and fear and permit truth to see the light."[8]

The encomium Lorraine gave for Du Bois had within it a question she kept asking herself, whether she was lecturing in Manhattan or convalescing in Croton: How, even in a state of infirmity, could she hold fast to her purpose? In various ways, in diaries and lectures, she kept this question alive. In one she wrote, "Do I remain a revolutionary? Intellectually—without a doubt. But am I prepared to give my body to the struggle?" She described looking at the acts and visages of freedom fighters: "They stand in the hose fire at Birmingham; they stand in the rain at Hattiesburg. They are young, they are beautiful, they are determined. When I get my health back I think I shall have to go into the South to find out what kind of revolutionary I am."[9]

Dying, though maybe she didn't know it, yet, Lorraine was still trying to live her commitment fiercely.

In her short play *The Arrival of Mr. Todog*, which riffed on Samuel Beckett's classic *Waiting for Godot*, Lorraine turns ambiguity into clarity. While waiting for "Mr. Todog," her two characters, unlike Beckett's, don't wait for God to provide answers; they realize if there is God at all, he is them and they are him. It is they who must act decisively to create the world. She lived this message, not only as a pupil but also a teacher and a creator, writing and speaking in bits and snatches whenever she could. She imagined architectures of liberation, visions and gestures from her sickbed. She also freed herself.

Or at least tried to. On March 10, 1964, Lorraine and Bobby obtained a divorce in Juarez, Mexico.

Five days later, she wrote a journal entry that she titled "Puzzle." It read:

> Having had a cup of hot tea and written a bit—my mind sweetens on life once again.
>
> The mercurial aspect of me! Why is it so extreme? No drug, not even aspirin, and yet my mood is as different from what it was 45 minutes ago as the Himalayas are from the Sahara. Why? What does it mean? Am I so utterly a creature of my juices? Entirely? It would seem so.[10]

And then there is a bit that seems strange for someone whose body was rapidly deteriorating: "We must get back to the physical body, methinks. Matter in motion, not mysticism. Chemistry to get a drip on mercury at last."[11] But maybe it isn't strange at all. Maybe in her suffering the stakes were even clearer. Perhaps it brought her even more intimately in contact with the woman who lay on the ground, an officer's boot upon her neck. Maybe her body in pain put her in communion with humanity. In any case, she held herself grounded, desperately, no drifting.

Two days later, on March 17, 1964, she wrote a letter to Bobby's parents. In it she describes her condition with another barely truthful explanation given to her by doctors: tendonitis. She says she is feeling better, but it is clear that also isn't entirely true when she tries to be philosophical about the whole thing: "You know, fate has a way of picking the worst thing to fit individual frustrations: Beethoven went deaf; Milton blind. Soooo, without implying equality with the company, it allows me a discomfort that makes it extremely difficult to sit at the typewriter for more than a little while."[12]

This was Lorraine's dusk. Reading her words as her body caved, reminds me of Edward Said's idea of "late style" in which he challenged any romantic ideas about how thinkers and artists tidily complete the arc of their thought in the final years. He raised the question, "What of artistic lateness not as harmony and resolution, but as intransigence, difficulty and contradiction? What if age and ill health don't produce serenity at all?"[13] It didn't in Lorraine. It deepened her restlessness. Dorothy came to Croton, tended to her, fed her, and nurtured her. Lorraine was frustrated and in pain, and under Dorothy's care, she did what she could with difficulty. Knowing what I do about pain (I have lived with chronic diseases for nearly half of my life), it shapes how I read the works Lorraine left from this time. There are many bits and pieces. But the fragments are something much more than their incompleteness. We cannot dismiss these artifacts that were not designated "done" as she lay dying. Lorraine worked and witnessed her own diminishing faculty. She saw in it a perverse poetry. Her late style was a stripping down to the bones, a building out of lumpy flesh, and a direction for us to follow. She worked on stories about the nineteenth-century feminist Mary Wollstonecraft and on a play, based on the Pulitzer Prize–winning novelist Oliver La Farge's *Laughing Boy*, about a young man caught between Navajo identity and a racist society. She posed profound questions about African independence in her play *Les Blancs* and imagined the life of the first monotheistic pharaoh, Akhnaton. She wrote a queer novel that she called *Martaslund*. These works are pictures of the past and future refracting her present. They are about freedom and faith and courage. They are about the sins of domination and the resilience of people. When her uncle Leo came to visit Lorraine in New York during one of her many hospital stays, he was stunned by her eagerness to hear about everything he was working on, thinking she should be resting. But no, she held on.

Works sometimes cohere on their own anyway, regardless of what the author says about them. The message in her final pieces, in the imaginative landscape she presented, was that new human relations—intimate, social, economic, national, and international, *just* relations—must be pursued and championed. Withering behind trees, mountains, and water she continued to believe in humanity.

Longtime Croton resident Cornelia Cotton wrote to me in the spring of 2017 and shared her one memory of Lorraine during this time, when she herself was very young. Cotton was delivering telephone books at a rate of seven cents a book, trying to turn a profit "in a race against gas spent driving from one isolated house to another in the backwoods of the town of Cortlandt." She described approaching Lorraine's house. At the glass panes of the entrance, Chaka and Spice were jumping and barking loudly. Cotton said, "Terrified, I stood at a distance, clasping her White and Yellow Pages. Miss Hansberry appeared in a robe, looking very frail—I did not know then that she was desperately ill—and, restraining the dogs, opened the door a crack. As I stepped forward to hand her the books, I shouted over the noise of the dogs, 'I loved your play!' Her worried expression gave way to a smile so beautiful that it repaid me handsomely for the ordeal of the dogs and the money lost in the delivery job, leaving me with a cherished remembrance of a lovely woman and writer."[14]

When Lorraine wasn't in Croton, she was giving the occasional speech or, increasingly, in the hospital. Renee Kaplan, her friend and one of her former lovers, recalled that for a time she stayed in the NYU Hospital: "Lorraine's room faced my building. . . . We used to wave to each other all the time. I was over there with great frequency."[15] As her body deteriorated further, Lorraine drank heavily to manage the depression, and she worked on her writing. She was running out of time and was donating her body, every bit of its strength, to the struggle, whether she realized it or not.

Illness for Lorraine, as is often the case, drew in sharp relief what the core of her intellectual and political concerns were; where the heart of her calling resided. She wrote to herself, "When I get my health back I really should probably visit Europe . . . but it's a curious thing. I cannot think seriously of being away from America. Everyone is always saying I 'must go' here or there—Greece, France, England, etc. I feel only that I must go to New England again, and to see the Pacific Northwest and the Coastline at Big Sur—and really very little else."[16]

Though she was an internationalist, and something of a Black nationalist, a Marxist, and a socialist, she was also deeply American. She understood that to be a thing of beauty and horror at once. She was disgusted by the war in Vietnam, and perhaps even more so at the passive acceptance of it by the American public. She saw in it the ease with which people could accept destruction as long as it wasn't too close to home.

In October, newspapers announced that Lorraine was dying.

The letters that came flooding in were a symphony of admiration and love. They came from every quarter: from schoolchildren, from activists, from friends. She lived the end of her life in choral eulogy of sorts. Weldon Rougeau, a member of SNCC, wrote her on October 23, 1964, "Lorraine, the strength I saw in your face and heard in your voice is enough to overcome almost anything. I know that strength will keep you from despairing. That strength will make you well; it will help restore you to good health and happiness."[17]

Most of the letter writers thanked her, and they told her with desperate passion that they wanted her to survive. Eve Merriam declared, "I hear that you are in the hospital, and this makes the world an even stupider place than before. Lorraine, all my wishes go to you. Your gifts have been so large that greedily we want more."[18]

She was still essential. Her high school friend James Forman stated simply, "Those in the movement and elsewhere need you." And Alex Haley reassured and implored her, holding up a mirror to her own steely countenance:

> A large plus in your corner, I think, is that your image for me, is courage dominated, with other allied qualities. I've done a fair amount of study of the metaphysical. I know there's mountains of evidence of how often medical science's miracles are catalyzed beyond our understanding by human courage. Also "square" as its[sic] appraised in far too much of our today world, I believe in praying, and I have petitioned in your behalf.
>
> Fight girl![19]

The letters from children were poignant. The genius of *A Raisin in the Sun* was that, notwithstanding its political nuance and sophisticated composition, it is a story even a child can seriously contemplate. The children told her they appreciated her. Their words were sweet, naïve, and sincere. A fourth grader from Oakland named Shawn Belvin wrote to her:

Dear Miss Lorraine Hansberry

I hope you get better. And I am in the fourth grade. Did you have a serious surgery? I wish you would come and see me sometimes when you feel better. Did you write many plays? Well, when you were well you could write plays like a dream.

And there were adults, strangers who didn't know her but felt moved to speak up about what she meant to them. A woman named Essie Barnes, whose written word is a quintessential voice from the Black South, wrote to Lorraine:

Little girl you must continue to trust in God, believe and trust him and wait until he reaches you. . . . I wrote you two weeks passed. . . . I am writing against you can write me if you want to, let me know how you feel by now. . . .

I am your friend, Essie Barnes
Your photo in the Jet is cute.[20]

"Little girl" is a moniker not unlike the designation "sweet" in Black Southern vernacular. It lets you know that you are cherished. Lorraine was by so many.

CHAPTER ELEVEN

Homegoing

In time of silver rain,
The earth puts forward new life again.
—*Langston Hughes,*
dedicated to Lorraine Hansberry[1]

Perhaps home is not a place but
simply an irrevocable condition.
—*James Baldwin*[2]

THE SIGN IN SIDNEY BRUSTEIN'S WINDOW opened at the Longacre Theatre on October 15, 1964. Lorraine moved into the Hotel Victoria so that she could be close to rehearsals as she lay dying. She developed shingles. Her nights were agonizing. Her legs went numb. She lost speech when the cancer entered her brain. Nina came to visit in December and played her a recording of "In the Evening by the Moonlight." Lorraine confessed that she wasn't ready to go. Nina remembered, "She raised her hands in front of her face and said 'Nina, I don't know what is happening to me. They say I'm not going to get better, but I must get well. I must go down to the south. I've been a revolutionary all my life, but I've got to go down there to find out what kind of revolutionary I am.'"[3]

In her diary just eleven months earlier, she had planned out her life; she dreamed it would be a year of writing and traveling.

I do not yet know what it is like to feel death descending. But having lived with chronic diseases, I know the tight pull of shingles around the perimeter of my flesh, the spastic paralysis of fatigue and sharp pain entangled, all the while knowing that I will not get well. A reckoning urgency, an inventory of your life: these are the things that take up space in the grief that accompanies your body's betrayal. I know Lorraine felt it all.

Nina's song took Lorraine, a daughter of migration, back to the South, back to the root. Nina had changed the lyrics, taking it from a mocking "coon song" written by James Bland in 1880 to a powerful evocation of intimate rural Black Southern life. That was their work: telling the true story. In the second stanza, the tempo picks up and the song turns from melancholy to buoyant. Nina testified to the energy and hope of the movement they were in, one that Lorraine wouldn't survive.

In Lorraine's final days, Dorothy and Bobby sat in vigil at her bedside. Her family visited and said their good-byes. Jimmy came to the hospital to see about her and then went to Europe. In Chicago, a controversy had brewed over Wright Junior College making his novel *Another Country* required reading. The queer and interracial sexuality were deemed "damaging" by angry parents. Jimmy was distressed, and rather than coming back to the States as he'd planned, he traveled to France. On the night of January 11, he came down with severe flu symptoms and a high fever that roiled his body all night. The next morning, at 8:50 a.m., January 12, 1965, Lorraine died. Jimmy told his brother David that his suffering and her passing were one.

The lights went down on *Sidney Brustein's Window* after 101 performances. It had been a struggle to keep it up. There was no show on the afternoon of the twelfth. Its run ended with Lorraine. Years later, Jimmy, in one of his reflections on her death, described Lorraine as a prophet and a martyr of her generation, though she did not die by a bullet. He wrote:

> I've very often pondered what she then tried to convey—that a holocaust is no respecter of persons; that what, today, seems merely humiliation and injustice for a few, can, unchecked, become terror for the many, snuffing out white lives just as though they were black lives; that if the American state could not protect the lives of black citizens, then, presently, the entire state would find itself engulfed. And the horses and tanks are indeed upon us, and the end is not in sight.[4]

Jimmy did not bemoan that Lorraine hadn't lived to see the progress, because he wasn't sure much progress had been made at all in
the decade after her death. Bitterly he wrote, "Perhaps it is just as
well, after all, that she did not live to see with the outward eye what
she saw so clearly with the inward one." She'd died for a cause that
was mightily resisted and had not been achieved, and according to
Jimmy, it was not "farfetched to suspect that what she saw contributed to the strain which killed her, for the effort to which Lorraine
was dedicated is more than enough to kill a man."[5]

Though Jimmy had seen her at the hospital as she was dying, she
was at that point rendered mute by the pancreatic cancer that had
metastasized. She could only smile and wave. So Jimmy remembered
another occasion as their last time together, a time when she was
still standing: "She was seated, talking, dressed all in black, wearing a very handsome wide, black hat, thin, and radiant. I knew she
had been ill, but I didn't know then, how seriously. I said, 'Lorraine,
baby, you look beautiful, how in the world do you do it?' She was
leaving. I have the impression she was on a staircase, and she turned
and smiled that smile and said, 'It helps to develop a serious illness,
Jimmy!' and waved and disappeared."[6]

She dazzled until the end.

Among the obituaries, wires, letters, memories, and encomiums
to Lorraine after her death there are poems. It is not uncommon for
very beautiful people, and by that I mean all sorts of beauty (and
she possessed all sorts), to inspire poetry. But also, I think, it was
the peculiar and wondrous collection of qualities she possessed that
made poetry—an impressionistic, descriptive form, one that offers
much more than logic or simple narrative—the form immediately
reached for by those who remembered her. On the day of her death,
Larry Pendleton wrote a poem titled "To Lorraine." In it he spoke of
her dying: "Whence come the bird that beats with sparrow wings /
against my windowpane / Futile are its efforts to reach the fair Lorraine, the aesthetic frail Lorraine."[7]

In contrast, Richard B. Moore, the Barbadian socialist intellectual
whose tribute appeared in the January 28 issue of *Workers World*,
remembered her in large, strong terms, not the withering form of her

last days.[8] Their testimonies were both true. Her body was ravaged in the final days. Her spirit seemed to live beyond it, at the very least in the feelings of those she left behind.

> Blow the trumpet blow
> On a frenzied note of anguish
> Keen and shrill and piercing
> With a long loud wail,
> Of rending, agonizing blues
> For sadly now we mourn
> The great deep loss
> Of one so young and beauteous
> Yet filled with deepest feeling
> For her crushed and struggling people . . .

Langston Hughes, Lorraine's model and mentor, who so deftly wove depth into simplicity, began his poem dedicated to Lorraine with the phrase "in time of" which in French is translated as "lors," approximating the beginning of her name. The rain is silver, according to Hughes, precious yet melancholy. He wrote of the bountiful earth because he saw in Lorraine a territory as well as the heavens yet also as the rain from the heavens feeding the seeded earth. He expected a blossoming after the sky had finished its weeping, all due to Lorraine's life and work.

The refrain in the poem repeats "of life of life of life." It is an incantation. I am reminded of Walt Whitman's words, "What good amid these, O me, O life?" And of the answer Whitman provides himself: "That you are here—that life exists and identity, / That the powerful play goes on, and you may contribute a verse."[9] I imagine Hughes was thinking of Whitman's words when he wrote them. The other great American bard was right. The play goes on. The plays go on. Verses have followed. Many decades later we have the playwrights who came later to show for it: August Wilson, Anna Deavere Smith, Suzan Lori Parks, Lynn Nottage . . . And we have the seekers and the freedom fighters, too, from their various walks of life.

The last word of Hughes's poem is "new." Assurance of the

eternal return, that Lorraine's seeds would yield fruit—that was his belief and that of many of her beloveds. They were trustworthy and trusting of her passions long after her passing. I am struck now, after digging through the archives about her and also her archives, that they knew back then what so many contemporary critics have failed to grasp. I am talking about those who have said that besides *Raisin* nothing is left of her but scraps, and about those who opine that the frailness of her body toward the end made a mess of her work. But I shouldn't be surprised, I guess. Even back then, right at the moment of her death, there were people eager to speak of her decline, to narrow her and stomp her into the past.

A cruel obituary in the conservative magazine the *National Review* stated, "In her last years she wasted time spitting angry clichés at pacifist meetings and race rallies. It may be said that this great selflessness of which good writers can so often convince themselves as well as others is the true thief of the gift that commercial self-seekers couldn't give away if they tried."[10] And Jerry Tallmer, despite calling himself "sympathetic" to Lorraine, said this about her: "She was an angry young woman; charming, good-looking, quick with a witticism, sophisticated, knowing and angry. The anger was so hard inside her that you could almost feel it like a rock. She tried to cover it with the charm etc., and with a cloud of tangential verbiage; indeed at times she spoke, except in her plays, with the muzziness of mysticism."[11]

Lorraine was not a mystic. That was a stupid claim. She believed in human action and responsibility. But she *was* angry, righteously so. However, calling a public Black person angry was then, as now, a dagger. It was used to suggest moral failure. Like the other passions, anger is often cast as reckless and useless when in the hearts and minds of Black people, perhaps because passion lies in opposition to passive acceptance. Passion moves and insists. Tallmer was wrong; it isn't a rock at all. It is living as a protest.

I woke up early on Memorial Day 2017, in the four o'clock hour, to write about Lorraine's funeral. She wasn't a soldier, but she certainly was a warrior and a veteran. It seemed right. Her services were held on January 16, 1965, at the aptly named Church of the Master in New York City. There was a blizzard outside. Most of the crowd of seven hundred who came to pay tribute stood through the storm, because there wasn't enough room in the church. Inside, attendees stood through scripture and prayer. They sang the hymn "Abide with Me," a song that stares death in the face:

> Shine through the gloom and point me to the skies.
> Heaven's morning breaks and earth's vain shadows flee;
> In life, in death, O Lord, abide with me.[12]

Outside as snow and wind whipped, I imagine the sound traveled.

The first speaker was James Forman, Lorraine's high school mate, then later her friend in the movement, who signed his letters to her with his old nickname, "Rufus." He said of Lorraine,

> I felt she was a person who believed in acting and believed in acting on her belief. . . . I think it's appropriate that we try to extract for ourselves some of the things that guided her through her life. . . . First of all, I think it was the commitment to action. . . . Those of us who are in this room today could perhaps have an everlasting memorial to Lorraine if in fact we continue the work that she so nobly began in trying to end segregation in the Deep South in the United States.[13]

Forman was followed by her mentor, Paul Robeson. Robeson marveled at such wisdom in one so young. He quoted the spiritual "Sometimes I Feel Like a Motherless Child." Of its various verses, he chose to end on this one: "Sometimes I feel like an eagle in the air." Like Forman he asked the congregation to follow Lorraine's guidance in life after her death: "At this farewell, Lorraine bids us to keep our heads high and hold on to our strength and power to soar like an eagle in the air."[14]

Hers was a death of inversion. Nannie, the mother, sat grieving her young daughter in the church. Her mentor mourned the mentored. And yet it was also clear that Lorraine was remembered as a teacher, a wise soul who became an ancestor in the blossoming of youth. It was in this spirit that Ruby Dee, who spoke as a representative of the artistic community, said, "She pointed the way to wider artistic horizons."[15]

Nina Simone was next. She sang and played the piano. Nina said of the funeral, "I didn't cry, I was beyond crying by that time."[16] She had finished a final performance at Carnegie Hall just twelve hours before coming through the storm to say good-bye to her dear friend Lorraine. She played "In the Evening by the Moonlight" again, and an Israeli folk song that she knew Lorraine loved. Jimmy wasn't there. He sent word though. The wire read in part:

> Lorraine and I were very good friends and I am going to miss her. Grief is very private I really can't talk about her or what she meant to me. We talked about everything under the sun and we fought like brother and sister at the very talk [*sic*] of our lungs. It was so wonderful to watch her get angry and it was wonderful to watch her laugh. We passed some great moments together. I am very proud to say and we confronted some terrible things. She is gone now. We have our memories and her work. I think we must resolve not to fail her for she certainly did not fail us.[17]

In the print obituaries written by journalists who knew her, Jimmy's words were echoed. They spoke of brilliance, beauty, flashing anger, and youthful laughter. Sylvester Leaks wrote in *Muhammad Speaks*, "The ingratiating warmth of her smile, the nimbleness of her intellect in debate or just plain discussions or the wrath of her indignation and anger were something to behold. She was one of two women . . . whose wrath I would never desire to be a victim of. She could peel you alive in one paragraph."[18] Joanne Grant wrote in the *Spectator*: "Two qualities for which I shall best remember Lorraine are her ability to get excited, stirred up over injustice, narrow mindedness, stupidity and her ability to laugh. These two aspects of her character were strikingly expressed in her two most outstanding physical characteristics—beautiful flashing eyes and a generous warm laugh."[19]

At the service, Nina's songs were followed by words from the actress Shelley Winters, who, while weeping, expressed trembling frustration that technology had sped up fast enough to build cutting-edge weapons but not a cure for Lorraine's cancer. It was a personal word, but also one that again captured Lorraine's values. She loved peace and people.

The last speaker was Leo Nemiroff, Bobby's brother. He spoke on behalf of the family. Leo quoted a letter written to Lorraine by a seventeen-year-old friend who, that past October, had learned of her terminal illness: "This letter is mainly being written so the hot ache I feel inside can be shared with yours. This terrible cruelty—what does it mean? After your call I was overcome with a sorrow I have never known." She wrote then of walking through the city, and an imaginary walk through humanity: "customs, language, struggle, suffering . . . throughout all, and creating all, and being all are people, people, people!"[20]

The human condition was Lorraine's obsession and commitment. She had confronted death not only literally but also philosophically and spiritually. Leo ended by quoting Lorraine's own observations about Marian Bachrach, an elder communist writer, as Marian lay dying. Lorraine had been deeply affected by their meeting at a cottage on the cliffs of Maine overlooking the ocean. Marian, she said, "was a woman who had lived such a purposeful and courageous life, and who was then dying of cancer." In her final days, Marian was still writing, had begun painting, and remained a dedicated American radical. She hadn't given up the cause of fighting for freedom. And, according to Lorraine,

> that was the way she thought of cancer—she absolutely refused to award it the stature of tragedy, a devastating instance of the brooding doom and inexplicability of the absurdity of human destiny . . . for this remarkable woman it was a matter of nature in imperfection. . . . It was an enemy but a palpable one, with shape and effect and source and if it existed it could be destroyed.[21]

But the "genius of man," as Lorraine called it, wasn't quick enough to save Marian. Or Lorraine.

Lorraine's prescience about death, as she witnessed the end of another radical woman's life, can and I think should be read alongside another one of her prophetic descriptions. Lorraine wrote a story

called "Renascence" under her pen name, Emily Jones, when she was
in her twenties. In it, a thirtysomething writer named Pip has died,
and her partner, Andrea, is left. Alone. By naming the dead woman
Pip, Lorraine made reference to the Black cabin boy in Herman Melville's *Moby Dick*. Cast about in the ocean, the boy loses his mind
and then becomes the intimate of and cabinmate to Captain Ahab. In
Melville's story, being cast about in the ocean was a harrowing con-
version experience, and the cabin boy was never the same:

> The sea had jeeringly kept his finite body up, but drowned the
> infinite of his soul. Not drowned entirely though. Rather car-
> ried down alive to wondrous depths, where strange shapes of
> the unwarped primal world glided to and fro before his pas-
> sive eyes. . . . Pip saw the multitudinous, God-omnipresent,
> coral insects, that out of the firmament of waters heaved the
> colossal orbs. He saw God's foot upon the treadle of the loom;
> and therefore his shipmates called him mad.[22]

Like Lorraine, who couldn't swim and feared being swept up into
the ocean like Melville's cabin boy, her character named Pip both
feared and loved the water. She waxed poetic about it, from a distance. Andrea remembers this about her lover. Over pages, Andrea is
reborn, baptized by watching the water flow after Pip's death. It is a
tragic end. And I mean that in the classic sense.

Lorraine dedicated the story to E.S.M., Edna St. Vincent Millay. I
do not know whether she ever met Millay. Maybe it was just her love
of Millay's art that inspired the dedication. Millay was, to Lorraine's
generation of Village lesbians, something of a heroine. She flouted
convention. She made her own life. And she took up space with her
pen. The title of Lorraine's story, "Renascence," is the same of that
of Millay's most famous lyric poem. Millay's poem is a meditation
on the sublime in nature and it is also about grief. In Millay's poem
the rain baptizes, turning grief into rebirth. In Lorraine's story, that is
what the ocean does for Andrea. In "Renascence," as with all of her
work, the fossils of what Lorraine read, what questions she wanted
to pose to the world, her answers, and her deepest desires emerge
with gentle dusting.

It is easy to think Lorraine predicted her own death in "Rena-scence." Like Pip, she was a writer who died under age forty and left behind a woman who loved her . . . and a man, too, and so many others. But the truth is more astonishing. Even as a young woman, Lorraine understood that this was part of the core of life: the plung-ing depths of death and the task of going on after the death of the beloved, not simply as endurance but as a baptism, a rebirth, a new beginning.

The honorary pallbearers at Lorraine's funeral included famous friends: Ossie Davis, the actress Diana Sands, Shelley Winters, Dick Gregory, John Oliver Killens, and Rita Moreno, as well as the women she loved privately, Renee Kaplan and, most intimately, Dorothy Secules. In the eulogy, delivered by Eugene Callender, a pastor and freedom fighter, he used Proverbs 20:27 as his guide: "The spirit of man is the candle of the Lord."

He spoke of her light shining on humanity, and serving as a guide on freedom's road:

> She brought the light of faith. . . . She believed in victory be-yond defeat; in triumph beyond tragedy; that in spite of shat-tered human hopes and man's inhumanity to man there are bright goals ahead worth every ounce of energy one has to give them. . . . She brought to us the light of truth. Truthful-ness for her was the central fact. . . . It meant the spirit of hon-esty and loyalty in personal relations, a basic respect for every man. . . . She brought to us the light of love. In her we saw a playful element sometimes overlooked in our thought about love. She knew also how to use the lighter touch to relax peo-ple in conversation and endeavor, and how to plant a fruitful thought while they smiled. But more than in any other way, her love for life was shown by the spirit of utter self-giving which marked her daily work.

Callender spoke of how Lorraine shone her light on others. I wonder now how we shine a light on her: how we not only remem-ber and marvel, and marvel we should, but also witness the seams of an exceptional and extraordinary person, to see with some depth and complexity the constitution of a life containing such gifts, generosity, and courage, such truth and love, without too much intrusion or sensation. Catching a likeness of Lorraine means to me, as witness to her life, telling as true a story as I know how, from the trifles to the hollows, from the heights to the depths. Communist activist Alice Jerome's wire after her death—"Your life renews our faith in youth and liberation. Even in death you are beautiful"—is as true today as it was at the hour of her death.[23] So too are Martin Luther King Jr.'s words: "Her creative ability and her profound grasp of the deep social issues confronting the world today will remain an inspiration to generations yet unborn."[24]

The funeral congregation filed out to the sounds of another hymn traditionally sung in Black churches, "Come Ye Disconsolate," written by the Irish poet Thomas Moore:

> Joy of the desolate, light of the straying,
> Hope of the penitent, fadeless and pure!
> Here speaks the Comforter, tenderly saying,
> "Earth has no sorrow that Heaven cannot cure."[25]

Someone risked his life to attend her funeral and milled about in the snow-covered crowd: Malcolm X. He was then in hiding and under constant death threats, yet frenetically trying to organize the Organization of Afro-American Unity. Like Lorraine, Malcolm was pursuing an anticolonial, internationalist model of freedom. Recently, they'd had some lovely moments together. She'd taken him to task for once berating her in public for marrying a white man. He apologized, and they talked about the world they both imagined could be, with struggle. They both ran out of time. Three weeks after Lorraine's funeral, on Nina's birthday, Malcolm was murdered. His death, her death, and, over the next three years, the deaths of so many others left a trail of grief.

Nina's and Jimmy's voices changed after that. Their anguish sent them into depressions and rage. Jimmy opined that all the world's problems that Lorraine was trying to fix undoubtedly wore her body down. They wore down Nina's mind.

The day after Lorraine's funeral there was a vigil in Harlem of a thousand people demanding an end to school segregation in New York. Lorraine was laid to rest in Croton. Days later, Nina wrote in her diary, "She's gone from me and I'm sure it'll take like many years to accept this thing. It's so far out." The next day she went on a cruise with her husband and said, "The rocking and rolling of the ship almost made me scream with pain."[26] Nina began to have suicidal thoughts. But in March, she was with Jimmy in Selma for the historic march over the Edmund Pettus Bridge. Time marched on. In the words of one of Lorraine's comrades, Ella Baker: "The struggle is eternal. The tribe increases. Somebody carries on."[27]

Nina wanted to do something more for her dear girlfriend, and so she wrote a song titled "Young, Gifted and Black." Those were Lorraine's words. They came from a speech Lorraine delivered to a group of young writers: "The Nation Needs Your Gifts." In it Lorraine made a specific call to Black youth to embrace their identities and the struggle, "though it be a thrilling and marvelous thing to be merely young and gifted in such times, it is doubly so to be young, gifted and black."[28] She told them, "You are . . . the product of a presently insurgent and historically vivacious and heroic culture, a culture of an indomitable will for freedom and aspiration to dignity."

The ode Nina wrote became an anthem for the next stage of the movement, a stage that in many ways finally matched the radical fire Lorraine had possessed all her life. Lorraine, once dismissed as bourgeois, was embraced by the Black Power generation. The militancy and radicalism of the 1930s, which had in many quarters lain dormant for years, came roaring back. Perhaps it was because the world was moving quickly, but not quickly enough. Perhaps it was because people finally caught up.

After her death, Bobby treated Lorraine's legacy with great care. He attempted to place stories she wrote in various magazines. He edited *Les Blancs* (which, somewhat ironically, was decried in the press as being anti-white) and put together a biography in her own words, also titled *To Be Young, Gifted and Black*. But her papers stayed private for years. Between the brevity of the record left behind, keeping her "in the closet," and the casting of Lorraine as a "before the movement" figure in the mainstream press and criticism, the wider public has lived with a truncated story of who Lorraine was for many decades. And yet there were always gestures to something more. There were always murmurs; murmurs about her sexuality, about her radicalism, about the work we'd never seen.

Murmurs become shouts. In 2014, when the Lorraine Hansberry Literary Trust, under the executorship of Joi Gresham, published some of Lorraine's most intimate thoughts, people were hungry for more. She had never gone away; after all, *Raisin* is still the most frequently produced work by a Black American playwright. It has had numerous revivals, a musical, and three film versions. But now people want more. And we deserve it. Her other work also deserves hearing, reading, and more performances. Her essays, her excerpts, her heart and mind put down on paper will be pored over. Her pages lie in state at the Schomburg Center for Research in Black Culture up in Harlem, right near the Speakers' Corner Lorraine once preached from. She is waiting for us.

Retracing, May 2017

Lorraine Hansberry was a giver. Bitterness never prevailed
long enough in her spirit to destroy the "lift" that was a such
a large part of her talent, and which comes naturally when
human beings are created on stage. Mostly we see shadows
being titillated into life, only to fall because their authors had
no lover for them. I hate and deplore her death. We cannot
afford such losses. As she once said of Baldwin: "We should
be grateful we have him." I say: we should be grateful we
had her. Although what the hell all these words give her now,
I don't know. Relieve my chest. A gift given too late.
—*Letter to the* New York Times *from
Camille Skirvanek of Brooklyn, published January 21, 1965*

IN THE TRADITION OF ALICE WALKER, who followed the literary and
literal maps of Zora Neale Hurston's home and life, I find myself
wanting to stand in the places Lorraine stood. I want to make sense
of the world in her spaces and on her terms. And I want to tell you
about it. It isn't so pretty. There is as much hell as heaven on this
other, after the movement, side. Much has changed, some for better, some worse. Walking in the aftermath teaches this lesson. In the
summer of 2017, I wonder as I wander, somewhat angrily at the absence of a marker for Lorraine in Greenwich Village. But in October
of 2017, a red plaque was embedded in the rust-colored brick at 112
Waverly Place, in honor of Lorraine. Still, the Village is no longer
hers. The multiracial lesbian bar (the only one that was multiracial in
New York in the 1950s) was a short walk away from her home, and
it is gone. It is now a Mexican restaurant, which I don't expect will
last much longer either. It isn't highbrow. Although the Village has a

queer history and present, Lorraine's presence is faint at best. She's not really here. Nor is the bohemia that once was, nor the poor who were there before that. They have been displaced by cool accumulation and edgy wealth.

I walk past the Ethel Barrymore Theatre. *Six Degrees of Separation*, a play about a Black gay conman who finagles his way into the New York elite, is up. *Hamilton*, a remix of American history in the vernacular of Black and Brown New York is playing nearby. So too is August Wilson's *Jitney*. All of them seem to have something to do with the space Lorraine left on the Great White Way. But it isn't visible to the untutored eye. History, after all, has to be told to count as such.

There's more of Lorraine uptown in Harlem, where she lived briefly and visited frequently. Langston's ashes are in the same building as her archive. And the question that remains is one Jimmy once asked: What do we do with all that beauty? How do we weave it all together? The answer is not for one person to give. It is, as she knew, a collective duty. The battles Lorraine fought are still before us: exploitation of the poor, racism, neocolonialism, homophobia, and patriarchy. She models some of what we must do to confront them: use frank speech, beauty, imagination, and courage. And be with the people.

In Ajijic and Provincetown, there are still tiny bohemian enclaves. But the rougher edges have been cleaned up, and the rougher people—locals—mostly expunged or cast on the margins. I have been to Provincetown many times. Its scent salt-soaked, and the pale gray light, even on sunny days, is intoxicating. Couples—two women, two men—hold hands everywhere. It is as beautiful as Lorraine said. I have yet to visit Ajijic or Montevideo. What I have written about them is based upon photographs and text. And dreams. All through my youth and young adulthood I had detailed colorful dreams, but then they ceased. Writing about Lorraine, they returned. My own memories of Latin America—Puerto Rico, Costa Rica, Mexico, La Republica Dominicana—are now tinged by Lorraine's thoughts. The writers, the radicals, the dreamers I've read have a landscape. Ocean waters baptizing revolutionaries, *la gente en las calles* with *palmas* on either side. Looking for Lorraine has, for me, conjured up a scenic hope and the romance of possibilities past.

Chicago remembers Lorraine. The home the Hansberrys integrated, where a racist's piece of concrete nearly caught her head, is a historic landmark. The neighborhood is also now a mostly Black community. There is even a Lorraine Hansberry Park nearby. A school and a theater bear her name. I remember Chicago. When I was a girl, in sweltering summers spent in the basement of a Y on the West Side, in the line of sight of the most infamous housing project in America, I learned what Lorraine knew about Chicago's ghettoized children. The West Side was then a step below the South Side because it was the dwelling place of more recent migrants with more country edges. We did syncopated cheers: songs about our zodiac signs and imagined lovers, stomping and clapping in rhythm. I braided hair early each morning for the children of exhausted mothers: cornrows, plaits, puffs, careful in response to the winces of the girls who were tender headed. We ran around the track and danced until we were drenched to the repeating bass and high hat of house music. And if anyone was insulted, he or she fought back.

Chicago remains segregated. Lorraine wouldn't be surprised. Police still seem, to many of its people, an occupying force that threatens more than it protects. She would agree. Families like the Hansberrys are not ghetto-bound, but those she admired are. And that matters. Lorraine's beloved Chicago is, however, only part of the story: vast, and the key place it reserves for her is necessary yet not enough. In the public relations record she is recollected in the way of Black firsts, one in a long line of great Black artists to emerge from Chicago, a hallmark of its renaissances, longer and more varying than Harlem's, and distinctively Chicagoan in the persistent concern with socially relevant writing. She is inspiration and role model. But in truth she ought to be remembered for all the ways she troubled the world then, and would have today too. Where would her place be? In Boystown—an expensive upper-crust queer community where her brownness would still be an oddity? Probably not. Although her love of women would be treated more kindly today, there is a good chance Lorraine's sexuality would be used to push her away from the center of American theater and thought. Her far-left radicalism, if she were alive today, would not only be decried, it would also make her the subject of constant skepticism. She wouldn't have been satisfied with the gains of Black elites while a million sit in cages and many millions go hungry. She would hate warmongering. And she would have that trite insult "hater" lobbed at her for criticizing the Ralph Bunches of today. She had no interest in tea at the White House when people were suffering. But others did and do. We know who they are. And I know Lorraine would be moaning the capitalism-assimilation blues. Perhaps she would leave this country, like Du Bois did. Though probably she would go to the Caribbean or Latin America and not farther. She was unrepentantly American, though in the broadest sense. Though her politics were global she was passionately attached to the New World.

I drove to her burial site in Croton-on-Hudson for her birthday in 2017. It is my father's birthday too. He is dead. I can't place a call. For him there is no gravesite to visit, no shiva to sit. I know I will honor him in honoring her. He would love it that way.

I wondered what sort of flowers I should bring her. And then I thought of Lily, the lone girl in Lorraine's story "What Use Are Flowers?" In the beginning of it, Lily is the hardest fighter among the feral children. But the girl silently, and I imagine wide-eyed, points at a flower, a lily, when choosing her name.

Lilies are flowers of resurrection or better yet, if I am to be true to Lorraine's vision of the world, rebirth. I have spent years working on this story of her life, wanting to force a bloom—pointing to the pages and pages and books and ideas of hers that have remains encased. But when I stop at the flower shop before getting on the highway, there are no more potted lilies. Easter is past. So I purchase a halfway blossomed bouquet and worry that the flowers will wilt too soon.

When I get to Bethel Cemetery, they are still fragrant and now tautly open. I drive around the perimeter, not sure where to enter. I decide to turn into the parking lot of the public library because it looks as though it was designed in the midcentury. I imagine that she must have visited that library frequently. After parking, I walk to the edge of the cemetery. A man is tending to graves and I ask him, "Do you happen to know where the headstone of Lorraine Hansberry is?" He is a solid man, one who I would have placed as a New Englander if I weren't in the Hudson Valley: red-faced, straw-haired, friendly. It is apparent that he works for a living. He moves about with confidence and muscle memory. I appreciate that he seems unbothered at my Blackness, but I can tell he is curious. He tells me that he tends to only a few of the headstones and asks if she is my teacher or grandmother. I don't quite know how to answer. The answer isn't exactly no, though it isn't formally yes. I mumble something purposefully unintelligible.

The caretaker tells me that the cemetery is seven acres and gives me the name of someone else to call who is not available today. I will have to come back, he guesses. Okay, I say. I will just walk around a bit. I have all day. He says the older deaths, ones dating back to the Revolutionary War, are in the center, so focus on the edges. I begin on a diagonal. As I start to walk, he warns me that I must tread carefully in a graveyard. It is easy to fall. I thank him and take a few more steps.

There it is, in my direct line of sight.

"There it is," I tell him. I want to say "There *she* is," but I am trying to be calm. He replies, "You've got to be kidding me." I am not. There she is.

It is hot. Ninety-one degrees. Birds are chirping in the bush directly behind me as I sit before Lorraine's headstone. Someone has left five pennies as an offering on top. I leave the lilies at the foot of the grave and ask for her blessing. On the left is another headstone, slightly behind hers, bearing my grandmother's maiden name. I pick up a silvery-charcoal rock for my altar at home.

I cannot stay at her gravesite long. My allergies are terrible. My eyes burn, my throat itches. The sun beats directly on my forehead. I go to the car, sit in the air conditioning and let the Benadryl work as I take notes. Then I drive to her house. It is difficult to find. I go around in circles at first because it is on a road with no visible sign. But finally I see the steep, tiny path and drive up. There isn't a place to park. I just stop the car and get out. Standing in front of Chitterling Heights, I can hear the lake water not many yards away. I do not want to make too much of coincidences, but the windows in her home remind me of my own. Windows that when you look out of them all you see is trees. I wonder if when she was bedridden she had her bed facing in a direction where she could see the trees. It is the one regret I have about the place where I live. When I am sick enough that I cannot get out of bed, my bed is not angled toward the trees. One day I will fix that.

The last stop I make before going into town is to the water. In the years since Lorraine's death, Black Rock Park residents can no longer swim in the water. But I imagine she once waded here with other Croton residents. I cannot go in. I am at the water's edge. The park is noisy with nature, but like everywhere I went in the town, the people are quiet. Someone plays with a dog, a man in a construction uniform writes in a journal. This is a place to think. To imagine.

The best words I ever read in memoriam of Lorraine are the words that keep me writing, not just about her but in her wake and light. They are words for all of us to remember her by, and to become and eventually perish and persist by too:

> She had said part of what she had to say, but there were other words burning inside of her so I wonder, as she takes her place in the great beyond, was she supposed to say it all or just put the lights on so that someone else might now step from the wings and continue the dialogue. . . . Give her her immortality, for it was justly earned in a never ceasing no man's land where the living is only easy in song.[1]

In the car, riding back to my own life, I smile. And I cry.

ACKNOWLEDGMENTS

This book was made possible by a community that believed in bringing Lorraine into greater view. I am especially grateful to my amazing editor, Gayatri Patnaik; editorial assistant Molly Velasquez; and the entire Beacon Press community. Elleza Kelly was the research assistant of my dreams. Steven Fullwood and Alexsandra Mitchell provided indispensable support and guidance with the Lorraine Hansberry Collections at the Schomburg Center for Research in Black Culture. The students in my Lorraine Hansberry 20th Century Master Course—Destiny Crockett, Nicky Steidel, Imani Ford, Imani Thornton, Alana Clark, Abigail Jean Baptiste, and Jennifer Bunkley—inspired me with their diligent study and active imaginations. Brilliant documentarian Tracy Strain and her crew gave me abundant information and encouragement and meaningful camaraderie. At a fortuitous meeting with the premier Hansberry scholar Margaret Wilkerson in the Bay Area, she gave me insight and encouragement, and that meant a great deal to me. The great Beverly Guy-Sheftall, a beacon and guide in Black feminist study, opened doors and shared important stories and details. My dear friend Theo Davis and the community of the Mahindra Center at Harvard were wonderful discussants as I wrote. My friend Ashon Crawley helped me distill the essence of Lorraine over hundreds of text messages and meditations on soul searching. My friends Michele Alexandre and Simone White held me down and lifted me up the many times the vagaries of life threatened to take me away from my calling. All of my friends listened and encouraged, especially Kathy Van Cleve, Farah Griffin,

Regina Bradley, Tarana Burke, Darnell Moore, Shantrelle Lewis, and Robert Garland.

And as always, being a part of my wonderful community in the African American Studies Department at Princeton facilitated and nurtured this project. I am especially grateful for my writing partner and interlocutor, Eddie S. Glaude Jr.; my Northwest Philly community café buddy and fellow Black feminist socialist, Keeanga-Yamatta Taylor; and the ever-organized, supportive, and delightful Dionne Worthy.

My family is always with me as I study and write. I attempt to honor my extended family and the legacy of our matriarch, Neida Garner Perry, in every effort. Throughout the book-writing process the guidance and support of my mother, Theresa Perry, was essential. My sons, Freeman Diallo Rabb and Issa Garner Rabb, who are gorgeous beings in every way, believe in my work and the importance of effort, craft, ideas, and art. That keeps me writing. My late father, Steve Whitman, gifted me with his love for Lorraine. What a gift!

Finally, this is a labor of love offered with gratitude to the many, the people whom Lorraine loved and I love, *our* people. In particular, I am indebted to the long genealogy of "Black queer genius," to riff on Steven Fullwood's book title and subject. Against all odds, facing enormous obstacles, Black queer genius has been sustained on pages, on stages, canvases and testimonies, ballrooms and battlefields, scores and clubs, indoors and out in the streets. Queer contributions to the tradition of Black thought and art are immense and essential. It is now time to bring Black queer work and stories from the margins to the center.

NOTES

INTRODUCTION: LORRAINE'S TIME

1. Lonne Elder, "Lorraine Hansberry: Social Consciousness and the Will," *Freedomways* 19 (1979): 213.
2. Michael Nash and Daniel J. Leab, "Freedomways," in *Red Activists and Black Freedom: James and Esther Jackson and the Long Civil Rights Movement*, ed. David Levering Lewis, Michael Nash, and Daniel J. Leab (London: Routledge, 2013), 62.
3. "Tribute Paid the Late Lorraine Hansberry: She Gave New Life to 'Negro' Drama," *Pittsburgh Courier*, January 23, 1965.

CHAPTER ONE: MIGRATION SONG

1. Robert Nemiroff, ed., *To Be Young, Gifted and Black: A Portrait of Lorraine Hansberry in Her Own Words* (New York: Samuel French, 1971), 12.
2. Ibid., 26.
3. Ibid., 29.
4. Richard Guzman, ed., *Black Writing from Chicago: In the World, Not of It?* (Carbondale: Southern Illinois University Press, 2006), 164.
5. Pat Curry, "Day in the Sun for Raisin Writer Home," *Chicago Tribune*, February 10, 2010, http://articles.chicagotribune.com/2010–02–10/news /1002090492_1_landmark-status-landmark-designation-black-family.
6. Lorraine Hansberry Papers (hereafter, Hansberry Papers), Schomburg Center for Research in Black Culture, New York, box 60, file 15.
7. Ibid.
8. Ibid.
9. Ibid.
10. Ibid.
11. Ibid.
12. Lorraine Hansberry, "The Black Revolution and the White Backlash," in *Black Protest: History, Documents, and Analysis, 1619 to the Present*, ed. Joanne Grant (New York: Fawcett Premier, 1968).
13. Melvin Tolson, "Dark Symphony," in *The Penguin Anthology of Twentieth Century American Poetry*, ed. Rita Dove (New York: Penguin, 2011), 109.
14. Nemiroff, *To Be Young, Gifted and Black*, 39.

15. Sidney Fields, "Housewife's Play Is a Hit," *New York Daily Mirror*, March 16, 1959.
16. Hansberry Papers, box 1, file 3.
17. James Forman, *The Making of Black Revolutionaries* (Seattle: University of Washington Press, 1972), 47.
18. Hansberry Papers, box 2, file 1.
19. Nemiroff, *To Be Young, Gifted and Black*, 42.
20. Ibid.
21. Englewood High School Yearbook, Hansberry Papers, box 1, file 4.

CHAPTER TWO: FROM HEARTLAND TO THE WATER'S EDGE

1. 1949 Mexico Poem, Hansberry Papers, box 1, file 1.
2. JoAnn Beier letter, Hansberry Papers, box 1, file 5.
3. Ibid.
4. Ibid.
5. Nemiroff, *To Be Young, Gifted and Black*, 51.
6. "Lorraine Hansberry Talks with Studs Terkel," on WFMT, May 12, 1959.
7. "1949," Hansberry Papers, box 1, file 1.
8. "Frank Lloyd Wright," Hansberry Papers, box 1, file 5.
9. Letter from JoAnn Beier, Hansberry Papers, box 1, file 5.
10. "1949 Mexico Poem," Hansberry Papers, box 1, file 1.
11. Ibid.
12. JoAnn Beier letter, Hansberry Papers, box 1, file 5.
13. Edythe Cohen letter to Robert Nemiroff, Hansberry Papers, box 1, file 5.
14. Robert Nemiroff letter to Edythe Cohen, Hansberry Papers, box 1, file 4.
15. Lorraine Hansberry letter to Edythe Cohen, Hansberry Papers, box 1, file 5.

CHAPTER THREE: THE GIRL WHO CAN DO EVERYTHING

1. "Tribute Paid the Late Lorraine Hansberry."
2. Steven R. Carter, *Hansberry Drama: Commitment amid Complexity* (Urbana: University of Illinois Press, 1991), viii.
3. Lorraine Hansberry, "Flag from a Kitchenette Window," *Masses and Mainstream* 3, no. 9 (1950).
4. Gwendolyn Brooks, "Kitchenette Building," *The World of Gwendolyn Brooks* (New York: Harper and Row, 1971), 4–5.
5. "1949," Hansberry Papers, box 1, file 1.
6. Ibid.
7. Ibid.
8. "Tribute Paid the Late Lorraine Hansberry."
9. Lorraine Hansberry letter to Edythe Cohen, Hansberry Papers, box 1, file 5.
10. Lorraine Hansberry, "The Outsider," *Freedom* (April 1953).
11. Lorraine Hansberry, "Gold Coast Rulers Go: Ghana Moves to Freedom," *Freedom* (December 1951).
12. Lorraine Hansberry letter to Edythe Cohen, Hansberry Papers, box 1, file 5.
13. "Louis Burnham," Hansberry Papers, box 2, file 13.
14. Lorraine Hansberry, "Lynchsong," *Masses and Mainstream* 4, no. 7 (July 1951): 19–20.

15. Jefferson School of Social Science advertisement, *New York Amsterdam News*, February 9, 1952.
16. Notes on W. E. B. Du Bois, Hansberry Papers, box 1, file 5.
17. Ibid.
18. "The Frederick Douglass Education Center," *Daily Worker*, March 26, 1952.
19. "Homecoming," Hansberry Papers, box 60, file 9.
20. Ibid.
21. Ralph Ellison, "Harlem Is Nowhere," *Harper's*, August 1964, 57.
22. Ibid.
23. "Homecoming," Hansberry Papers.
24. Lorraine Hansberry, "A Negro Woman Speaks for Peace," *Sunday Worker*, June 22, 1952.
25. "Lorraine Hansberry," "F.B. Eyes Digital Archive: FBI Files on African American Authors and Literary Institutions Obtained Through the U.S. Freedom of Information Act (FOIA)," FBI file NY 105–40092, http://omeka.wustl.edu/omeka/exhibits/show/fbeyes/hansberry.

CHAPTER FOUR: BOBBY

1. Hansberry Papers, box 2, file 1.
2. Hansberry Papers, box 1, file 5.
3. Hansberry Papers, box 2, file 1.
4. Ibid.
5. Ibid.
6. Dwight D. Eisenhower, Statement by the President Declining to Intervene on Behalf of Julius and Ethel Rosenberg, June 19, 1953, Public Papers of the Presidents of the United States: Dwight D. Eisenhower, 1953.
7. Ilene Philipson, *Ethel Rosenberg: Beyond the Myths* (New Brunswick: Rutgers University Press, 1993), 352.
8. David Levering Lewis, Michael Nash, and Daniel J. Leab, eds., *Red Activists and Black Freedom: James and Esther Jackson and the Long Civil Rights Movement* (London: Routledge, 2013), 96.
9. Ibid.
10. "The Trial of Jomo Kenyatta," *The Reporter*, Hansberry Papers, box 63, file 26.
11. Ibid.
12. "Lorraine Hansberry Tribute to Paul Robeson," Hansberry Papers, box 56, file 20.
13. "My Own Dear Husband," Hansberry Papers, box 2, file 1.
14. Ibid.
15. Hansberry Papers, box 2, file 1.
16. Ibid.
17. Ibid.
18. Ibid.
19. Ibid.
20. Dan Wakefield, *New York in the '50s* (New York: Open Road Media, 2016), 157.
21. John Oliver Killens, "The Literary Genius of Alice Childress," in

Black Women Writers 1950–1980: A Critical Evaluation, ed. Mari Evans (Garden City, NY: Anchor Books, 1984), 129.

22. Hansberry Papers, box 2, file 1.
23. Hansberry Papers, box 3, file 1.
24. Joan Sandler, a friend of Lorraine's, was an African American actress and activist in New York.
25. Hansberry Papers, box 1, file 1.
26. Hansberry Papers, box 60, file 2.
27. Ibid.
28. "1956," Hansberry Papers, box 60, file 2.
29. Ibid.
30. Herman Melville, *Moby Dick; or, the White Whale* (Boston: St. Botolph Society, 1892), 39.
31. "Annie," Hansberry Papers, box 50, file 3.
32. "Simone de Beauvoir and The Second Sex—An American Commentary," 1957, Hansberry Papers, box 59, file 1.

CHAPTER FIVE: SAPPHO'S POETRY

1. Theresa Cha, *Dictee* (Berkeley: University of California Press, 2001), 1.
2. Hansberry Papers, box 5, file 7.
3. *Ladder* 1, no. 8 (May 1957): 26.
4. Ibid.
5. Marcia Gallo, *Different Daughters: A History of the Daughters of Bilitis* (New York: Seal Press, 2007), 42–43.
6. Hansberry Papers, box 2, file 1.
7. Lorraine Hansberry letter to Robert Nemiroff, Hansberry Papers, box 2, file 1.
8. Ibid.
9. Elise Harris, "The Double Life of Lorraine Hansberry," *OUT Magazine*, September 1999.
10. Lorraine Hansberry [Emily Jones, pseud.], "The Anticipation of Eve," *ONE Magazine* 6, no. 12 (December 1958): 22.
11. Ibid.
12. Hansberry, "The Anticipation of Eve," 24.
13. Ibid.
14. Ibid., 25.
15. Ibid., 27.
16. Ibid., 28.
17. Ibid.
18. Ibid., 29.
19. Ibid.
20. Ibid.
21. Hansberry Papers, box 59, file 1.
22. Hansberry, "The Anticipation of Eve," 29.
23. Hansberry Papers, box 59, file 1.
24. Ibid.
25. Colm Toibin, "The Unsparing Confessions of Giovanni's Room," *New Yorker*, February 26, 2016.

26. Lorraine Hansberry [Emily Jones, pseud.], "Chanson Du Konallis," *Ladder* 2, no. 12 (September 1958).

27. Ibid., 6.

28. Ibid., 10.

29. Ibid., 20.

30. Hansberry Papers, box 59, file 1.

31. Gene Smith, "Telling the Truth of People's Lives," *American Legacy* (Spring 1997): 7.

32. Mary Oliver and Molly Malone Cook, *Our World* (Boston: Beacon Press, 2009), 4.

33. Ibid., 81.

34. "Lorraine Hansberry," FBI file.

35. Autobiographical Notes, Hansberry Papers, box 1, file 1

CHAPTER SIX: *RAISIN*

1. W. E. B. Du Bois, *The Souls of Black Folk* (Chicago: A. C. McClurg, 1903), 206.

2. William J. Maxwell, *F.B. Eyes: How J. Edgar Hoover's Ghostreaders Framed African American Literature* (Princeton, NJ: Princeton University Press, 2015), 103.

3. "Lorraine Hansberry," FBI file.

4. Robin Bernstein, "Inventing a Fishbowl: White Supremacy and the Critical Reception of Lorraine Hansberry's A Raisin in the Sun," *Modern Drama* 42, no. 1 (1999): 23.

5. James Baldwin, "Sweet Lorraine," *The Price of the Ticket: Collected Nonfiction 1948–1985* (New York: St. Martin's Press, 1985), 444.

6. Ossie Davis, *Life Lit by Some Large Vision* (New York: Atria Press, 2006), 99.

7. Ibid., 103.

8. Amiri Baraka, "A Wiser Play Than Some of Us Knew," *Los Angeles Times*, March 22, 1987.

9. "Lorraine Hansberry," FBI file.

10. Fields, "Housewife's Play Is a Hit."

11. Lorraine Hansberry, "We Have So Much to Say," transcript of interview with Ted Poston, *New York Post*, March 22, 1959.

12. Esther Edwards, "Hit a Raisin in the Sun," *Philadelphia Inquirer*, February 7, 1959.

13. Walter Kerr, "Raisin in the Sun at American," *St. Louis Post Dispatch*, February 12, 1961.

14. Lorraine Hansberry, author's reply, *New York Times*, June 28, 1959.

15. Lorraine Hansberry, "An Author's Reflection: Willie Loman, Walter Lee, and He Who Must Live," *Village Voice*, August 12, 1959.

16. Ibid.

17. Ibid.

18. Ibid.

19. Ibid.

20. Ibid.

21. Ibid.

22. Phillip Rose, *You Can't Do That on Broadway* (Milwaukee: Hal Leonard Corporation, 2001), 150.

23. "Brandeis Lecture," Hansberry Papers, box 56, file 3.
24. Ibid.
25. "Swarthmore Lecture," Hansberry Papers, box 56, file 15.
26. Norman Mailer, "The White Negro," *Dissent* (Fall 1957).
27. Ibid.
28. "Brandeis Lecture."
29. Lorraine Hansberry, "Thoughts on Genet, Mailer, and the New Paternalism," *Village Voice*, June 1, 1961.
30. Ibid., 14.
31. Ibid.
32. Ibid.
33. Langston Hughes letter to Lorraine Hansberry, Hansberry Papers, box 63, file 15.
34. LeRoi Jones letter to Lorraine Hansberry, Hansberry Papers, box 63, file 15.
35. Ibid.
36. Ibid.
37. Harry J. Elam Jr., "Cultural Capital and the Presence of Africa: Lorraine Hansberry, August Wilson and the Power of Black Theater," in *The Cambridge History of African American Literature*, ed. Maryemma Graham and Jerry Ward Jr. (Cambridge, UK: Cambridge University Press, 2011), 685.
38. Lorraine Hansberry, "About Billie Holiday," *New York Post*, July 27, 1959.
39. Lorraine Hansberry, "What Could Happen Didn't," *New York Herald Tribune*, March 26, 1961.
40. Ibid.
41. Original prospectus for the John Brown Theatre ("Toward a Harlem Community Theatre"), Hansberry Papers, box 56, file 12.

CHAPTER SEVEN: THE TRINITY

1. Baldwin, "Sweet Lorraine," 444.
2. Ruth Feldstein, *How It Feels to Be Free: Black Women Entertainers and the Civil Rights Movement* (Oxford, UK: Oxford University Press, 2013), 103.
3. Lorraine Hansberry letter to Robert Nemiroff, Hansberry Papers, box 1, file 1.
4. "Lorraine Hansberry Talks with Studs Terkel."
5. Baldwin, "Sweet Lorraine," 444.
6. David Leeming, *James Baldwin: A Biography* (New York: Skyhorse, 2015), 195.
7. James Baldwin letter to Lorraine Hansberry, Hansberry Papers, box 63, file 15.
8. Letter from Lorraine Hansberry to James Baldwin, James Baldwin Papers, Schomburg Center for Research in Black Culture, New York, box 3a, folder 20.
9. Smith, "Telling the Truth of People's Lives."
10. Baldwin, "Sweet Lorraine," 443.
11. Ibid.
12. Nathan Glazer, "Liberalism and the Negro: A Round-Table Discussion," *Commentary* 37 (March 1, 1964), https://www.commentarymagazine.com

/articles/liberalism-the-negro-a-round-table-discussion. Participants were James Baldwin, Nathan Glazer, Sidney Hook, and Gunnar Myrdal.

13. Ibid.

14. Ibid.

15. Lorraine Hansberry, *A Raisin in the Sun* (New York: Samuel French, 1984), 127.

16. James Baldwin, "Everybody's Protest Novel," *The Price of the Ticket*, 33.

17. James Baldwin letter to Lorraine Hansberry, Hansberry Papers (2), box 63, file 15.

18. James Baldwin letter to Lorraine Hansberry, Hansberry Papers, box 63, file 15.

19. Nadine Cohodas, *Princess Noire: The Tumultuous Reign of Nina Simone* (Durham: University of North Carolina Press, 2010), 138.

20. Ibid., 139.

21. Ibid.

22. Ibid.

23. Nina Simone with Stephen Cleary, *I Put a Spell on You: The Autobiography of Nina Simone* (orig. 1991; Cambridge, MA: Da Capo Press, 2003), 87.

24. Joe Hagan, "I Wish I Knew How It Would Feel to Be Free," *Believer*, August 2010.

25. Simone, *I Put a Spell on You*, 87.

26. Nina Simone, "Mississippi Goddam," *Nina Simone Live in Concert*, Philips Records, 1964.

27. Nemiroff, *To Be Young, Gifted and Black*, 148.

28. Jane Howard, "Doom and Glory of Knowing Who You Are," *Life*, May 24, 1963, 89.

29. "Diary," Hansberry Papers, box 1, file 1.

30. Ibid.

CHAPTER EIGHT: OF THE FAITH OF OUR FATHERS

1. Nemiroff, *To Be Young, Gifted and Black*, 20.

2. James Baldwin, *Notes of a Native Son* (orig. 1955; Boston: Beacon Press, 1984), 85.

3. "Slum Play Author Sued as Slumlord," *New York World Telegram*, June 13, 1959.

4. Helen Dudar, "To a Raisin in the Sun," *New York Post*, July 1, 1959.

5. Truman K. Gibson, *Knocking Down Barriers: My Fight for Black America* (Evanston, IL: Northwestern University Press, 2005), 48.

6. St. Clair Drake and Horace R. Cayton, *Black Metropolis: A Study of Negro Life in a Northern City* (Chicago: University of Chicago Press, 2015), 232.

7. "Lorraine Hansberry Talks with Studs Terkel."

8. Lorraine Hansberry, *Les Blancs: The Collected Last Plays of Lorraine Hansberry* (New York: Vintage 1994), 88.

9. Ibid., 107.

10. "Brandeis Lecture."

11. Lorraine Hansberry, "Village Intellect Revealed," *New York Times*, October 31, 1964.

12. Lorraine Hansberry, *The Sign in Sidney Brustein's Window: A Drama in Two Acts*, rev. stage ed. (New York: Samuel French, 1993), 161.

13. Ibid.
14. Ibid.
15. Ibid., 88.
16. Ibid., 89.
17. Ibid., 106.
18. Ibid., 107.
19. Ibid., 108.
20. Ibid., 112.
21. Ibid., 114.

CHAPTER NINE: AMERICAN RADICAL

1. Baldwin, "Sweet Lorraine," 445.
2. Lorraine Hansberry, "Stanley Gleason and the Lights That Need Not Die," *New York Times*, January 17, 1960.
3. "JFK and the Student Airlift," John F. Kennedy Presidential Library and Museum, 1960.
4. Lorraine Hansberry, "Congolese Patriot," *New York Times*, March 26, 1961.
5. Ibid.
6. "Lumumba, Bunche, Baldwin," Hansberry Papers, box 63, file 21.
7. Letter from Julian Mayfield to Lorraine Hansberry, Hansberry Papers, box 63, file 15.
8. Ibid.
9. "Metamorphasis [*sic*]," Hansberry Papers, box 60, file 12.
10. Ibid.
11. *Lorraine Hansberry Speaks Out: Art and the Black Revolution* (Caedmon Records, 1972), audio recording.
12. Ibid.
13. "Lorraine Hansberry," FBI file.
14. Letter to Daniel Thompson, March 22, 1963, Hansberry Papers, box 56, file 10.
15. Ibid.
16. Ibid.
17. Ibid.
18. Ibid.
19. Baldwin, *Notes of a Native Son*, 38.
20. James Baldwin, *The Cross of Redemption: Uncollected Writings*, ed. Randall Kenan (New York: Knopf, 2010), 137.
21. Ibid.
22. Ibid., 138.
23. Ibid., 139.
24. Jerome Smith, "A Freedom Rider's First Stand," *AARP*, May 3, 2011.
25. Ibid.
26. Ibid.
27. "Rally to Support the Southern Freedom Movement," Croton, New York, June 1963, Hansberry Papers, box 56, file 16.
28. Lorraine Hansberry, *The Movement: Documentary of a Struggle for Equality* (New York: Simon and Schuster, 1964), 13–14.

29. Ibid., 26.
30. Ibid., 98.
31. Ibid.
32. Nemiroff, *To Be Young, Gifted and Black*, 72.
33. Ibid.
34. Ibid., 21.
35. Ibid.
36. *Muhammad Speaks*, December 20, 1963.
37. James Wechsler, editorial, *New York Times*, June 22, 1964; "Racial Debate at Town Hall Gets Nowhere," *New York Post*, June 16, 1964, both in Hansberry FBI file.
38. Hansberry, "The Black Revolution and the White Backlash," in Grant, *Black Protest*.
39. Ibid.
40. Simone, "Mississippi Goddam."
41. Hansberry, "The Black Revolution and the White Backlash," in Grant, *Black Protest*.
42. Ibid.
43. Wechsler editorial, *New York Times*; "Racial Debate," *New York Post*.

CHAPTER TEN: THE VIEW
FROM CHITTERLING HEIGHTS

1. Edward W. Said, *On Late Style: Music and Literature Against the Grain* (New York: Knopf, 2007), 7.
2. Hansberry, *The Sign in Sidney Brustein's Window*, 32.
3. Lorraine Hansberry letter to Evelyn Goldwasser, Hansberry Papers, box 4, file 3.
4. Ibid.
5. Ibid.
6. Lorraine Hansberry speech for W. E. B. Du Bois memorial, Hansberry Papers, box 56, file 21.
7. Ibid.
8. Hansberry Papers, box 63, file 15.
9. Nemiroff, *To Be Young, Gifted and Black*, 249–50.
10. "Puzzle," Hansberry Papers, box 1, file 1.
11. Ibid.
12. Letter to Mae and Motya, Hansberry Papers, box 2, file 8.
13. Said, *On Late Style*, 7.
14. Email to author from Cornelia Cotton.
15. Harris, "The Double Life of Lorraine Hansberry," 175.
16. Nemiroff, *To Be Young, Gifted and Black*, 102.
17. Hansberry Papers, box 4, file 5.
18. Hansberry Papers, box 4, file 4.
19. Letter from Alex Haley to Lorraine Hansberry, November 7, 1964, Hansberry Papers, box 4, file 5.
20. "Homegoing," Hansberry Papers, box 4, file 8.

CHAPTER ELEVEN: HOMEGOING

1. Langston Hughes, *The Collected Works of Langston Hughes: The Poems: 1941–1950*, ed. Ramona Bass and Arnold Rampersad (Columbia: University of Missouri Press, 2001), 124.
2. James Baldwin, *Giovanni's Room* (New York: Dial Press, 1956), 121.
3. David Brun-Lambert, *Nina Simone: The Biography* (London: Aurum Press, 2009), 134.
4. Baldwin, "Sweet Lorraine," 447.
5. Ibid.
6. Ibid.
7. Larry Pendleton, "To Lorraine," January 12, 1965, Hansberry Papers, box 68, file 2.
8. Richard B. Moore, "For Lorraine Hansberry," *Richard B. Moore, Caribbean Militant in Harlem: Collected Writings, 1920–1972* (Bloomington: Indiana University Press, 1988), 312.
9. Walt Whitman, "O Me! O Life!," *Leaves of Grass* (1892), https://www.poetryfoundation.org/poems/51568/o-me-o-life.
10. Lorraine Hansberry obituary, *National Review* 17, no. 4 (January 26, 1965): 54.
11. Hansberry Papers, box 68, file 5.
12. Henry Francis Lyte, "Abide with Me" (1861).
13. James Forman eulogy, Hansberry Papers, box 68, file 2.
14. Paul Robeson eulogy, Hansberry Papers, box 68, file 2.
15. Ruby Dee eulogy, Hansberry Papers, box 68, file 2.
16. Simone, *I Put a Spell on You*, 87–88.
17. James Baldwin telegram to Robert Nemiroff, Hansberry Papers, box 68, file 5.
18. Sylvester Leaks, "The Legacy of Lorraine: Requiem for a Remarkable Woman," *Muhammad Speaks*, February 3, 1965.
19. Joanne Grant, quoted in Leaks, "The Legacy of Lorraine."
20. Leo Nemiroff eulogy, Hansberry Papers, box 68, file 2.
21. Ibid.
22. Herman Melville, *Moby Dick; or, the White Whale* (Boston: St. Botolph Society, 1892), 391.
23. Lorraine Hansberry Papers, box 68, file 2.
24. Martin Luther King Jr. telegram, Hansberry Papers, box 68, file 5.
25. Thomas Moore, "Come Ye Disconsolate" (1816).
26. Cohodas, *Princess Noire*, 168.
27. Ellen Cantarow et al., *Moving the Mountain: Women Working for Social Change* (New York: Feminist Press, 1980), 93.
28. The speech was published as an article, quotes from Lorraine Hansberry, "Memo to Negro Youth: The Nation Needs Your Gifts," *Negro Digest*, August 1964, 26.

CONCLUSION: RETRACING MAY 2017

1. "Tribute Paid the Late Lorraine Hansberry."

INDEX

NOTE: LH refers to Lorraine Hansberry; RN to Robert Nemiroff; *Raisin* to *A Raisin in the Sun*; and *Sign* to *The Sign in Sidney Brustein's Window*

"Abide with Me" (hymn), 191

Abioseh (character in *Les Blancs*), 141–43

activism, radical: and activities in Harlem, 47–48, 50–52; and armed struggle, 142, 168–71; Black nationalist vision, 2, 44, 161–62; and the Daughters of Bilitis, 80–81; early exposure to, 4, 19, 24; emphasis on direct action, 89, 160; fiction reflecting, 54, 57; and fight against cancer, 193; and friendship with Simone, 117, 129–30; the Inter-American Peace Conference, 57–59; at 1963 AAF forum, 171–73; at 1963 RFK meeting, 163–65; O'Casey's revolutionaries, 30; as response to despair, nihilism, 180; support for Wallace, 34. *See also* anticolonial internationalism; Baldwin, James Arthur; communism; Du Bois, W. E. B.; feminism

Actors Studio, New York, 118

aesthetics, personal, 31, 95, 119, 130. *See also* beauty; nature; writing craft

African independence movements. *See* anticolonial internationalism

Airlift Africa, 1960, 152–53

Ajijic, Mexico: changes since the 1950s, 200; poetry written at, 38–40; summer art program, LH at, 35–38

Algren, Nelson, 110

All the Dark and Beautiful Warriors (Hansberry), 124

Alton (character in *Sign*): experience of racism, injustice, 146–47; mocking of romanticism, 175

ambition, 32, 119, 135

The Amen Corner (Baldwin), 120

American Labor Party, 50

American Negro Exposition, 18

American Negro Theater, 53

American Student Movement, 46–47

Andrea (character in "Renascence"), mourning of lover by, 194

anger, rage, 3, 14–15, 59, 68, 154, 162–165, 190, 192. *See also* activism, radical

"Annie" (Hansberry), 77

Another Country (Baldwin): comparison with *Sign*, 128–29; controversies caused by, 128, 187; exploration of intimacy and grief in, 128; letter to LH about, 127

"The Anticipation of Eve" (Hansberry), 84–87

anticolonial internationalism: and apartheid, 67; Beneatha Younger's interest in, 140; and the Inter-

American Peace Conference, 57–59; and the joy of freedom, in *Raisin*, 140; LH's commitment to, 48, 150, 196; Malcolm X's commitment to, 196; ongoing support for African independence movements, 152–57; in SNCC, 168; and uprisings in Latin America, 58, 65, 157; and worldwide ghettoization, 22

Antoine (character in *400 Blows*), LH's love for, 96

Árbenz de Guzmán, Jacobo, 65

"Arnold" (Hansberry), 75–76

The Arrival of Mr. Todog (Hansberry), 180

art, as political, 47, 52, 161. *See also* social criticism; writing craft

assimilationist politics: Bunche as symbol of, 154, 159, 161, 202; and criticisms of *Raisin*, 112–13; LH's rejection of, 122–23, 179, 202; and the popularity of *Raisin*, 100

Association of Artists for Freedom (AAF), 170–72

Atkinson, Brooks, 107

Attie, David, 102–3

Avon Books, 73–74

Bachrach, Marian, 193

Baker, Ella, 197

Baldwin, David, 136

Baldwin, David, Jr., 163

Baldwin, James Arthur (Jimmy): and the AAF, 171; on art in the struggle for liberation, 16; on Wright, 123; basis for friendship with, 118–19, 127; critique of Gide, 129; critique of Wright, 124–25; descriptions, memories of LH, 117, 119, 121, 150, 162–63; echoes of *Les Blancs*, 143; father, David, 136; on impact of *Raisin* on Black audiences, 100; on LH as a martyr, 187–88, 196; LH's admiration for, 117–18; "Liberalism and the Negro" roundtable, 122–23; literary give-and-take with LH, 120, 123–27;

loneliness, 134; message read at LH's funeral, 192; and Nation of Islam, 159–60; at 1963 RFK meeting, 162–63; personality, similarities to LH, 127–28; politics, 125; post-movement life, death, 135; questioning of American Christianity, 126; recounting of LH at 1963 meeting with RFK, 162–64; respect for LH's intellect and character, 119. *See also specific works by Baldwin*

Baltimore Afro-American, 47

Bandele Matoseh (character in "Metamorphosis"), exploration of politics of, 156–57

Baraka, Amiri (LeRoi Jones), 101, 111–12, 171

Barnes, Essie, 185

Beat writers, hipsters, views on, 109–10

beauty: in Ajijic, 36; Black, LH's appreciation for, 54; Camp Unity, 68–69; Croton-on-Hudson home, 176–78; female, LH's appreciation for, 87–88; importance in the Emily Jones writings, 87; Millay's "Renascence" as meditation on, 195; natural, as solace and rebirth, 2–3, 38, 52, 68–69, 82, 86–87, 130, 176, 194

Beckett, Samuel, 180

"begging," in Black vernacular, 120

Beier, JoAnn, 27–29, 33, 40

Belafonte, Harry, 53, 163

Belgian Congo, 51–52, 153. *See also* colonialism, imperialism; Lumumba, Patrice

"The Belgian Congo: A Preliminary Report on Its Land, Its History and Its Peoples" (Hansberry), 51–52

Belvin, Shawn, 184–85

Bendiner, Elmer, 57

Beneatha Younger (character in *Raisin*): ambitions, 97, 139; Cruse's questioning verisimilitude of, 113–14; as self-portrait, 126

Bennett, Gwendolyn, 51

Bergman, Ingrid, 40

Berry, Edwin, 163

Betsy Ross Elementary, Chicago, 20

Bigger Thomas (character in *Native Son*): Baldwin's critique, 124–25; *Raisin* as answer to, 124; as result of racism, 20

A Big White Fog (Ward), 139

Birmingham, Alabama, 167

Black Americans: beauty of, 54; housing discrimination, 9, 12–13, 17, 27; humanity and strength, LH's sensitive depictions of, 76–77; 105, 124–25, 149, 154, 160; and mother wisdom, 138–39; perceptions of white Americans, 100–11; realities faced by, LH's portrayals, 14, 105, 151, 160; stereotyping, 132; as survivors, 89, 105; working class, admiration for, 3–4, 19, 23. *See also* the ghetto; *specific characters and writings*

"Blackbird" (Simone), 134

Black elites. *See* Black middle class

Black Left: criticisms of *Raisin*, 102, 111–13

"Black Magic" (song), as LH's favorite song in high school, 20–21

Black masses, and LH's Black "man of the people," 157

Black Metropolis (WPA Negro in Illinois publication), 104, 139

Black middle class: and acceptance by whites, 103–4, 159; Carl Hansberry's business success, 9, 11; and Carl Hansberry's activism, 17; and the civil rights movement, 167; and criticisms of *Raisin*, 104, 112–13; expectations for women, 26, 90; ghettoization of, 104, 113; LH's experience of, 9, 11, 24; and life insurance, 113; "success of," as excuse for inaction, 161

Black radical traditions: and the Black Power movement, 197; calls for radical militancy, 170–73; and efforts to work within the system, 17, 170; LH's writings as reflection

of, 14, 24–25, 100–10, 154–55, 158–59, 174; and LH's views on need for militancy, 170–73; "Pirate Jenny," Simone's version, 133; and "radical" as term of praise, 150; separation from mainstream Black politics, 66–67; and the slowness of progress toward liberation, 187–88. *See also* activism, radical; Du Bois, W. E. B.; liberation

Black Renaissance, 17–18

"The Black Revolution and the White Backlash" forum (AAF), 171–73

The Blacks (Genet), LH's response to, 110

Black vernacular: "begging," 120; "down home" talk, 121–22; "little girl," 185; "Mr. Charlie," 126, "Sweet Lorraine," 119, 121

Black writers, artists: American Negro Theater, 53; special challenges faced by, 100, 106–7, 111, 117; and today's Broadway theater, 200. *See also* racism; *specific writers/artists*

Bleeker Street apartment, 94

Blues for Mr. Charlie (Baldwin), 126

Bontemps, Arna, 178

Bradley, Omar, 32

Brandeis University, Martin Weiner Distinguished Lecture, 107–8, 110

Brecht, Bertolt, 108, 132–33

brilliance, genius, LH's, 96, 118, 121, 137, 180, 192

Brooks, Gwendolyn: and Black women's writing tradition, 88; influence on LH, 44; "Kitchenette Building," 44, 98; "Negro in Illinois" WPA project, 18

Brown v. Board of Education, 65–67, 168

Buck, Pearl, 21

Bunche, Ralph: dismissal of protests following Lumumba assassination, 154; interest in among Ghanaians, 48; as symbol of assimilationist politics, 154, 159, 161, 202

Burgum, Edwin, 82
Burnham, Louis, 46–47. *See also*
  Freedom (newspaper)
Butterlin, Ernesto (Linares), 37–38

Callender, Eugene, 195
Camp Unity, Wingdale, NY, 68–69
cancer, pancreatic cancer: activist
  view of, 193; LH diagnosis and
  treatments, 177–78; LH's death
  from, 186–87
Cane (Toomer), 89
capitalism: Brecht's rejection of, 132–
  33; Chicago as reflection of, 36;
  debates about during LH's youth,
  21; LH's experience and rejection
  of, 49, 56, 138, 150, 153, 159. *See
  also* Hansberry family
Cayton, Horace, 18–19
Cha, Theresa (Sappho), 79
Chakamoi, Oyil, 159
Chaney, James, 173
"Chanson Du Konallis" (Hansberry),
  88–90
Charlie (character in *Les Blancs*), as
  white liberal, 142
Chicago, Illinois: American Negro
  Exposition, 18; arts scene in the
  1930s, 17–21; Black press in, 17–
  18; Hansberry home in, 201; housing discrimination in, 9, 12; LH's
  birth in, 9; LH's returns to, reflections on, 45, 69, 74; segregation
  in, 201; tryouts for *Raisin* in, 97.
  See also childhood, LH's; Hansberry family; South Side, Chicago
childhood, LH's: admiration for
  working-class children, 3, 19, 23,
  61; cultural experiences, 17–19;
  elementary and high school, 20;
  intellectual home environment, 4,
  10–11, 19, 66, 214; leadership activities, 19; Mother, May I game,
  10–11; political debates, 21–22;
  shame experienced during, 11, 24;
  teenaged heroes and preferences,
  20–21; trauma and violence experienced during, 12–14

Childress, Alice: at Camp Unity, 68;
  friendship with LH in Harlem, 53;
  production of plays written by,
  72–73
Childress, Alvin, 53
"Chitterling Heights," Croton-on-
  Hudson, New York, 175, 203–4
Christianity, American, Baldwin's
  questioning of, 126
Church of the Master, New York,
  190–91
"Cindy, Oh Cindy" (Nemiroff and
  D'Lugoff), 74
Civil Rights Act of 1964, John Kennedy's proposal for, 165
civil rights movement: and *Brown v.
  Board of Education*, 65, 168; JFK's
  views, 165; LH's critique of, 179;
  as long-term, messy struggle, 174;
  portrayal of, in *Raisin*, 102; and
  questioning of nonviolence, 142,
  168–69. *See also* activism, radical
Clark, Kenneth, 163–64
Cohen, Edythe: letters from LH, as
  source material, 41; LH letter to,
  about passion for racial justice, 49;
  LH letter to, mentioning coming
  marriage, 60
Colbert, Sonya, 7
college education: Beneatha's ambitions for, 113–14, 124; as expected
  within the Hansberry family, 9;
  Navy Pier campus of the University
  of Illinois, 113–14; New School for
  Social Research, 43. *See also* University of Wisconsin
colonialism, imperialism: *Freedom*'s
  focus on, 47; and LH's activism
  against, 66, 150–51; and LH's
  global perspective, 22, 24–25,
  65–67
"Come Ye Disconsolate" (hymn),
  196
Commentary magazine, "Liberalism
  and the Negro" roundtable, 122
Committee for the Negro in the Arts,
  47
communism: Camp Unity, 68;

Ellison's distancing self from, 55–56; and the execution of the Rosenbergs, 63–64; LH's attraction, commitment to, 32, 47, 49, 52; and the 1930s Chicago art scene, 18, 21; youthful debates about, 22, 32–33, 42. *See also* Community Party; Inter-American Peace Conference; Robeson, Paul

Communist Party: Burnham's affiliations with, 46–47; Foley Square Trial treason trial, 34–35; Ray Hansborough's membership in, 21; and Jefferson School of Social Science, 51; LH's retreat from, 68; LH's support for, 56; and Robeson, 57, 68. *See also* US State Department

Congress of Racial Equality (CORE): LH's Croton fund-raiser for, 166–67, 173; shooting of Goodman, Schwerner, and Chaney, 173; "Stall In," critiques of, 170

Cook, Molly Malone, 91–93

Cordero, Ana Livia, 155–56

Cotton, Cornelia, 182–83

courage, fearlessness: depictions of, in *Les Blancs*; depictions of, in *Raisin*, 139, 142–44; Du Bois's, 179; Carl Hansberry's, 136; LH's, 127–28, 170, 184. *See also* activism, radical

The Crisis of the Negro Intellectual (Cruse), 113

critical essays on art and politics: on art as illumination, 108; LH's skill at, 106–7; on liberalism, 172–73; response to responses to *Raisin*, 107–8, 100, 112–14; support for Baldwin's work, 119; Provincetown art show opening, 82; views on Ellison, 54, 99, 113; views on Wright, 123–24. *See also* Freedom (newspaper); *specific writings and writers*

Croton-on-Hudson, New York: LH's gravesite, 197, 202–3; LH's home,

175–76, 203–4; radical activists in, 176

Cruse, Harold, 113

Cuban Revolution, 157–58

Curtis Institute, Philadelphia, 131

Daily Worker (newspaper), 82, 84

Daley, Richard M., 137

Danny Rogers (character in *A Big White Fog*), as villainous entrepreneur, 139

"Dark Symphony" (Tolson), 19

Daughters of Bilitis, 79–80

David (character in *Sign*), homosexuality of, 147–49

Davis, Ossie: and the AAF, 171; Carnegie Hall memorial for Du Bois, 178; as pallbearer at LH's funeral, 195; support for LH's radical voice, 155; as Walter Lee Younger in *Raisin*, 101

Death of a Salesman (Miller), 105–6

de Beauvoir, Simone: disparagement of female beauty, 87; LH essay on, 89; *The Second Sex*, impact on LH, 75, 77–78

Dee, Ruby: and the AAF, 171; and the American Negro Theater, 53; as Ruth Younger in *Raisin*, 98; tribute at LH's funeral, 191

depression, emotional ups-and-downs: efforts to manage during illness, 183; LH's frequent experience of, 45–46, 99, 134–35, 181; reflection of in letters to RN, 68–70, 74–75; and response to Provincetown, 81–82; and the short story "Arnold," 76–77

diary, datebook entries: about intellectualizing deep emotions, 79; about desire to remain active despite illness, 180; lists of likes and dislikes, 95–96, 115; and mood swings, 181; nostalgia for Chicago, 45; plans for year before her death, 186; and self-exploration, questioning in, 69–71, 95–96, 107, 129; writings about lovers and love, 93–94. *See also* depression; personal qualities

Dirty Hands (Sartre), 170

D'Lugoff, Art, 72

D'Lugoff, Burt, 74

dogs, 176, 183

domestic workers, 113

Drake, St. Clair, 18

Drama Critics Circle Award, 1, 98

drawing skill, 28

The Drinking Gourd (TV series, Hansberry), 158–59

Du Bois, Shirley Graham, 178

Du Bois, W. E. B.: on art as political, 48, 52; Carnegie Hall memorial, 178; on the day of Awakening, 97; death, 178; LH's admiration for, tributes to, 52, 178–80; mentorship of LH, 48, 51–52; mentorship of Leo Hansberry, 51; passport revocation, 56; split from the NAACP, 66–67

Dufty, William, 114

dying, death: Carl Hansberry's, 22, 195; LH's illness and final days, 182, 184–85, 187, 195. *See also* cancer

Edmund Pettus Bridge, Selma, Alabama, 197

education. *See* college education; Englewood High School, Chicago

Eisenhower, Dwight D., 63

Elbein, Joseph, 42

Ellison, Ralph: distancing from Communist Party, 55–56; "Harlem Is Nowhere," 54, 99; *Invisible Man*, 55; LH's criticisms of, 54, 99, 113

Emily Jones (Hansberry pseudonym): "Chanson Du Konallis," 88–90; explorations of gender and lesbian sexuality, 83–84, 87; "Renascence," 194; separation of race from sexuality, 88

Englewood High School, Chicago: academic performance at, 20; debates and discussions, 22, 24–25; inscriptions in LH's yearbook,

25–26; integration of, 23; strike by white students at, 23

Eric/Ngedi (character in *Les Blancs*), homosexuality and courage, 141–43

Ethel Barrymore Theatre, New York, 98, 200

Excelsior (Mexico City newspaper), 157

fame, stardom: and cultural diplomacy, 151–52; desire for, changing views, 119, 135; impacts of, 95–96; and the *Raisin* film, 115–16. *See also Raisin in the Sun*

Fast, Howard, 47

Faulkner, William, 55, 123

Fauset, Jessie, 88

FBI surveillance: concerns about *Raisin*, 99; decision not to interview LH, 99–100; following the Montevideo conference, 59; of LH's Greenwich Village apartments, 94; physical description of LH, 102

fears and vulnerabilities, 91

Federal Negro Theater, 53

feminism: connection with lesbianism, 81; criticisms of Gide's misogyny, 129; criticisms of LH's use of strong male voices, 140–41, 144; and female activism at the Montevideo conference, 58; and female roles in "The Anticipation of Eve," 84–86; and male vs. female artists, 72; messages about in LH's and Simon's work, 133–34; and *The Second Sex*, 77–78; and women's intellectual rights, 81. *See also* the *Ladder*; lesbians, lesbianism

Fields, Sidney, 103

The Fire Next Time (Baldwin), 125, 136–37

Fisher, Eddie, 74

"Flag from a Kitchenette Window" (Hansberry), 44, 98

Florence (Childress), 72–73

Flowers for the General (Hansberry), 79

"Foreign paper told me about Miss Bergman" (Hansberry), 40

Forman, James (Rufus), 21–22, 184, 191

For Whom the Bell Tolls (Hemingway), 62–63

400 Blows (Truffaut), 95–96

Fourteenth Amendment, 17

Franklin, John Hope, 178

Frederick Douglass Educational Center, New York, 53

Freedom (newspaper): content, 47; coverage of Nkrumah's election, 48; critique of *Invisible Man* in, 113; LH's book and movie reviews, 47–48; LH's hiring, 46; LH's resignation from, 65; LH's writings about international politics, 48

Freedom Negro History Festival pageant, 53

freedom riders, 166–67

funeral, 190–93, 195

Garcia Lorca, Federico, 29, 30

gay and lesbian people. *See* lesbians, lesbianism

gender: early concerns about, 14; explorations of, *Les Blancs* example, 144; and male vs. female artists. *See also* feminism

generosity of spirit, LH's, 71–72, 192, 195, 199

Genet, Jean, 95, 110. *See also Les Blancs*

George Murchison (character in *Raisin*), assimilationist perspective, 140

Ghana, 48. *See also* Pan–Africanism

the ghetto: and the Black middle class, 9, 104, 113; international ghettoization, 22; LH's experience of, 9–10, 23; and *Native Son*, 124; and potential for violence, and *Raisin*, 97–99, 103–4, 115; vignettes portraying, 14–15; violence in, 3, 13–15, 169–70; West Side,

Chicago, 201. *See also* housing discrimination; segregation, South Side, Chicago

Gibson, Truman J., Jr., 138

Gibson, Truman, Sr., 18

Gide, André, 129

Giovanni, Nikki, 130

Giovanni's Room (Baldwin), 88, 118–19

globalism. *See* colonialism, imperialism

Gloria (character in *Sign*): truths spoken by, 148–49; work as prostitute, 146

Gold Through the Trees (Childress), 73

Goldwasser, Evelyn (Evie), 177

Gonçalves, Carlos, 159

Goodman, Andrew, 173

"good uncolored," 14

Goss, Margaret Taylor, 18

Go Tell It on the Mountain (Baldwin), 119, 136

Grant, Joanne, 192

Great Depression, 9, 11, 17–18, 139

Great Migration, 10, 16, 54–55, 139

"green land. Dark land." (Hansberry), 27, 38–39

Greenwich Village, New York: artistic and personal freedom, 43; dominance of whites in, 88; gentrification, 200; Washington Square Park, 45

Gregory, Dick, 195

Gresham, Joi, 7, 198

Grifalconi, Ann, 93

Guare, John, 200

Haitian Resolution against racial discrimination in the Americas, 39

Haley, Alex, 184

Hamilton (Miranda), 200

Hannibal, 21

Hansberry, Carl: at the Chapultepec Conference, 39; consciousness of race, 12; death, 22; education, 9; enduring impact of LH's life and work, 22, 98, 136–38; experience

of being swindled, 138; LH
mourning for at Ajijic, 38–39; as
middle class capitalist, 9, 11; parenting style, 11–12; patriotism, 22,
39, 170; Rhodes Avenue property
dispute, 12–13, 17
Hansberry, Elden, 4
Hansberry, Mamie, 13
Hansberry, Nannie Perry: birth of
Lorraine, 9; education and teach-
ing career, 9; illness, LH's care for
during, 74; LH letter to about *Raisin*, 98; at LH's funeral, 191; parenting style, 11–12; references to in
LH's poetry, 50; response to LH's
marriage, 65
Hansberry, William Leo: Du Bois's
mentorship of, 48, 51, 66; founder
of African Studies, 4; friends, LH's
exposure to as child, 11, 66; teach-
ing career, 26; visit to LH in hospital, 182
Hansberry family: commitment to,
desire to remain in touch with,
71–72, 149; as middle class, 9, 11,
24; intellectual interests, 4, 10–11,
19, 66, 214. *See also* 6140 Rhodes
Avenue
Hansberry Foundation, 138
Hansberry v. Lee, 17
Hansbrough, Ray, 21
"Harlem" (Hughes), 98
Harlem, New York: artist community
in, 53; Frederick Douglass Educational Center, 53; LH's move to,
46; modern, echoes of LH in, 200;
rioting in following police shooting
of Powell, 173; vigil demanding
end to school segregation, 197
"Harlem Is Nowhere" (Ellison),
54–55, 99
Harry (character in "Metamor-
phasis"), internalized racism of,
156–57
Hemingway, Ernest, 62
Hentoff, Nat, 122
Higashida, Cheryl, 6
Hiroshima (film), 47

Holiday, Billie, 114
homosexuality: embracing of term
by LH, 125; and LH's and Simon's
struggles with, 131; in the Village
during the 1950s, 43. *See also* lesbians, lesbianism
honesty, importance to LH and Baldwin, 3, 31, 45, 125, 195
Hoover, J. Edgar, 99
Horne, Lena, 163
housing discrimination: Carl Hansberry's approach to, 9, 17; racially
restrictive covenants, 12–13; racism and, 27; at the University of
Wisconsin, 27–28. *See also* ghettos; kitchenettes
Hovey, Serge, 70
"How to Write a Play" (Kerr), 109
Hudson Valley, New York, culture,
176
Hughes, Langston: American Negro
Exposition, 19; ashes, 200; Childress's dramatizations of stories by,
73; "Harlem," 98; on new paternalism, 111; poetic tribute to LH,
186, 189–90; on the quandary of
Black artists, 100
human nature, messiness of: LH's focus on, 182, 193; O'Casey's skill at
portraying, 30
humor, wit, and charm, LH's, 2, 28–
29, 62, 91, 107, 192
Hunton, Alphaeus, 52–53
Hurston, Zora Neale, 199

illnesses, chronic disease, 177–78,
182, 186–87
"I Loves You Porgy" (Gershwin),
Simone's rendition, 129, 132
"In the Evening by the Moonlight"
(Simone), 186–87, 192
indigenous culture, exposure to in
Mexico, 37
Ingram, Rosalee, 50
inheritance. *See* paternal legacy
integration. *See* racism; segregation;
white supremacy
Inter-American Conference on

Problems of War and Peace,
Chapultepec, Mexico, 39
Inter-American Peace Conference,
Montevideo, Uruguay, 57–59, 58,
59
interior spaces, role in LH's work as
Emily Jones, 87
international perspective. *See* antico-
lonial internationalism
interracial intimacy: Baldwin's and
LH's explorations of, 126–28, 187;
in bohemian culture, 43, 72; in
Smith's *Strange Fruit*, 20. *See also*
Nemiroff, Robert (Bobby)
Invisible Man (Ellison), 55, 113
Iris Brustein (character in *Sign*), re-
jection of Sidney's paternalism,
134, 146
Irish culture, O'Casey's skill at capturing, 30

Jackson, Roosevelt "Rosie," 61
Jefferson School of Social Science,
New York, 51
Jenny Reed (discarded character
from *Sign*), 144
Jerome, Alice, 196
Jimmy (character in *The Fire Next
Time*), on costs of white suprem-
acy, 125
Jitney (Wilson), 200
John Brown Community Theatre,
prospectus for, 115–16
John Henry (Hansberry pseudonym),
84
Jonas, Irma, 36–37
Jones, Emily. *See* Emily Jones (Hans-
berry pseudonym)
Jones, Claudia, 52–53, 73
Jones, LeRoi. *See* Baraka, Amiri (Le-
Roi Jones)
Joseph Asagai (character in *Raisin*):
commitment to African indepen-
dence, 140; as LH's voice and fa-
vorite, 140; and the "religion" of
activism, 143
Journal of Negro Education, 160
journals. *See* diaries, datebooks

Julien, Isaac, 4
Juno and the Paycock (O'Casey),
29–30

Kaplan, Renee, 83, 183, 195
Kennedy, John F., 152–53, 165
Kennedy, Robert F., 162–64
Kenyatta, Jomo, 65–66
Kerr, Walter, 109
"The Kerry Dance" (song), 21
Killens, John Oliver: and the AAF,
171; description of *Trouble in
Mind*, 73; on LH's politics, 2; as
narration for Freedom Negro His-
tory Festival, 53; as pallbearer at
LH's funeral, 195
King, Martin Luther, Jr., 167–69,
196
kitchenettes: "Flag from a Kitchen-
ette Window" (Hansberry), 44, 98;
"kitchenette building" (Brooks),
44, 98; and *Raisin*, 98; as solution
to Black housing problem, 9. *See
also* Hansberry, Carl
Kitt, Eartha, 95–96
Konallia Martin Whitside (character
"Chanson Du Konallis"), sexuality
of, 89–90

Labor Youth League, *New Challenge
Magazine*, 65
the *Ladder* (Daughters of Bilitis):
"Chanson Du Konallis," 88–90;
LH's letters to, 80–81; story pub-
lished in, 83
La Farge, Oliver, 182
Langdon Manor, University of Wis-
consin, 27–28
Larsen, Nella, 88
Latin American politics, 157
Laughing Boy (La Farge), 182
leadership abilities, LH's, 19–20, 35
Leaks, Sylvester, 180, 192
Lee, George, 21
leftist politics. *See* activism, radical;
communism
legal system, as vehicle for change,
cynicism about, 17, 160, 168

Lena Younger (character in *Raisin*): affirmation of Black humanity, 124; desire for own home, 97, 139–40; Marxist messages, 139; strength, 141

lesbians, lesbianism: "The Anticipation of Eve," 84–85; among Black women, 89; connection with feminism, 81; exclusion from cultural mainstream, 201–2; in *Flowers for the General*, 79; LH's embracing of term, 125; lovers and love as inspiration, 93–94; Molly Cook, 91–93; RN's saving of LH's writing on, 83; Dorothy Secules, 83, 93–95, 182, 187, 195; writings about, characteristics, 87. *See also* Emily Jones (pseudonym); Simone, Nina

Les Blancs (Hansberry): as "call and response" with Baldwin, 126; early notes, original focus on women, 144; homage to Lumumba in, 156; and interracial relationships, 142–43; and the revolutionary moment, 143–44; RN's editing of, 197; theme of inheritance in, 141; work on during illness, 182

liberalism: anticommunist stance, 35; Ellison's move toward, 56; Hansberry's parents adherence to, 56; LH's criticisms of, 142, 172–73; "Liberalism and the Negro" roundtable (*Commentary* magazine), 122–23; portrayal of, in *Les Blancs*, 142

liberation, freedom: and armed self-defense, 168–69; dreams of, while in Mexico, 38–39; importance for both LH and Baldwin, 129; Simone's militancy, 131; slowness of progress toward, 187–88; and "the Village" of the 1950s, 43. *See also* activism, radical; Black radical traditions

Liberation Committee for Africa, 159

life insurance, importance for working-class Blacks, 113

lilies, symbolism of, 202

Lily (character in "What Use Are Flowers?"), as fighter, 133, 202

loneliness, sense of isolation: LH early experience of, 12; reflections of in journal writing, 45–46; as shared by LH, Baldwin, and Simone, 121–22, 130, 134–35

Looking for Langston (film, Julien), 4

Lorraine Hansberry Literary Trust, 198

Lorraine Hansberry Park, Chicago, 201

L'Ouverture, Toussaint, 21

Louys, Pierre, 80

Low-Dive Jenny (character in *The Three-Penny Opera*), anger of, 132

Lumumba, Patrice, 153–54

"Lynchsong" (Hansberry), 50

Lyon, Phyllis, 80–81

Lysistrata (Aristophanes), 29

Madame Nielsen (character in *Les Blancs*), as representative of the revolutionary moment, 143–44

Madison, Wisconsin, LH reflections on, 45–46. *See also* University of Wisconsin

Mailer, Norman, 109–12

The Making of Black Revolutionaries (Forman), 21–22

Malcolm X: Airlift Africa, 1960, 152; assassination, 196; "by any means necessary" speech, 169; at LH's funeral, 196

"Male Prison" (Baldwin), 129

male voice, LH's use of, 140–41, 144

March on Washington for Jobs and Justice, 1963, 177–78

marriage: *Chicago Defender* article on, 63; complexity of, ambivalence about, 69–70; divorce, 181; and execution of the Rosenbergs, 64; LH's employment following, 65. *See also* Nemiroff, Robert

Marshall, Burke: at 1963 meeting with RFK, 163; efforts to get Smith

and the freedom riders to stop
their protests, 166
Marshall, Paule, 171
Martaslund (Hansberry), 182
Martin, Del, 80–81
Martin, Helen, 53
Martin, Vince, 74
Martin Weiner Distinguished Lecture
(Brandeis University)
Masses and Mainstream (magazine):
"Flag from a Kitchenette Win-
dow," 44; "Lynchsong," 50
Mau Mau, 66
Mavis (character in *Sign*): racism
shown by, 146–47; view of father,
146
Mayfield, Julian, 155–56, 162
McCarran Act, 67–68
McComb, Mississippi, Smith's beat-
ing in, 163, 166
McCullers, Carson, 123
McGee, Willie, 48, 50
Medina, Harold, 34–35
Mekas, Jonas, 110
Melville, Herman: Pip in *Moby Dick*,
194; sense of vocation, 76–77
Merida, Carlos, 37
Merriam, Eve, 184
"Metamorphasis [*sic*]" (Hansberry),
156
Mexico: Ajijic experience, 35–40;
Chapultepec Conference, 39; Carl
Hansberry's death in, 22; reloca-
tion of Blacks to, 22
middle class. *See* Black middle class
migrants from the South: Ellison's
disparagement of, 54–55, experi-
ence of, 10, 16; as the Great Mi-
gration, 139. *See also* the ghetto
Millay, Edna St. Vincent, 194
Miller, Ann, 27
Miller, Arthur, 105, 106
Miller, Monica, 7
Mirine Tige (character "Chanson Du
Konallis"), and portrayal of lost
love, 89–90
"Mississippi Goddam" (Simone), 172
mob violence. *See* violence

Moby Dick (Melville), 194
Montgomery, Alabama, bus boycott,
73
Moore, Richard B., 188
Moore, Thomas, 196
Moreno, Rita, 195
Mother, May I game, 10–11
Mother Courage and Her Children
(Brecht), 133
Mount Airy section, Croton-on-
Hudson, New York, 176
The Movement (Baldwin and Hans-
berry), 167
Mr. Rector (fictional character), sad-
ness, impotence of, 15
Muhammad Speaks (newspaper),
Leaks's obituary for LH, 192; LH's
tribute to Du Bois, 180
Murphy, George B., 47
Museum of Natural History, New
York City, racist depictions of
Blacks, 151

National Association for the Ad-
vancement of Colored People
(NAACP): expulsion of Du Bois
from, 66–67; and *Hansberry v.
Lee*, 12–13; and representation of
Blacks in the media, 48; represen-
tative from, at LH's funeral, 67;
separation from the radical left,
67, 155, 160
National Negro Commission, 21
National Negro Congress, 47
National Review, obituary for LH,
190
Nation of Islam, 159–60
"The Nation Needs Your Gifts"
(Hansberry), 197
Native Son (Wright), 20, 123–25
nature, out-of-doors. *See* beauty;
nature
"The Negro Artist and the Racial
Mountain" (Hughes), 100
"Negro History in Poetry and Prose"
presentation (Hansberry), 53
"Negro in Illinois" project (WPA), 18
Nemiroff, Leo, 192–93

Nemiroff, Robert (Bobby): appreciation for LH's genius, 72; "Bob Rolfe" pseudonym, 65; "Cindy, Oh Cindy," 74; divorce from LH, 181, 183; friendship with D'Lugoff, 72; first meeting with LH, 60; hiding of LH's cancer diagnosis from, 178; letter from Edythe Cohen to, 41; LH letter to, about Camp Unity, 69; letter to, about Provincetown art opening, 82; LH letter to, about their differences, 59; LH letter to, complaining about Tubbs, 71; LH letter to, declaring her love, 61–62; letter to, complaining about Chicago 74; mother, LH's affection for, 65; promotional work for Avon Books, 73–74; as protector of LH's life and legacy, 59, 61–62, 72, 84, 92, 131, 197–98; pseudonymous songwriting, 73–74; vigil at LH's deathbed, 187; wedding to LH, 63–64
New Challenge Magazine (Labor Youth League), 65
New School for Social Research, New York, 43
New York City: Black theater world, 53; LH's early poems written in, 44; move and returns to, 42, 72. *See also* Greenwich Village, New York; Harlem, New York; theater
New Yorker (magazine), 75
New York Post, LH letter praising Dufty, 114
New York Times: criticisms of CORE "Stall In," 170; LH article on radical activism, 170; LH article on *Sidney*, 145; LH letter about Lumumba assassination, 154; Skirvanek letter about LH, 199; "Stanley Gleason and the Lights That Need Not Die," 150–51; "Willie Loman, Walter Younger, and He Who Must Live," 105
New York University, protest of racial discrimination, 60
New York World-Telegram, "Slum Play Author Sued as Slumlord," 137
Nkrumah, Kwama, 48
nonviolence. *See* activism, radical; civil rights movement
Nottage, Lynn, 189

O'Casey, Sean, 29–30, 104
Oliver, Mary, 91–93
ONE (homophile publication), "The Anticipation of Eve" in, 84–86
Organization of African American Unity, 169
The Outsider (Wright), 47, 113

Painter, Mary, 27
Pan-Africanism: and the Black diaspora, 65–66; Du Bois's, 179; LH's, 153–54, 159
Parker, Theodore, 168–69
Parks, Gordon, 99
Parks, Suzan Lori, 189
passport revocations, 56–57, 59
paternal legacy, inheritance: as theme in *Les Blancs*, 141, 143; as theme in *Raisin*, 139–41; as theme in *Sign*, 144, 146–49
paternalism, paternalists: complexity of, for LH, 139; LH's characterizations of Beat writers as, 110–11
paternal legacy: reflections of, in *Sign*, 144; as theme throughout *Sign*, 146–49
patriarchy: and Alton's character in *Sign* as reflection of, 146–47; and Beat writers, 110–11; questioning of, 118; in "What Use Are Flowers?," 133
patriotism, uncritical: Carl Hansberry's, 22, 170; LH's rejection of after father's death, 22–23; Vincent Tubbs's, 71; at the University of Wisconsin, 32
Paul Whitside (character in "Chanson Du Konallis"), sexual appetites, 90
Pendleton, Larry, 188
People's Rights Party, 50–51

Perry grandmother, childhood visit
to, in Tennessee, 16
personality, force of, 28–29, 34,
162–65
Philadelphia, PA, tryouts for *Raisin*
in, 97
physical appearance: beauty, 3, 28,
102; FBI description, 102; photographs, 2, 63, 91, 99, 102–32
Pip (character in both *Moby Dick*
and "Renascence"), 194
"Pirate Jenny" (Brecht), Simone's
version, 132
Poitier, Sidney: and the American Negro Theater, 53; in cast of *Raisin*,
97; LH's views on, 115; as narrator for Freedom Negro History
Festival pageant, 53
police racism, LH's portrayal of, 15
police violence, depictions of, 14–15,
24, 55
politics, political views: evolution of,
12, 21, 44, 81; Carl Hansberry's,
170; holistic perspective, 77–78,
91, 100, 130; integrating with art,
107–9, 115–16; LH's commitment
to racial justice, 24, 47, 49, 129;
LH's, compared with Baldwin's,
125; and LH's connection with
Simone, 131–31; LH's increasing
militancy, 126, 150, 159, 169–73;
and LH's sense of purpose and
responsibility, 21, 134, 168, 170,
179, 190. *See also* activism, radical; Black radical traditions; communism; liberation, freedom
"Pomp and Circumstance," 21
Poston, Ted, 103
Potpourri (Nemiroff family restaurant), 65, 72
Powell, James, 173
Price, Leontyne, 161
private papers and writings of LH,
publication of, 198
the professor (character in "What
Use Are Flowers?"), as symbol of
the patriarchy, 133
Provident Hospital, Chicago, 9

Provincetown, Massachusetts: as bohemian enclave, 200; Cook's photographs of LH, 91; description of
first visit to, 82
Publicists Guild of America, 71

racial justice, importance, 24, 47,
49, 149
racism: anger, rage as response to,
14–15, 56; apartheid, 67; and
the challenges facing Black artists, 106–7; childhood lessons,
12; Childress's indictment of, 73;
in critical assessments of LH and
Raisin, 103–4; global/holistic perspectives, 77–78, 88, 129, 145,
160; Carl Hansberry's bitterness
and pessimism about, 22; and
LH friendship with JoAnn Beier,
33; lynch-law and Jim Crow
courts, 50; resistance to through
writings, 23–24, 118–19, 146–47;
and the "romantic racism" of
the Beats, 110; as structural and
need for radical change, 173.
See also activism, radical; Black
radical traditions; the ghetto;
segregation
"radical," as term of praise, 150
A Raisin in the Sun (Hansberry):
autobiography and memory in,
13, 98, 137–38; awards and honors, 1, 98; as both conventional
and radical, 100–102; Broadway
production, 97–98; criticisms of
as racist, 102–6; critical evaluations, 100, 104, 198–99, 112–14;
early draft, 92; enduring fame and
popularity, 1, 99, 100–104, 198;
faithful depictions of characters'
dreams and aspirations, 98–99,
139–40; FBI investigation trig-
gered by, 99; film version, 114–15,
158; LH's response to misunderstanding of, by critiques, 113–14;
LH's views on weaknesses of, 106;
Marxist and radical influences,
104; plot, 97; presentation of

diversity of Black Americans, 140; tryouts for, 93, 97, 119
rat metaphor, 124
real estate, and the fight over integration, 13
realism, O'Casey's artistic model, 30–31
religion, rules of, questioning of, 118
"Renascence" (Hansberry), as story of loneliness and grieving, 194
"Renascence" (Millay), 195
Reporter (magazine), LH's letter to supporting Kenyatta, 65–66
Republican Party, Hansberry family affiliation with, 11
restlessness, distractibility, LH's, 52, 62, 68–69, 99, 137, 181–82
the revolutionary moment, 143–44
Rhodes Avenue, Chicago: Carl Hansberry's purchase of property at 6140, 12; eviction of Hansberry family from property at 6140, 12–13, 16–17; *Hansberry v. Lee*, 17; mob violence against the Hansberry family, 13–14, 98
Richards, Lloyd, 97, 120
"The Riot" (Hansberry), portrayal of Black resistance in, 24
Rivera, Diego, 37
River George (Lee), 21
Robeson, Eslanda Goode, tribute at Du Bois memorial, 178
Robeson, Paul: and the Communist Party, 57, 68; eulogy at LH's funeral, 191; passport revocation, impacts, 56, 67; as publisher, editorial-writer of *Freedom*, 47; taped greeting to delegates at the Inter-American Peace Conference, 58
Rochester (character on the *Jack Benny Show*), as racial stereotype, 156
Roosevelt University, Chicago, 42
Rose, Philip, 92, 97, 107
Rosenberg, Julius and Ethel, 63–64
Rougeau, Weldon, 184
Rowe, Izzy, 7

Rufus Scott (character in *Another Country*), interracial romance, 128
Russak, Mary, 57
Ruth Younger (character in *Raisin*): desire for own home, 97, 139–41; quietness, silence of, 141

Said, Edward, 175, 181–82
Sands, Diana, 195
Sanford, Isabel, 53
Sarah (fictional character), in LH's story about childhood trauma, 16–17
Sartre, Jean-Paul, 95, 145, 170
Schomburg Center for Research in Black Culture, Harlem, New York, LH's papers at, 7, 198
Schwerner, Michael "Mickey," 173
The Second Sex (de Beauvoir), 75, 77–78, 86
Secules, Dorothy: care of LH during illness, 182; love affair with LH, 83, 93–95; as pallbearer at LH's funeral, 195; residence at 112 Waverly Place, 94; vigil at LH's deathbed, 187
segregation: continuation of, in Chicago, 201; and Jim Crow laws in the South, 12, 17, 50, 167–68; sustaining through ghettoization, 160, 167; and violent responses to integration, 13. *See also* racism
self-criticism, self-exploration, 69–71, 95–96, 107, 129
Selma, Alabama, Edmund Pettus Bridge march, 197
sexuality, sex: ambiguities about, 79; and LH's love for women, 79–80. *See also* lesbians, lesbianism
Shagaloff, June, 163
Sidney Brustein (character in *Sign*): as failed radical, 144; paternalism and sexism of, 134, 146
Sighted Eyes/Feeling Heart (Strain, documentary), 7
The Sign in Sidney Brustein's Window (Hansberry): Broadway opening, closing, 186–87; comparison

with *Another Country*, 128–29;
focus on a father's legacy in, 144;
LH article about, 145; on need for
action as well as dreams, 175; portrayal of countercultural politics,
145; portrayal of sexism, 134; reviews, criticisms of, 144–45
Signoret, Simone, 131
Silberman, Charles, 171, 173
"Simone," as a name, 131
Simone, Nina: "Blackbird," 134; creative discipline, musical brilliance
of, 131–34; depression and rage after LH's death, 196–97; friendship
with LH, 117–18; "I Loves You
Porgy," 129, 132; "In the Evening
by the Moonlight," 186–87, 192;
LH as godmother to daughter, 130;
on LH's influence, 129–30; loneliness of, 134–35; "Mississippi Goddam," 172; musical background
and style, 131; "Pirate Jenny,"
132; political awakening, 129,
132; post-movement life, death,
135; "Sinnerman," 105; songs and
eulogy at LH's funeral, 192; struggles around sexuality, 131; visit
with the dying LH, 186; "Young,
Gifted, and Black," 197
Simple Speaks His Mind (Hughes),
Childress's dramatic adaptation
of, 73
"Sinnerman" spiritual (Simone), 105
Siqueiros, David Alfaro, 157
Six Degrees of Separation (Guare),
200
Skirvanek, Camille, 199
slave rebellions, white reactions to,
170
slavery: and Black female adornment
with, 87; escape from by LH's
grandfather, 16; impact on Black
American perspectives, 172–73;
slave rebellions, white fears about,
170
slum landlord accusations, impact on
LH, 137–38
"Slum Play Author Sued as

Slumlord" (*New York World–
Telegram*), 137
smile, laugh, LH's, 103, 107, 121,
135, 164, 183, 188, 192
Smith, Anna Deavere, 189
Smith, Gene, 120
Smith, Jerome, 163–66
Smith, Judith, 6
Smith, Lillian, 20–21
social criticism. *See* critical essays on
art and politics
"social dramatist" label, 108–9
socialism, LH's ongoing belief in,
150. *See also* communism; politics,
political views
Social Security, exclusion of domestic
workers from, 113
Son (character in *All the Dark and
Beautiful Warriors*), as answer to
Wright's Bigger Thomas, 124
The Songs of Bilitis (Louys), 80
the South: and Jim Crow laws, violence against Blacks, 12, 17, 50,
163, 167–68; LH's rootedness in,
16; and limitations of Southern
white writers, 123; reflection of, in
Simone's music, 131; as symbol of
struggles past and to come, 16
South African apartheid, protests
against, 67–68
South Side, Chicago: depiction of, in
Raisin, 97, 101, 137; Hansberry
family in, 28, 104, 115; LH's child-
hood and youth in, 9–26; LH's
return visits to, 84; Wright's description, 20
Spartacus (Fast), 47
Spectator, 192
Spingarn, Arthur, 178
Spottswood, Stephen Gill, 178
stagecraft, staging, LH's natural skill
at, 91–92
"Stanley Gleason and the Lights That
Need Not Die" (Hansberry), 151
Starborin, Joseph, 82
station wagon, purchase of, for
CORE, 167, 173
Strain, Tracy, 7

Strange Fruit (Smith), 20–21
A Street in Bronzeville (Brooks), 44
Stroud, Andrew (Andy), 130–31
Student Nonviolent Coordinating
    Committee (SNCC), 161, 167–68.
    See also activism, radical
Supreme Liberty Life Insurance, 12,
    113
Susskind, David, 115, 171
Swarthmore College, LH lecture at,
    108
"Sweet Lorraine," 119, 121

Tallmer, Jeremy, 190
tendonitis, 181
Tennessee, visit to grandmother in,
    16
Terkel, Studs, 117
theater: American Negro Theater,
    53; Childress's refusal to change
    Trouble in Mind, 73; Federal
    Negro Theater, 53; John Brown
    Community Theatre prospectus,
    115–16; LH's influence on, 200;
    O'Casey's influence, 29–30, 104;
    opening of *Raisin* on Broadway,
    97; opening of *Sign* on Broadway,
    186; skill at staging, stagecraft,
    91; studies at the University of
    Wisconsin, 28–29
Theory of the Leisure Class (Veblen),
    104
Thompson, Daniel, 160
Thoreau, Henry David, 176
"Thoughts on Genet, Miller, and the
    New Paternalism" (Hansberry),
    110
Till, Emmett, 73
To Be Young, Gifted, and Black
    (Hansberry and Nemiroff), 5, 6–7,
    24, 197
"To Lorraine" (Pendleton), 188
Tolson, Melvin, 19
Toomer, Jean, 89
Torn, Rip, 163
Torres, Angel, 57
toughness, admiration for, 19–20,
    201

trauma, LH's repeating of in fiction,
    14–15
trauma, childhood: LH's recreations
    of 16; story about, 16
Trouble in Mind (Childress), 73
Truman, Harry, 33–34
Tshembe (character in *Les Blancs*),
    and debates about revolution,
    141–43
Tshombe, Moise, 156
Tubbs, Mamie Hansberry, 12–13,
    71–72
Tubbs, Vincent, 71–72

United States Progressive Party,
    33–34
United States of America: Carl Hans-
    berry's disillusionment with, 22,
    170; hypocrisy about freedom in,
    158; LH's commitment to, 183;
    role in Lumumba's assassination,
    153. *See also* activism, radical; pa-
    triotism, uncritical; politics
University of Illinois, Navy Pier cam-
    pus, 113–14
University of Wisconsin: diaries,
    journals written at, 31; Frank
    Lloyd Wright's lecture at, 31–32;
    Langdon Manor housing, 27–28;
    LH's decision to attend, 26; racial,
    political tensions at, 28, 32–33;
    theater studies at, 29–31; World
    War II veterans at, 32
US presidential election, 1948, 33–34
US State Department: Airlift Africa,
    1960, 152–53; criminalization of
    the Inter-American Peace Confer-
    ence, 59; revoking passports of Du
    Bois, Robeson and LH, 56–57, 59
US Supreme Court, *Hansberry v.
    Lee*, 17

Veblen, Thorstein, 104
Vietnam War, 172
Village Voice: Cook's photogra-
    phy for, 91; "Thoughts on Genet,
    Miller, and the New Paternalism"
    in, 110

violence: against activists, civil rights workers, 163, 173; against Black women, 13–14; and colonialism, 143, 148; as commonplace in the ghetto, 13–15, 169–170; LH's childhood experience of, 13–16, 98; police violence, 14–15, 24, 55; and racism, 50, 109, 126. *See also* the ghetto

Vivaldo (character in *Another Country*), interracial bisexuality, 128

Vogue magazine, article about LH, 102–3

Waiting for Godot (Beckett), *The Arrival of Mr. Todog* as answer to, 180

Walker, Alice, 199

Walker, Margaret, 18

Wallace, Henry, 33–34

Wally (character in *Sign*), on need for action as well as dreams, 175

Walter Lee Younger (character in *Raisin*): ambitions, yearnings, 97, 104, 139; comparison of with Willie Loman, 105–6; essential dignity of, 105; LH frustration with critics' misunderstanding of, 106; swindling of, 138

Ward, Douglas Turner, 53, 61, 162

Ward, Theodore, 139

Washington, Mary Helen, 6

Waverly Place, New York, LH residence at, 94, 199

Wechsler, James, 171, 173

Western intellectualism, postwar, reflections of in *Sign*, 145

West Side, Chicago, 201

"What Use Are Flowers?" (Hansberry), 132–33

White, Charles, 18

White, Walter, 48

"The White Negro" (Mailer), 109–10

white supremacy: Baldwin's excoriation of, 125–26; and Black perceptions of whites, 110–11; LH's writings on, 56, 142–43; and

limitations of Southern white writers, 123; whites' need to accept responsibility for, 142

Whitman, Steve, 4, 6

Wiener, Ed, 82

Wilkerson, Margaret, 7

Williams, Robert, 168

"Willie Loman, Walter Younger, and He Who Must Live" (Hansberry), 105–7

Willy Loman (character in *Death of a Salesman*), comparison with Walter Lee Younger, 104

Wilson, August, 3, 189, 200

Winters, Shelley, 192–93

Wolfe, Thomas, 70

Wollstonecraft, Mary, 182

women. *See* feminism; lesbians, lesbianism

Woodlawn Property Owners Association, 16

Workers World (newspaper), tribute to LH in, 188–89

working class: fighting, resistance by, LH's admiration for, 3, 9, 61; importance for effecting change, 165; LH's portrayals of, 14, 113; mischaracterizations of LH as, 51, 104; work in New York on behalf of, 60–61

"Working Class Poets of the Negro People," 51

Works Progress Administration (WPA): American Negro Exposition, 18; Federal Negro Theater, 53; Negro in Illinois project, 18

World War II, political discussions following, 22, 32–33. *See also* communism

Wright, Frank Lloyd, 31–32

Wright, Richard: American Negro Exposition, 19; Baldwin's and LH's criticisms of, 123–24; fame and influence, 20; LH's review of *The Outsider*, 47, 113; mentorship of Baldwin, 123; Negro in Illinois project, 18; social determinism of, 139

Wright Junior College, controversy over *Another Country* at, 187
writing craft: aesthetics of, appreciation for, 87; anger and rage in, 14; attention to detail, 1, 76–77, 82–83, 98, 113–14; experimentation, 13–14, 54–55, 57, 99; impact of fame on, 95–96; O'Casey's influence, 30–31; and respect for skill and quality, 44–45, 120, 130; reworking themes in multiple forms, 13–14; self-criticism, 69–71, 95–96, 107, 129; and sense of vocation, mission, 1, 24, 46, 61–62, 76–77, 120, 182;

skill at verbal portraiture, 91, 105, 148, 151; struggles with focus, 62, 71–72, 74; synthesis of politics and art, 77; work process, 75. *See also* Emily Jones (Hansberry pseudonym); *specific works*

Yerma (Garcia Lorca), 9
You Can't Go Home Again (Wolfe), 70
"Young, Gifted and Black" (Simone), 6, 197
Young Communist League, 46–47
Young Progressives of America, 33–34

ABOUT THE AUTHOR

Imani Perry is the Hughes-Rogers Professor of African American Studies at Princeton University, where she is also affiliated with the Programs in Gender and Sexuality Studies and Law and Public Affairs. Perry is the author of five books and numerous scholarly articles. Her fields of inquiry include legal history, cultural studies, literary studies, and music. She holds a PhD from Harvard in American Studies, a JD from Harvard Law School, an LLM from Georgetown University Law Center, and a BA from Yale College. She is also a creative nonfiction essayist and a book reviewer. A native of Birmingham, Alabama, Perry spent most of her childhood in Massachusetts, as well as time in Chicago. Perry currently lives in the Philadelphia area with her two sons.